Richard Davi Sams    9/12/16
Sheppards 1

MW00608281

# 1 & 2 CORINTHIANS

the Smart Guide to the Bible™ series

BE SMART · BE INSPIRED ·

**Dewey Bertolini**

**Larry Richards**, General Editor

Thomas Nelson
*Since 1798*

NASHVILLE   DALLAS   MEXICO CITY   RIO DE JANEIRO   BEIJING

*1 & 2 Corinthians*
The Smart Guide to the Bible™ series
© 2009 by GRQ, Inc.

All rights reserved. No portion of this book may be reproduced, stored in a retrieval system, or transmitted in any form or by any means—electronic, mechanical, photocopy, recording, scanning, or other—except for brief quotations in critical reviews or articles without the prior written permission of the publisher.

Published in Nashville, Tennessee, by Thomas Nelson. Thomas Nelson is a trademark of Thomas Nelson, Inc.

Thomas Nelson, Inc. titles may be purchased in bulk for educational, business, fundraising, or sales promotional use. For information, please e-mail SpecialMarkets@ThomasNelson.com.

Scripture quotations are taken from the New King James Version® (NKJV), copyright © 1982 by Thomas Nelson, Inc. Used by permission. All rights reserved.

Additional Scripture quotations have been taken from:
The Holy Bible, King James Version (KJV)

(NIV) Holy Bible, New International Version®. NIV®. Copyright © 1973, 1978, 1984 by International Bible Society. Used by permission of Zondervan. All rights reserved.

(MSG) *The Message* by Eugene H. Peterson, copyright © 1993, 1994, 1995, 1996, 2000, 2001, 2002. Used by permission of NavPress Publishing Group. All rights reserved.

(CEV) The Contemporary English Version. Copyright © 1991, 1992, 1995 by American Bible Society. Used by permission.

(NLT) *Holy Bible*, New Living Translation, copyright © 1996, 2004. Used by permission of Tyndale House Publishers, Inc., Wheaton, Illinois 60189. All rights reserved.

To the best of its ability, GRQ, Inc., has strived to find the source of all material. If there has been an oversight, please contact us, and we will make any correction deemed necessary in future printings. We also declare that to the best of our knowledge all material (quoted or not) contained herein is accurate, and we shall not be held liable for the same.

General Editor: Larry Richards
Managing Editor: Michael Christopher
Scripture Editor: Deborah Wiseman
Assistant Editor: Amy Clark
Design: Diane Whisner

ISBN 10: 1-4185-1013-0
ISBN 13: 978-1-4185-1013-8

Printed in the United States of America
09 10 11 12 RRD 9 8 7 6 5 4 3 2 1

# Introduction

There is something about a letter. Something personal yet remote; something intimate yet formal; something urgent and unavoidable yet much easier to deal with than a finger in the face. And, if you were a frequent traveler throughout the known world of some two thousand years ago, it could also be just about your only reliable form of communication with those you loved when you could not be there in person. If you were also a teacher, a guidance counselor, and a spiritual mentor for the people in several separate congregations, you might have to depend on letters even more.

For all those reasons, Paul's letters to the church he founded in Corinth are among the most fascinating in the Bible. But they are also hugely instructive, not only for what they tell us about the basic theology of Christianity itself but also for what they tell us about ourselves.

Yet in spite of all that, people sometimes claim that the Bible is no longer relevant today. They claim that we have somehow "moved beyond" any kind of meaningful application to our lives here in the twenty-first century. But on the contrary, as 1 and 2 Corinthians make so very plain, though many things have changed in the last twenty centuries the nature of mankind and the main function of letter-writing have not.

If people are fouling things up and you have something you really need to say, and if you want to make sure the folks on the other end will get the point, you need to write it down!

## Facing Up to Godly Solutions

Paul's two surviving letters to the church in Corinth give us the perfect proof. The problems those people had, balanced against the godly solutions Paul made them face up to, over and over until they finally got the message, have all been repeated down through history, too many times to count.

The Corinthians were human. They were easily influenced by outside forces. They were sometimes weak, sometimes vain and proud, sometimes willing to believe the most hideous lies because the truth seemed nowhere near as exciting.

In other words they were just like us, and that's exactly why the books of 1 and 2 Corinthians are so meaningful today. That's why they seem so much like gold mines of eternal truth, basic spiritual guidance, and those "human" touches that make the people of that era seem so up-close and personal in ways we cannot deny.

In the pages ahead we will look at both of Paul's letters to the Corinthians from all these different perspectives. Paul had a huge job on his hands, keeping the Corinthians on the right path even as others worked so hard to pull them sideways and undermine everything he had done in founding their church and building them up in the first place. It's no fun when someone comes in and tries to undo every good thing you've set out to accomplish within your own family. Indeed, most fathers and mothers know what it means to pour themselves out to knit together a family unit they can be proud of. It's even harder to create something that functions reliably on a day-to-day basis but also honors the important truths they want their family to remember.

## Where Was Paul Coming From?

This is where Paul was coming from throughout much of what he wrote to the Corinthians. But if anything, he was probably dealing with "outside influences" that were just as intrusive and just as relentless as they are today. Perhaps even more so, for there were still a few things going on in Corinth that even the most decadent members of modern society will not embrace in public.

So far, at least.

In Corinth, the general population had almost no inhibitions and very few commonly accepted rules of behavior. But fortunately for us, Paul did not deal with all these things by relying on his own knowledge or his own sense of right and wrong. Paul was probably the ultimate practical theologian of his era, and perhaps of all time. Because, even though he was a profound thinker with far more formal education than almost anyone he talked to on a regular basis, he was also among the most pragmatic people in history.

But that doesn't mean he shaded the truth to accommodate the guy on the other end. Paul was able to explain huge concepts in simple, clear words of unmistakable clarity and uncompromised integrity that hit with the force of bullets. But then, before the bleeding could even start they enveloped the reader in a big ray of sunshine that made all the pain go away in a rush of revelation, clear as a summer day yet as limitless, hopeful, and energizing as the boundless sky above.

Someone once described satire as "kicking a guy's teeth out but making him smile while you do it." Paul was definitely not writing satire, but it's still impossible not to smile just a little bit inside, even as many of the Corinthians must have done. That's what happens when you realize that someone cares so much about you that he's willing to lay on the line every ounce of personal capital he's built up with you, to make sure you understood where your wanton ways are leading you.

Only a father or a mother could care so much. And, only a father or a mother could take such risks and do such hard, painful, potentially unrewarding work. Likewise, Paul was human. He was no lowercase god of any kind whatsoever. Yet he probably came closest to imitating God the Father Himself in his approach to the Corinthians. For God is the ultimate father, the ultimate disciplinarian, and the ultimate source of love in the entire universe.

Paul was just a man. But oh my goodness! Such a man! Such a tender yet firm voice of admonition! Such a fountain of brotherly and sisterly love, so strong it could stand up to the most gut-wrenching tests and pass without flinching, so that others could know the truth and not find ways around it.

That was Paul, and that was how he dealt with the Corinthians. But he did not do so alone, and chances are good that many of those he wrote to in these two letters felt the unmistakable presence of the same God who looked over Paul's shoulder as he wrote. It's also quite likely that the same God then peeked over the top of the words as they were read, checking out the response.

It's also been said many times that God can do whatever He wants, but He chooses on purpose to work through men so that His message will directly connect to those who need it most. Paul was one of those men, and though he certainly had to suffer along the way he did an incredible job of delivering the message God entrusted to him.

## Why Am I Writing, Too?

My goal in writing this book is to help you read the "Paul of Corinthians" and understand him better than ever before. It's also possible that you might read him and weep, not for sadness but for the simple joy of knowing that God is capable of raising up men like Paul. God empowers His own to take care of His own! Thus, 1 and 2 Corinthians present Paul at his most practical, being used by God like a hammer in a cushioned glove, not necessarily a glove made of velvet but not of horsehide either. His words come to our senses like divinely inspired responses to real situations that precisely mirror what the people in Corinth were facing two thousand years ago. Yet they are also duplicated just down the street, even today.

Corinthians is not just for the humble or the proud, the weak or the strong, the rich or the poor. It's certainly for me, but it's also for you.

We all owe Paul so much that I'm sure he'll be smothered in hugs when we meet him Above.

## About the Author

To say that Dewey Bertolini has a huge heart for people would be a sizable understatement. As the teaching pastor of New Hope Christian Fellowship in McMinnville, Oregon, Dewey delights in being a "spiritual cheerleader," working tirelessly to enable individuals to reach their full potential in Christ. A much-in-demand Bible teacher and conference speaker, every year Dewey speaks to thousands of parents, pastors, students, and youth workers across North America. Dewey and Rebecca, his wife of thirty-one years, have two grown children, Dave and Ashley, who along with their spouses, Amy and Dandy, love the Lord and are active in youth and children's ministries.

## About the General Editor

Dr. Larry Richards is a native of Michigan who now lives in Raleigh, North Carolina. He was converted to Christianity while in the Navy in the 1950s. Larry has taught and written Sunday school curriculum for every age group, from nursery through adult. He has published more than two hundred books that have been translated into twenty-six languages. His wife, Sue, is also an author. They both enjoy teaching Bible studies as well as fishing and playing golf.

# Understanding the Bible Is Easy with These Tools

To understand God's Word you need easy-to-use study tools right where you need them—at your fingertips. The Smart Guide to the Bible™ series puts valuable resources adjacent to the text to save you both time and effort.

Every page features handy sidebars filled with icons and helpful information: cross references for additional insights, definitions of key words and concepts, brief commentaries from experts on the topic, points to ponder, evidence of God at work, the big picture of how passages fit into the context of the entire Bible, practical tips for applying biblical truths to every area of your life, and plenty of maps, charts, and illustrations. A wrap-up of each passage, combined with study questions, concludes each chapter.

These helpful tools show you what to watch for. Look them over to become familiar with them, and then turn to Chapter 1 with complete confidence: You are about to increase your knowledge of God's Word!

# Study Helps

The thought-bubble icon alerts you to commentary you might find particularly thought-provoking, challenging, or encouraging. You'll want to take a moment to reflect on it and consider the implications for your life.

Don't miss this point! The exclamation-point icon draws your attention to a key point in the text and emphasizes important biblical truths and facts.

**death on the cross**
Colossians 1:21–22

Many see Boaz as a type of Jesus Christ. To win back what we human beings lost through sin and spiritual death, Jesus had to become human (i.e., he had to become a true kinsman), and he had to be willing to pay the penalty for our sins. With his <u>death on the cross</u>, Jesus paid the penalty and won freedom and eternal life for us.

The additional Bible verses add scriptural support for the passage you just read and help you better understand the <u>underlined text</u>. (Think of it as an instant reference resource!)

How does what you just read apply to your life? The heart icon indicates that you're about to find out! These practical tips speak to your mind, heart, body, and soul, and offer clear guidelines for living a righteous and joy-filled life, establishing priorities, maintaining healthy relationships, persevering through challenges, and more.

This icon reveals how God is truly all-knowing and all-powerful. The hourglass icon points to a specific example of the prediction of an event or the fulfillment of a prediction. See how some of what God has said would come to pass already has!

What are some of the great things God has done? The traffic-sign icon shows you how God has used miracles, special acts, promises, and covenants throughout history to draw people to him.

Does the story or event you just read about appear elsewhere in the Gospels? The cross icon points you to those instances where the same story appears in other Gospel locations—further proof of the accuracy and truth of Jesus' life, death, and resurrection.

Since God created marriage, there's no better person to turn to for advice. The double-ring icon points out biblical insights and tips for strengthening your marriage.

The Bible is filled with wisdom about raising a godly family and enjoying your spiritual family in Christ. The family icon gives you ideas for building up your home and helping your family grow close and strong.

**Isle of Patmos**
a small island in the
Mediterranean Sea

something significant had occurred, he wrote down the substance of what he saw. This is the practice John followed when he recorded Revelation on the **Isle of Patmos.**

What does that word really mean, especially as it relates to this passage? Important, misunderstood, or infrequently used words are set in **bold type** in your text so you can immediately glance at the margin for definitions. This valuable feature lets you better understand the meaning of the entire passage without having to stop to check other references.

the big picture

**Joshua**

Led by Joshua, the Israelites crossed the Jordan River and invaded Canaan (see Illustration #8). In a series of military campaigns the Israelites defeated several coalition armies raised by the inhabitants of Canaan. With organized resistance put down, Joshua divided the land among the twelve Israelite

How does what you read fit in with the greater biblical story? The highlighted big picture summarizes the passage under discussion.

what others say

**David Breese**

Nothing is clearer in the Word of God than the fact that God wants us to understand himself and his working in the lives of men.[5]

It can be helpful to know what others say on the topic, and the highlighted quotation introduces another voice in the discussion. This resource enables you to read other opinions and perspectives.

Maps, charts, and illustrations pictorially represent ancient artifacts and show where and how stories and events took place. They enable you to better understand important empires, learn your way around villages and temples, see where major battles occurred, and follow the journeys of God's people. You'll find these graphics let you do more than study God's Word—they let you *experience* it.

# Chapters at a Glance

# 1 Corinthians

## Part One: Seven Contagious Compromises

# 2 Corinthians

## Part Three: Seven Essential Concepts

# 1 Corinthians

# Part One
# Seven Contagious Compromises

# 1 Corinthians 1:1-16
# Fracturing the Family

**Chapter Highlights:**
• Sin City
• For Good Things
• Speaking Authority
• True Endearment
• About a Bad Thing
• Divide and Conquer

## Let's Get Started

The bumper sticker read, "Christians aren't perfect, just forgiven." Whoever mounted that pithy platitude on the back of his Ford Focus might have recently read 1 Corinthians. If you want to talk about an imperfect passel of confused and confusing Christians, meet the members of the First Church in Corinth, a church that wasn't perfect yet a church that God loved—a church that God did, indeed, forgive!

Paul was in <u>Ephesus</u> when he received a disheartening <u>report</u> of the distressing goings-on in the Corinthian congregation. As the founder of the church, he felt compelled to write them a rather pointed letter in which he took on their many issues head-on. First Corinthians represents Paul's best attempt to confront and correct their problems, heal their divisions, and answer their questions.

At the time Paul put pen to parchment, in or around AD 56, the church in Corinth seemed hopelessly divided. The leaders turned a blind eye to charges of gross immorality within the membership. They even boasted about their tolerance of such appalling behavior. Not surprisingly, they refused to exercise proper church discipline of disobedient members. And, because prostitution and perversion were pervasive throughout the city, many marriages within the church were a shambles. Confusion reigned concerning what constituted appropriate conduct during the worship services. Some members had become disruptive; others were even getting drunk by drinking the **Communion** wine.

Instead of acting like a caring and nurturing band, the members of the Corinth congregation had completely forgotten how to love one another as brothers and sisters. The church family fractured into factions. Sibling rivalries erupted over their jealousies of each other's

**Ephesus**
1 Corinthians 16:8

**report**
1 Corinthians 1:11

**Communion**
an observance that calls to mind Christ's death on the cross

**go to**

teaching
Acts 18:11

carnality
1 Corinthians 3:1

apostle
a person chosen by
God to represent
Him to others

isthmus
narrow strip of land
bordered on two
sides by water con-
necting two larger
land masses

carnality
to live according to
one's fleshly desires

spiritual gifts, even as individuals competed with each other for prominent positions of power in the church. Some members were even suing other members in open court. Likewise, many doubted the resurrection of Christ and were spreading confusion regarding the eternal destinies of beloved Christians who had recently died, upsetting many grieving friends and family members in the process.

Mind you, none less than the illustrious **apostle** Paul had started the church in Corinth. He devoted a full year and a half to estab-lishing and <u>teaching</u> the Word of God to this infant Christian com-munity. How then, you might ask, had this particular church fallen from such stellar heights to such unspeakable lows? The answer can be found in an understanding of the cultural context within which this church struggled to exist.

## Sin City Corinthian-Style

Say the name "Corinth" during New Testament times and you would have received the same reaction then as if you said "New York," "Chicago," or "Los Angeles" today. Corinth was *that* pow-erful.

If then was now, *CSI: Corinth* would be a Nielsen ratings bonanza. This notorious city-by-the-sea was the single most important metropolis in all of Greece.¹ It was a hustle and bustle of worldwide commerce, an economic powerhouse perched on a narrow **isthmus** between the Aegean and Adriatic Seas, connecting the Peloponnesus to the mainland of Greece. Forty-eight miles due west of Athens, Corinth boasted not one but two thriving seaports. Thus, it was per-fectly positioned to export its economic firepower far and wide throughout the ancient world of the Mediterranean, while import-ing the cultural corruptions of her many neighbors, including North Africa, Italy, and Asia Minor.

Given its prime location, the population of Corinth swelled to a self-indulgent collection of 700,000 sin-crazed citizens, which con-stituted a huge city at that time. Corinth hosted the Isthmian games, second only to the Olympics in prestige and popularity, thereby turning the spotlight of the world on this cesspool of <u>**carnality**</u>.

Corinth was a city in serious spiritual and moral decline, a lawless town that sounds like a throwback to the worst of our Wild, Wild

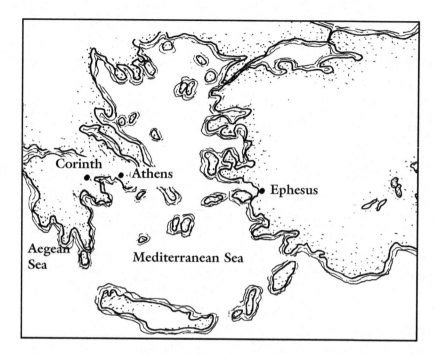

**Location, Location, Location**—Corinth was perfectly positioned to influence and to be influenced by the world.

West. Indeed, to call someone a "Corinthian" was to suggest that he was given over to gross immorality or drunken debauchery.

For one thing, Corinth was filled to capacity with shrines and temples. Its legendary Temple of Aphrodite, "the goddess of love," dominated the skyline as it towered 1,800 feet above and in full, alluring view of every thoroughfare and back alley of the city. Worshippers indulged their every fantasy with her 1,000 "priestesses," or temple prostitutes, who descended into the city every night, offering their services to Corinth's male citizens and the constant flow of foreign visitors.

As a cult goddess, Aphrodite was no newcomer to the ancient Mediterranean world. Her family tree had many branches, going back hundreds of years. Indeed, Aphrodite had a festival of her very own, the *Aphrodisia*, which was celebrated all over Greece, but particularly in Athens and—you guessed it—Corinth. Her Roman equivalent was Venus; her Mesopotamian counterpart was Ishtar; her Egyptian alternative was Hathor. In the Holy Land, Aphrodite's alter ego was Astarte, referred to numerous times in the Bible as "Ashtoreth," a deliberate conflation of Astarte and the Hebrew word *boshet*, which means "shameful" and gives us a clear indication of God's contempt for this detestable "sensuality" cult.

go to

**riotous**
Acts 18:17

**hedonism**
the pursuit of
pleasure, sensual
self-indulgence

As one example, we read this scathing rebuke of the Israelites who had given themselves over to this reprehensible religion: "Then the children of Israel again did evil in the sight of the LORD, and served the . . . Ashtoreths. . . . So the anger of the LORD was hot against Israel" (Judges 10:6–7 NKJV).

Keep in mind that Aphrodite worship flourished on the streets of Corinth as its nightly fare. The Aphrodite cult consisted of an especially perverse form of paganism, a direct affront to the God of the Bible. In Corinth, Aphrodite represented the height of **hedonism**. Intercourse with Aphrodite's priestesses was encouraged as central to the worship of this particularly sensuous goddess. Corinth thus became the epicenter of this amalgam of perverted sex and idolatrous religion. Imagine the parents who tried to raise their sons and daughters with some semblance of morality against this cultural/religious backdrop. If there had been an *Aphrodite Worship for Dummies* book in print at the time, it would have been published in Corinth.

Sadly, the citizens of Corinth fully and willingly embraced their own culture of triple-X-rated entertainment, vice, crime, and corruption unparalleled in the ancient world. Debauchery of every sort was the order of the day.

This was a city given over to a <u>riotous</u> mob-rule utterly intolerant of, and violently antagonistic toward, anything even remotely Christian. As you might expect, everything going on outside the halls of the Corinthian church eventually came inside to further corrupt the congregation in a big way. It's no wonder that the Christians in Corinth struggled in their spiritual lives, and that the church Paul planted in the midst of this morass faced significant challenges.

If you . . .

- have ever struggled to make right choices,
- are ever tempted to make wrong choices,
- have issues in your life with which you have yet to deal,
- sometimes feel confused or confounded by doubts about God or the Bible,
- have ever felt spiritually inadequate or inferior, have ever been assaulted by the corruption of our culture, by temptations that seem at times irresistible,

• ever fear that as a Christian you are a failure . . .

Then you have picked up the right book. First Corinthians was written to provide instruction, inspiration, and encouragement to struggling Christians everywhere. Christians just like you and me. Christians who are not perfect, but who *are* forgiven. So open your Bible and your heart, and let's learn and grow together.

**Aquila**
Acts 18:2

## As One Who Speaks with Authority

1 CORINTHIANS 1:1 *Paul, called to be an apostle of Jesus Christ through the will of God, and Sosthenes our brother,* (NKJV)

The first epistle of Paul to the Corinthians follows the customary letter-writing formula of Paul's day. This template typically included the sender's name and office (or his title), the name of the addressee, a personal greeting to the letter's intended recipient(s), a wish for personal prosperity or well-being, the main body of the letter (which, in the case of several of Paul's letters, tended to be much longer than typical epistles), a farewell that often included a closing greeting, and well-wishes to specific individuals, and sometimes the author's signature.

Anticipating that portions of this letter would tread on the toes of several of his readers, Paul immediately seized the initiative by stating right up front his credentials as an apostle appointed by God. Therefore his words carried the weight of divine authority. Indeed, given the confrontational tone of this letter, Paul put his readers on notice that his words carried the full endorsement of heaven itself.

Paul then gave Sosthenes a ringing endorsement when he attached this beloved brother's name to his own. Rightly so. Sosthenes's was a rather remarkable résumé. He factored prominently in the founding of the church in Corinth, the story of which goes like this.

When Paul first entered Corinth during his second of three missionary journeys (Acts 15:36–18:32), he met Aquila and his wife, Priscilla. They became fast friends and associates in the tent-making business. During his time in Corinth, Paul regularly testified to both Jews and Gentiles that "Jesus is the Christ" (Acts 18:5 NKJV). The citizens of Corinth were so violently opposed to Paul's preaching that this otherwise fearless apostle feared bodily harm. God had to assure him, "Do not be afraid, but speak, and do not keep silent; for

**ruler**
Acts 18:17

I am with you, and no one will attack you to hurt you; for I have many people in this city" (Acts 18:9–10 NKJV). This was a clear indication that there were a number of Corinthians who would receive Christ in response to Paul's preaching. These early believers soon formed the nucleus of the "church of God which is at Corinth" (1 Corinthians 1:2 NKJV).

Paul might have been assured that no one would attack him, but Sosthenes wasn't so fortunate. When Paul was put on public trial for his preaching, a riot broke out. In the spontaneous combustion of the moment, Sosthenes, the <u>ruler</u> of the synagogue in Corinth, was seized by the bloodthirsty mob and beaten senseless. Sosthenes later became a follower of Christ and Paul's "brother" in the Lord. By invoking the name of Sosthenes, Paul added to his letter the hefty weight of his partnership with this consummate Corinthian insider, a recognized and respected leader in that city's Christian community.

First Corinthians is God's written word to us, its credibility buttressed by apostolic authority. As such, it is authoritative, infallible, trustworthy, and true. It is as relevant to our lives and as authoritative as it was the day Paul penned it. This is a book well worth our study and obedience.

## A Not-So-Subtle Reminder

> 1 CORINTHIANS 1:2 *To the church of God which is at Corinth, to those who are sanctified in Christ Jesus, called to be saints, with all who in every place call on the name of Jesus Christ our Lord, both theirs and ours:* (NKJV)

Paul told his readers who he was: an apostle. He then reminded them of who they were: the church of God, sanctified saints who call Jesus their Lord. That's quite a mouthful. Let's break it down into a few digestible bites.

***Church of God:*** *Ekklesia,* the New Testament word translated "church," conveys an especially beautiful and intensely personal concept. It literally means "to call out of." "The church of God which is at Corinth" refers to those individuals whom God specifically "called out of" the mire of a contaminated Corinthian culture to be a people of His very own. If you think of the church as a circle, then the many corruptions we have earlier described take place outside

——— **The Smart Guide to the Bible** ———

that circle. Inside the circle is a divinely chosen family of people who have committed their lives to Jesus, and to one another.

*Sanctified:* "To separate (or set apart) from the **secular** for **sacred** use and purposes."[2] In other words, God separated His people from the filth of their former lives, and replaced their perversions with His heavenly purposes. He set them apart "to glorify God and enjoy Him forever."[3]

*Saints:* A word that speaks of purity. God now confers upon the Corinthian Christians this lofty though humbling title that conveys the notion that they are now a people whom God has cleansed completely and made spotlessly new, the *purified* people of God.

*Who call Jesus their Lord:* Until they met Jesus, these Corinthians were followers of their flesh. Perverse pleasure was their priority. Their appetites ruled their lives and determined their decisions. Lust was their Lord. Then Jesus came along. In His mercy, He offered them a brand-new start, a brand-new life. No longer were they enslaved to their sensual pleasures. They now had a new Master, Jesus.

**secular**
sinful practices

**sacred**
God-honoring

## the big picture

### God's Calling You!

If you put the pieces together, the implication of Paul's not-so-subtle reminder could not be clearer. It's as if Paul shouted from the rooftops for all the world to hear: "Hear ye, hear ye, Corinthian Christians one and all: God called you out of the contemptible culture of compromise in which you have been living to be His very own. He separated you from the filth of your sins and replaced your perversions with His heavenly purpose. He purified you and cleansed you completely. He gave you a brand-new start with a brand-new Master. So live like it!" For the next sixteen chapters, he will tell them exactly how to do that.

key point

## what others say

### James Montgomery Boice

Sin abounds! But it is precisely in that context and against that dark and tempestuous background that the mercy of God flashes forth like lightning.[4]

**abundantly**
Romans 5:15

**persecutor**
Acts 9:1

**thorn**
2 Corinthians 12:7

**blasphemer**
one who speaks
against or defames
God

**persecutor**
one who inflicted
pain or death on
Christians

**insolent**
overbearing or
contemptuous

# Terms of Endearment

1 CORINTHIANS 1:3 *Grace to you and peace from God our Father and the Lord Jesus Christ. (NKJV)*

Consistent with the letter-writing formula of his day, Paul next inserted a warm, friendly greeting to his readers. However, unlike typical letter writers of his day, Paul highlighted two uniquely Christian terms of endearment: "grace" and "peace."

By invoking the word *grace*, Paul reminded his readers that they were the recipients of God's undeserved, unearned, and unlimited favor, which He <u>abundantly</u> bestowed on each of them. God looked with delight upon the believers in Corinth. He favored them with His pleasure. So central was grace to Paul's personal Christian experience that he used the term 87 times in his 13 letters. He reveled in God's grace. As he told his young pastoral protégé Timothy, "Although I was formerly a **blasphemer**, a **persecutor**, and an **insolent** man . . . the grace of our Lord was exceedingly abundant" (1 Timothy 1:13–14 NKJV). Paul could not get over God's gracious favor in his life, grace that transformed a murderous man into one of God's elite emissaries. He never lost the wonder of a holy God who love, forgave, and blessed a sinner like himself. It's almost as if he basked every day in the glow of God's grace. Paul so wanted the believers in Corinth to do the same.

"Peace" speaks of the practical result of God's grace in our lives, a general sense of well-being that transcends our circumstances, a peace anchored in our intimate relationship with the God of the universe. For no matter how painful our problems or hopeless our challenges may be, God will never abandon us to face them alone.

Indeed, at a time when Paul hit rock bottom, tormented by what he described as a <u>thorn</u> God assured him, "My grace is sufficient for you, for My strength is made perfect in weakness" (2 Corinthians 12:9 NKJV). Armed with that realization, Paul was actually able to thank God for his problems, "that the power of Christ may rest upon me" (12:9 NKJV). That is "the peace of God, which surpasses all understanding" (Philippians 4:7 NKJV), the peace he conferred upon his Corinthian readers, and upon us as well.

# Thankful for the Good Things

**1 CORINTHIANS 1:4** *I thank my God always concerning you for the grace of God which was given to you by Christ Jesus, (NKJV)*

The church in Corinth had a lot of things going for it. For that matter, so do we. Before getting into the nitty-gritty of the alarming report that Paul received about Corinthian carnality, Paul burst forth with thanksgiving to God for the blessings He had lavished upon the Christians in Corinth. He thanked God for Christ's grace, His gifts, and His glorious return.

go to

**gospel**
1 Corinthians 15:1
**born**
John 3:3

**gospel**
God's "good news" that we can be saved from our sins by Christ's death and resurrection

the big picture

### Did Paul Love the Corinthians?

Make no mistake about it: Paul loved the church in Corinth. He probably invested more of his time and energy there than in any other church that he founded during his three missionary journeys. For a solid year and a half he taught, nurtured, and guided the church. He witnessed firsthand the dramatic impact the **gospel** had in the lives of people like Sosthenes, Aquila, and Priscilla. Paul saw evidence of God's grace that transformed them and many others from sinners into saints. They were now "a new creation; old things have passed away; behold, all things have become new" (2 Corinthians 5:17 NKJV).

In other words, they weren't the same people anymore. Their old ways of life, marred by the sinful choices that they had regrettably made, no longer existed. They who were "dead in trespasses and sins," God "made alive" (Ephesians 2:1 NKJV). They were given a brand-new life, a brand-new start, so much so that it was like being <u>born</u> all over again. Now that's grace!

Their many sins—past, present, and future—were now removed from them "as far as the east is from the west" (Psalm 103:12 NKJV). God buried their sins in "the depths of the sea" (Micah 7:19 NKJV). God even went so far as to say, "I, even I, am He who blots out your transgressions for My own sake; and I will not remember your sins" (Isaiah 43:25 NKJV). Now *that's* grace *too*!

GOD AT WORK

what others say

### Michael Card

To say that Jesus is the Word is another way of saying he is God speaking to us. While we struggle with our many "clumsy

**scattered**
1 Peter 1:1

words," God needs only one Word to perfectly communicate the depth and mystery, the passion and the overwhelming grace of who he is. By that Word, Light became a living being. Manna became man. Wisdom became a person. In Him, Life came to life; all that God is came to us in that One Final Word we call Jesus.[5]

## Beyond Their Wildest Dreams

1 CORINTHIANS 1:5–7a *that you were enriched in every thing by Him in all utterance and all knowledge, even as the testimony of Christ was confirmed in you, so that you come short in no gift,* (NKJV)

The Christians in Corinth were wealthy beyond their wildest dreams, not necessarily in terms of their bank statements or stock portfolios but in the things that really mattered. In a gush of heartfelt emotion, Paul emphasized that Christ had "enriched" these believers "in every thing." This statement certainly echoes the sentiment expressed in Ephesians 1:3 where Paul wrote, "Blessed be the God and Father of our Lord Jesus Christ, who has blessed us with every spiritual blessing in the heavenly places in Christ" (NKJV). In other words, every blessing that heaven has to offer has been showered down upon us without limit, so much so that we are declared to be "complete in [Christ]" (Colossians 2:10 NKJV).

When Peter wrote to suffering saints who, under the heavy hand of persecution, had lost everything, he reminded them that "we have everything we need to live a life that pleases God. It was all given to us by God's own power, when we learned that he had invited us to share in his wonderful goodness" (2 Peter 1:3 CEV). On a human level, Peter's original readers were impoverished, driven from home and hearth, and <u>scattered</u> throughout the Mediterranean world, some escaping the vicious onslaught that befell the Christian community with barely the clothes on their backs. It's important to note that Peter wrote 2 Peter from his death-row jail cell in Rome just weeks or even days before he himself lost his head to the sword of Nero, a Roman emperor of a particularly vicious and violent nature who hunted down and executed Christians relentlessly.

The paradox is apparent: Those who had nothing had everything. They were "enriched in every thing" in a general sense. They were also "enriched in every thing" in a specific sense—"in all utterance and all knowledge" (1 Corinthians 1:5 NKJV). Let's consider these things in reverse order.

*Knowledge:* The problems manifest in this troubled congregation belied their immaturity, not their ignorance. This was a church grounded in solid biblical truth, delivered over an eighteen-month span of time by none other than the illustrious apostle himself.

**doers**
James 1:22–23

**doctrine**
the teachings of the Bible

This church knew **doctrine** on a level that few others had achieved. They understood far more than just the basics of the Christian life. Their biblical foundation had been carefully laid by none other than the illustrious apostle.

*Utterance:* They knew the truth, and were in the perfect position to speak the truth throughout a city that desperately needed a word from God. Paul used the same term when he asked the Christians in Ephesus to pray "for me, that utterance may be given to me, that I may open my mouth boldly to make known the mystery of the gospel" (Ephesians 6:19 NKJV). That's what the church of Corinth should have been doing. They had the knowledge. They certainly had a city full of opportunities. And, as we'll see in a moment, they had the God-given gifts to enable them to make a lasting, life-changing impact in their city for the glory of God. Corinth was perfectly placed to export God's "good news" to the far reaches of the Mediterranean world.

Yet, with all of this, Paul lamented, "I, brethren, could not speak to you as to spiritual people but as to carnal, as to babes in Christ" (1 Corinthians 3:1 NKJV). As we will learn throughout this study, the Christians of Corinth were hearers of the Word, but not <u>doers</u> of the Word. How sad. Put this down as an opportunity squandered: an opportunity to make a lasting positive impact on their city, an opportunity to have an impact throughout the Mediterranean world. Instead of doing so, the church in Corinth eventually died, the city ultimately died, and today Corinth lies in the shadow of the ruins of the Temple of Aphrodite in a windswept pile of rubble.

## Faithful to the Very End

1 CORINTHIANS 1:7b–9 *eagerly waiting for the revelation of our Lord Jesus Christ, who will also confirm you to the end, that*

**go to**

**eagerly waiting**
Romans 8:19, 23, 25;
1 Corinthians 1:7;
Galatians 5:5;
Philippians 3:20;
Hebrews 9:28

**imminent**
something that
could happen at
any moment

*you may be blameless in the day of our Lord Jesus Christ. God is faithful, by whom you were called into the fellowship of His Son, Jesus Christ our Lord. (NKJV)*

"God is faithful." The Corinthian Christians might have failed to be faithful to their God, but God did not fail to be faithful to them, even to the very end.

These verses reveal two topics that are somewhat complex yet critically important, both resting on the rock-solid foundation of God's faithfulness: the **imminent** return of Christ and the eternal security of every true follower of Jesus.

*The imminent return of Christ:* The word translated "<u>eagerly waiting</u>" is used seven times in the New Testament and conveys the notion of an eager and active anticipation of an event that is certain to take place. This imminent return of Christ, often referred to as the *rapture of the church*, is most clearly described in 1 Thessalonians 4:16–18: "The Lord Himself will descend from heaven with a shout, with the voice of an archangel, and with the trumpet of God. And the dead in Christ will rise first. Then *we* who are alive and remain shall be caught up together with them in the clouds to meet the Lord in the air. And thus we shall always be with the Lord. Therefore *comfort* one another with these words" (NKJV, emphasis added).

Prophecy

Note that Paul included himself in the word *we*, giving evidence that it seemed perfectly plausible to Paul that he might live to see Jesus's return. So real to Paul was this possibility that he found much "comfort" in the thought.

what others say

**Wilda Green**

The Christian has mainly three points of view. Looking back to the cross, he sees his salvation accomplished in the Atonement made by Jesus as his High Priest. Looking forward, he envisions Christ's return when he will come to rule (Heb. 9:28); and this view gives meaning to all things. Looking upward between these two, he beholds his High Priest interceding continually on his behalf.[6]

*The eternal security of every true believer in Christ:* There is some level of controversy regarding the doctrine of "Eternal Security," the teaching that once a person becomes a *true follower* of Jesus, he is eternally secure in that relationship. In other words, he cannot lose his or her salvation.

The subject of the Eternal Security of the Believer opens up a whole spectrum of opinions about whether someone can lose his salvation. On the one side of this spectrum is the view that "once saved, always saved." Taken to an extreme, this view can lead one to believe that once he has "received Christ" he is going to heaven no matter how he lives post-conversion.

At the other extreme, some believe that we can never be sure of heaven because certain sins can cause us to lose, or forfeit, our salvation. Thus they live in mortal fear of committing such a sin. Within this camp, some believe that a person can lose his salvation but then get it back by "getting saved" all over again. Others teach that once you lose it you have lost it forever.

This is obviously an important issue. But let us remember to whom Paul wrote 1 Corinthians 1:8. The lives of most of Corinth's Christians were marred by behavior that was downright contemptible. May I suggest that if anyone was in danger of losing his or her salvation it would have been many of the individuals who made up this congregation of compromise? Yet, Paul assured his readers that God would faithfully "confirm [them] to the end . . . blameless" (1 Corinthians 1:8 NKJV). What exactly did he mean by that statement?

The term translated "confirm" means "to establish" as a fact, to anchor, as though to build something upon an unshakable foundation. If we think of the cross of Christ as the unshakable foundation of our salvation, our eternal destiny rests securely on Christ's death, burial, and resurrection, and thankfully not on the insecurity of our failure to live a totally obedient, consistently sin-free life. This is the *confirmation* of our security.

"To the end," means simply that the security of our salvation is without end. The security of our salvation is therefore confirmed, established upon the unshakable foundation of the cross of Christ. This security is eternal, in that it will stand forever, "to the end."

**loves**
John 14:15

**hates**
Romans 7:15

And the outcome of our security is that for all time God declares us to be "blameless." This is eternal security!

At the same time, lest we think that we can throw caution to the wind and live any way we want to live, let us be reminded that our friend Paul had some pretty strong words regarding this mistaken notion. He wrote the believers in Rome, "So what do we do? Keep on sinning so God can keep on forgiving? I should hope not!" (Romans 6:1–2 MSG). A true follower of Christ longs to obey the Savior he loves. A true follower of Christ hates making choices that displease Jesus. If a person maintains a sinful lifestyle, it isn't that he has lost his salvation. It may be that he never had it in the first place. Consequently, Paul concluded his last letter to the Christians of Corinth with this warning: "Examine yourselves as to whether you are in the faith. Test yourselves" (2 Corinthians 13:5 NKJV). In other words, a true follower of Jesus cannot lose his or her salvation. But a "Christian" who defiantly determines to live a rebellious lifestyle calls into question whether or not he is *truly* a follower of Christ.

**what others say**

**Revell Bible Dictionary**

Salvation then is God's work, by which He completely changes the moral condition of the believer, not only releasing him from sin and the prospect of divine wrath, but even making the believer able to do truly good works.[7]

## Concern About a Bad Thing

As if the Christians in Corinth didn't face enough challenges *outside* the church, it wasn't long before the problems *inside* the church started to rear their ugly heads. This was a church in crisis. A war was on for its soul. Its very existence was threatened, so much so that its founder and first pastor, the apostle Paul, wrote at least three letters to correct and confront the compromises and corruptions within. Two of these three have been preserved in his two letters to the Corinthians.

The first issue that Paul confronted head-on had devastated this young church. He addressed the age-old problem of divisions in the church. Paul did not randomly decide to tackle this one first. He understood the principle that, in spiritual warfare, just as in military warfare, "united we stand; divided we fall." There was no way this church could withstand the cultural corruptions assailing it from the outside if the church members were not united on the inside.

## Divide and Conquer

1 CORINTHIANS 1:10–11 *Now I plead with you, brethren, by the name of our Lord Jesus Christ, that you all speak the same thing, and that there be no divisions among you, but that you be perfectly joined together in the same mind and in the same judgment. For it has been declared to me concerning you, my brethren, by those of Chloe's household, that there are contentions among you.* (NKJV)

It was precisely their imperfections, their sin natures, that caused all kinds of complications within the church in Corinth. Cracks began to appear that threatened to cause this church to crumble. Paul received this disturbing report concerning their contentions from "Chloe's household," a probable reference to a prominent family in the church who wrote Paul or visited him in Ephesus with this troublesome news. Paul pleaded with the people to immediately cease and desist from further splintering the congregation, and did so invoking the holy name "of our Lord Jesus Christ," a clear implication that Jesus was as concerned about their divisions as Paul was.

Paul had good reason to be so concerned. This church had fragmented on three levels:

1. The church was divided doctrinally. They were no longer speaking "the same thing" with regard to their core beliefs.

2. The church was divided organizationally. The word translated "divisions" comes from the Greek word *schisma*, from which we get the word *schism*. It denotes a cleft or a rent, like the tearing of a piece of cloth in half. In other words, the church family had been torn into opposing factions vying for control.

3. The church was divided organically. No longer were they "perfectly joined together," a medical term referring to the setting of a broken bone. Rather than functioning fluidly like a healthy body, they were now stumbling badly, like a running back who fractures his leg. They were no longer united in mind around a

**Jew**
Acts 18:24

**Messiah**
the Savior promised
to the Jews in the
Old Testament

**apologist**
one who effectively
defends the faith

common purpose (translated "judgment"), the passionate pursuit of Jesus's Great Commission to "go therefore and make disciples of all the nations, baptizing them in the name of the Father and of the Son and of the Holy Spirit, teaching them to observe all things that I have commanded you" (Matthew 28:19–20 NKJV). Having lost their sense of purpose, this church was about to lose its very soul.

## Personality Plus

1 CORINTHIANS 1:12–16 *Now I say this, that each of you says, "I am of Paul," or "I am of Apollos," or "I am of Cephas," or "I am of Christ." Is Christ divided? Was Paul crucified for you? Or were you baptized in the name of Paul? I thank God that I baptized none of you except Crispus and Gaius, lest anyone should say that I had baptized in my own name. Yes, I also baptized the household of Stephanas. Besides, I do not know whether I baptized any other. (NKJV)*

As if things weren't dicey enough in the Corinthian assembly, each faction tried to out-spiritualize the others by claiming their own patron saints. Personality cults sprang up like mushrooms after a summer downpour.

Some in the church aligned themselves around the apostle Paul, author of 1 and 2 Corinthians and the founding pastor of the church. No doubt some of these people tried to pull rank on the others by virtue of the fact that their loyalty went all the way back to the church's beginning.

Others thought Apollos was the guy to follow, and that for some compelling reasons. As an Alexandrian-born <u>Jew</u>, Apollos was baptized by John the Baptist. Our friends Aquila and Priscilla took a special interest in him and "explained to him the way of God more accurately" (Acts 18:26 NKJV), leading him to receive Jesus as the **Messiah**. Apollos was noted for his keen intellect, accurate Bible teaching, and eloquence in speaking. He was quite the **apologist**, "vigorously . . . showing from the Scriptures that Jesus is the Christ" (Acts 18:28 NKJV). We can see why some would want to hitch themselves to his wagon.

Then there's Cephas, more commonly known as the apostle Peter. Peter, after all, was the leader of the pack when it came to the disciples. He was arguably the most outspoken of the disciples. And he was instrumental in the birth of the church, preaching the first-ever evangelistic sermon on the Day of <u>Pentecost</u>, on which some three thousand people repented of their sins and received Christ as their Savior. Indeed, the church was born with a bang, not a whimper. So Peter became the patron saint of some Corinthian believers.

And then there were the super-spiritual saints who claimed not to follow any man, but to follow Jesus only. We can assume from the tone of Paul's rebuke that these people held that fact over the heads of all others, by claiming spiritual superiority.

Paul about came unglued when he heard about these divisions. Christ isn't divided, Paul reminded his readers. Paul even depreciates his own importance by pointing out to his followers that he did not die for them! Nor were they baptized in the name of Peter. His point could not be plainer—personality cults have no place in Christ's church. We all ought to follow Christ, and Him alone.

As a personal aside, Paul expressed his thankfulness that he didn't baptize more of the Corinthian Christians, lest they follow him too. In fact, he only baptized <u>Crispus</u>, the leader of the synagogue in Corinth, who, along with his family, received Christ under Paul's preaching; <u>Gaius</u>; and the household of Stephanas, mentioned only this one time in Scripture.

Paul found the cracks within the Corinthian congregation quite vexing. The fact that one of the factions identified itself with him was especially disturbing. For Paul's mission, the purpose statement that defined his life was not to draw people to himself but to draw people to his Savior only. That's what he lived for, and that's what he <u>died</u> for. Which begs the question, "What is the purpose statement of our lives?" For the remainder of 1 Corinthians and all of 2 Corinthians, Paul will do just that—seek to draw his readers, including us, into a deeper relationship with the Savior.

**Pentecost**
Acts 2:1, 14–40

**Crispus**
Acts 18:8

**Gaius**
Romans 16:23

**died**
2 Timothy 4:6–8

# Chapter Wrap-Up

- In the first century AD, Corinth itself was a thriving seaport. But it was also a city of disturbing corruption at all conceivable levels.

- Paul's first letter to the Corinthians came in response to disturbing rumors about what was going on within their church.

- The negative things Paul heard about had arisen from purely "human" sources, reflecting sins of various kinds, at various levels. They also reflected the debased culture that surrounded the people in the congregation.

- The sins of Corinth—and of the people in the Corinthian church—though "ancient," are also quite modern, for they have been repeated uncountable times in the two thousand years since Paul wrote 1 Corinthians, and undoubtedly will be again. For much of the human condition tends to stay about the same, despite God's glorious provisions for redemption through His Son, Jesus Christ.

# Study Questions

1. How would you describe the moral climate in ancient Corinth, in one sentence? How about one word?

2. What was the Greek name of the Goddess of Love that the pagan population of Corinth worshipped?

3. Can you name at least one person whom Paul endorsed as a good, honest, spiritual leader in the church at Corinth?

4. What are the chances that the problems in Corinth could ever be repeated today?

## Let's Get Started

Webster defines *philosophy* as "a search for a general understanding of values and reality by chiefly speculative rather than observational means." Frankly, that definition does nothing for me. But you'd better know that it did a lot for the Corinthians. They *loved* their philosophy. Rather than centering their lives around God's revealed truth, they titillated themselves with meaningless dialogue about what truth is. They defined their lives by their never-ending debates about all things philosophical. Philosophy was their passion, their religion. Endless debate ad infinitum, ad nauseam about all things **existential** became their amusement of choice.

**existential**
based on their personal experience of existence

### what others say

**Jonathan Swift**

The various opinions of philosophers have scattered through the world as many plagues of the mind as Pandora's box did those of the body; only with this difference, that they have not left hope at the bottom.[1]

## Trivial Pursuit

The Athenians were cut from the same cloth as the Corinthians. Sister cities in this regard, the Athens-Corinth connection became quite the juggernaut of the ancient world's obsession with all things speculative.

You might recall how Paul engaged the philosophy-crazed citizens of this grand seaport city-to-the-south in a rather pointed discussion of their flawed ruminations. Paul stood high atop Mars Hill, literally in the shadow of the famed Acropolis, and declared to the Areopagus, "Men of Athens, I perceive that in all things you are very religious; for as I was passing through and considering the objects of your worship, I even found an altar with this inscription: TO THE

UNKNOWN GOD. Therefore, the One whom you worship without knowing, Him I proclaim to you" (Acts 17:22–23 NKJV).

The Athenians welcomed this type of dialogue. Indeed, at the conclusion of Paul's presentation, which, by the way, included a discussion of Christ's resurrection, "some mocked, while others said, 'We will hear you again on this matter'" (Acts 17:32 NKJV). They loved this stuff. And so did the Corinthians.

The Greek word *Areopagus* literally means, "Rock of Ares." Also known in antiquity as "Mars Hill" (Mars and Ares are both names for the Greek god of war), the site was used as the meeting place of the ruling council before Athens became a democracy in 620 BC. Mars Hill lies just below the Acropolis and just above the **agora**. The hill rises some 380 feet above the ground below. An ancient stairway carved into the rock leads to the top, where the intellectual elites of the day met regularly to debate all things philosophical.[2]

However, at some point, both sets of citizens—those in Athens and Corinth—crossed a fine line. Their philosophy—and this is key—ceased to be a sincere pursuit of the truth motivated by their passionate desire to know the one true God. Instead, their knowledge itself became their god.

It also seems that the entire Roman Empire was infected with this same insidious disease of the soul. As Paul wrote of the Romans, "Although they knew God, they did not glorify Him as God, nor were thankful, but became futile in their thoughts, and their foolish hearts were darkened. Professing to be wise, they became fools, and changed the glory of the incorruptible God into an image made like corruptible man—and birds and four-footed animals and creeping things" (Romans 1:21–23 NKJV). Ironically, their streets and alleyways were indeed lined with temples and shrines. Tragically, so were their hearts.

## the big picture

### Keeping It Simple

Not surprisingly, the sheer simplicity of the gospel message became for the Corinthians a stumbling block of massive proportions. Even many of the parishioners in the church at Corinth who acknowledged Jesus as their Lord continued to complicate their Christian lives by adding human "wisdom" to, and elevating it above, biblical revelation.

# A Fool's Errand

*1 Corinthians 1:17–19 For Christ did not send me to baptize, but to preach the gospel, not with wisdom of words, lest the cross of Christ should be made of no effect. For the message of the cross is foolishness to those who are perishing, but to us who are being saved it is the power of God. For it is written: "I will destroy the wisdom of the wise, and bring to nothing the understanding of the prudent." (NKJV)*

Superlatives abound in Paul's writings. He spared no expense when it came to getting his point across. Such is the case here when he handpicked the word translated as "foolishness." The word in the original is *moría*, from which we get our word "moron." In other words, Paul made the point loud and clear that "to those who are perishing" (which includes those who have yet to embrace God's saving grace, those who, in Jesus's words, are on the broad road "that leads to destruction" [Matthew 7:13 NKJV]), and those who have set themselves against God and His revealed truth, the precious message of the cross that we so cherish is moronic, something that only a moron would believe.

key point

Sounds like an over-the-top indictment until we pause to ponder exactly what Paul was saying. For example, to many people, believing in the reality of God's existence is moronic. The notion of a holy God holding us accountable for our sins is also moronic. The concepts of an eternal heaven and hell are moronic. The idea that a thirty-three-year-old carpenter's son is, in fact, God's "only begotten Son" (John 3:16 NKJV), that He was born of a virgin, that His humiliating death as a common criminal at the hands of the Roman legions paid the penalty for all of our sins—all of this is totally moronic. Likewise, the story that three days later this same Jesus walked out of a tomb alive and well is to them moronic. To identify Jesus as a great teacher who proclaimed good moral ethics is surely a notion universally embraced; but to believe Him to be "our great God and Savior" (Titus 2:13 NKJV) is moronic. You get the idea.

Note the line of demarcation by which the apostle divides the human race—a distinction based solely on each individual's view of the "message of the cross." There are "those who are perishing," and those of "us who are being saved" (1 Corinthians 1:18 NKJV). Which begs the question: Into which category do we each fall? Let's consider these two groups of people separately.

**destruction**
Matthew 7:13

**wrath**
Psalm 2:5, 12;
John 3:36;
Romans 9:22;
Ephesians 5:6

*Those who are perishing:* The verb tense chosen by Paul indicates that these individuals are in a *present-tense* state of being or condition, the inexorable result of which will be their complete ruin. He stressed the present tense because, until the day they die, there is yet time for them to repent of their sins and receive Jesus Christ, who died on that cross. Present-tense perishing does not necessarily equate to future-tense eternal <u>destruction</u>. We pray for our loved ones in that sorry condition of soul to receive Christ as we did. That being said, these are individuals who, apart from "the message of the cross," are in the present tense completely lost. As Paul reminded the believers in Ephesus, "It wasn't so long ago that you were mired in that old stagnant life of sin. You let the world, which doesn't know the first thing about living, tell you how to live. You filled your lungs with polluted unbelief, and then exhaled disobedience. We all did it, all of us doing what we felt like doing, when we felt like doing it, all of us in the same boat. It's a wonder God didn't lose his temper and do away with the whole lot of us" (Ephesians 2:1–3 MSG).

Paul got even more pointed in his opening statements to the believers in Rome when he described in some detail the present-tense condition of "those who are perishing." Or as he designates them in Romans 1:18, those to whom "God shows His anger" (NLT). Not a pleasant topic of discussion, to be sure, but one of eternal importance. Note what Paul says. See if this sounds like anyone you know and love: "The wrath of God is revealed from heaven against all ungodliness and unrighteousness of men, who suppress the truth in unrighteousness" (Romans 1:18 NKJV).

God's <u>wrath</u> or anger is never a random outburst capriciously aimed at innocent bystanders who just happened one day to tick God off. Rather, God's anger is the appropriate, determined, settled response of a holy God toward an individual's sinful choices. As he did in 1 Corinthians 1:18, Paul here in Romans 1 speaks in the present tense. That is, willfully sinful people will not only face God's anger in the future, but also, by their willfully rebellious choices, they are rendering themselves objects of God's anger in the here and now.

Paul continues, "Since what may be known about God is plain to them, because God has made it plain to them. For since the creation of the world God's invisible qualities—his eternal power and divine nature—have been clearly seen, being understood from what has been made, so that men are without excuse" (Romans 1:19–20 NIV).

In other words, God has granted to every person an inborn, innate knowledge of Himself. The fact that there is a God is "plain to them." It's as if God placed within every human heart a heart-shaped vacuum that only He can truly fill. However, as long as an individual refuses to allow God to fill that space, he will continue on a desperate search for something, anything, that will give his life meaning. Take God out of the equation and life becomes absurd. Why? Because in the depths of our guts, in the very marrow of our bones, we know that there is a God. That's the knowledge that God placed on the *inside* of us.

God has also revealed Himself on the *outside* of us. All anyone needs to do is step out of his or her house or apartment and look up, down, or around, and the proof of God's existence is literally everywhere to behold.

Think of it this way: You believe in Rembrandt, yes? Yet, you have never met him. And, you have never met anyone who has. Yet there is no doubt in your mind that Rembrandt walked this planet until his death. How do you know that he lived? What proof do you offer? How would you convince a skeptic of his existence?

Rembrandt left the evidence behind him, a portfolio of paintings, a lifelong legacy of art that to this day gives mute testimony to the undeniable reality of his existence.

Look outside. What do you see? Paintings! A breathtaking sunset that splashes a brilliant red across a darkening blue sky. Ocean waves crashing upon the seashore. Trees of every description fluttering their leaves in the gentle breeze. Pinpoints of light twinkling in the night sky above, flaming suns glowing from vast distances that our finite minds cannot begin to comprehend.

If you never looked at a Bible in your life, you could draw some rather amazing conclusions about the God who painted all of this. The vastness of space demands a large God (theologians call this "**omnipresence**.") The variety of design demands an intelligent designer ("**omniscience**"). The power unleashed in a single lightning bolt, or felt in the rumble of thunder, demands a powerful God ("**omnipotence**").

Now look into a mirror. Think about what you see. First, consider the fact that we humans can communicate. Does this not demand a Creator who Himself can communicate? Next, think about our

**omnipresence**
everywhere present

**omniscience**
all-knowing, limitless knowledge

**omnipotence**
all-powerful

**go to**

image
Genesis 1:26

proof
Acts 1:3

capacity to love, to show compassion, to forgive, and to give to others. These characteristics, or *attributes* as Bible students like to call them, are proof-positive that the One who created us is, by His very nature, loving, compassionate, forgiving, and generous. In the vocabulary of the first chapter of the first book of the Bible, we are created in God's <u>image</u>. We bear within our being a divine spark.

Every man or woman who graces this planet is confronted every day of his or her life with undeniable <u>proof</u> that God exists. We see His paintings!

God has blessed us with both an inward and outward knowledge of Himself, knowledge that demands a response. No one can be neutral, or claim indifference, to such knowledge. We either accept it or reject it. "Those who are perishing" are in a present-tense state of rejecting it, putting a lid on it, extinguishing it from their lives.

The result? "Although they knew God [in the sense that they knew He exists], they did not glorify Him as God, nor were thankful, but became futile in their thoughts, and their foolish hearts were darkened" (Romans 1:21 NKJV). To put it another way, they become moronic in their thinking. Rather than acknowledge that God exists, and that they have a moral obligation to honor and obey Him, they chose to believe that those of us who love and serve this God are morons.

Such is the condition of all who are presently "perishing." That's the bad news. Such was our sorry state before we believed "the message of the Cross" and placed our faith in Christ to save us. And therein lies the glad news.

what others say

**Ravi Zacharias**

If mankind were only mind or intellect, evidence from the physical world would be all that mattered. But there is a depth to our being; a spiritual essence that goes deeper than our intellect. That essence hungers for intimacy. The spiritual, not the physical, is the essence of our being, and . . . only communion with the living God satisfies.[3]

***Those of us who are being saved:*** Our response to the "message of the cross" is vastly different from "those who are perishing." So much so that you can go back to Romans 1:18–21 and turn each of those verses inside out to see how diametrically different our responses to the truth really are.

For instance, rather than placing a lid on the truth to extinguish it, we have centered our lives on it. Rather than rejecting the truth by making wicked choices, we strive with every fiber of our being to obey the truth by making choices that please God. We understand that God is without limit in His amazing attributes, and we stand in awe of His greatness. While the "wicked" grope about in the darkness of their minds to make sense of this crazy thing we call "life," we who love the truth are illuminated by the insights that only God's Word can provide. The very fact that I am writing and you are reading this book indicates that we long to look deeply into God's Word in order to learn as much of its truth as we can. Why? Because we recognize the central place and sheer power that God's Word ought to hold in our lives.

key point

As Peter points out so succinctly, "'All men are like grass, and all their glory is like the flowers of the field; the grass withers and the flowers fall, but the word of the Lord stands forever.' And this is the word that was preached to you" (1 Peter 1:24–25 NIV). Or as Paul reminded the Christians of Corinth when he quoted God speaking in this passage: "Behold, I will again do a marvelous work among this people, a marvelous work and a wonder; for the wisdom of their wise men shall perish, and the understanding of their prudent men shall be hidden" (Isaiah 29:14 NKJV).

## The Folly of Worldly Wisdom

1 CORINTHIANS 1:20–21 *Where is the wise? Where is the scribe? Where is the disputer of this age? Has not God made foolish the wisdom of this world? For since, in the wisdom of God, the world through wisdom did not know God, it pleased God through the foolishness of the message preached to save those who believe.* (NKJV)

One cannot help but read between the lines in Paul's indictment of those who consider themselves to be worldly wise. He no doubt remembered the days, not so long ago, when he himself fell into that category. I mean, if ever a guy thought he had a corner on the market when it came to being a wise guy, it was Paul! A reading of his abbreviated résumé punctuates the point perfectly. He writes, "I also might have confidence in the flesh. If anyone else thinks he may have

**died**
Genesis 48:7

**Benjamin**
1 Kings 12:21

confidence in the flesh, I more so: circumcised the eighth day, of the stock of Israel, of the tribe of Benjamin, a Hebrew of the Hebrews; concerning the law, a Pharisee; concerning zeal, persecuting the church; concerning the righteousness which is in the law, blameless" (Philippians 3:4–6 NKJV).

Let's break this down. The newborn Paul was circumcised according to Jewish Law as outlined in Leviticus 12:3. We can deduce from this that Paul came from good God-fearing stock, an observant Jewish family. Paul possessed an enviable pedigree, being a pure-born Jew, a direct descendant of Abraham, Isaac, and Jacob.

Of course, scores of Jews could have easily claimed these first two particular line items on Paul's curriculum vitae. It's when we get to this third bullet point that things get interesting: Paul was of the tribe of Benjamin.

Benjamin was the second-born son of Jacob's favorite wife, Rachel. Tragically, Rachel <u>died</u> while giving birth to Benjamin. That Benjamin held a special place in his dad Jacob's heart is revealed by this one fact: Even though with her dying breath Rachel named him Ben-Oni (Son of My Sorrow), Jacob renamed him Benjamin (Son of My Right Hand; Son of My Strength; the Son I Place in the Position of Privilege in My Family). One further tidbit of historical context: When the nation of Israel split in two—with ten tribes forming the Northern Kingdom, and two tribes (Judah and Benjamin) coalescing into the Southern Kingdom—only those tribes of Judah and <u>Benjamin</u> remained loyal to the Davidic Dynasty. In the annals of Jewish lore, Benjamin justifiably holds a place of highest honor. As do those who, like Paul, can properly claim a lineage that boasts such a legacy.

You've perhaps heard phrases like, "He's a man's man," or "She's a teacher's teacher," or something similar. In Paul's case, he was a "Hebrew of the Hebrews," meaning that he was a Jew's Jew. Paul possessed in abundance all the essential attributes that make a good Jew a Jew. He was thoroughly committed to all things Jewish, and observed his religion faithfully, with a dedication that set him apart as an elite follower of Judaism.

**key point**

As far as our discussion of worldly wisdom is concerned, Paul writes that he was a Pharisee, a lofty title that placed him in the rarified air of philosophical scholarship. A Pharisee was one who devoted his life to study, not just of Old Testament Law but of the volumes of traditional thought compiled over the centuries by Judaism's brightest scholars.

But please don't misunderstand. To be a student of the Scriptures is a good thing. To be a student of the Scriptures apart from the Christ of the Scriptures is a meaningless thing. And that's precisely Paul's point. Sure, he could pass the tests. He could recite chapter and verse, not only of the Scriptures but also of the centuries of man-made traditions developed by the great thinkers who went before him. Subtract Christ from the equation, however, and you're left with nothing. As Jesus Himself said, "You search the Scriptures, for in them you think you have eternal life; and these are they which testify of Me" (John 5:39 NKJV). Talk about being unable to see the forest for the trees, this was studying the **Torah** through eyes that could not see.

**Torah**
Usually considered the first five books of the Bible, although the same word is also sometimes used to refer to the physical scroll that contains those five books. It can also refer to the entire Jewish Bible, plus the entire body of commentary on the same, both written and of oral tradition.

Paul not only rejected Christ, he became Public Enemy Number One to the followers of Christ. Paul himself admitted, "concerning zeal, persecuting the church" (Philippians 3:6 NKJV). Paul boasted of his self-appointed role as a Christian bounty hunter. When he finally did submit his life to Jesus, there he was en route to the modern-day capital of Syria with one single purpose in mind: "Saul was uttering threats with every breath and was eager to kill the Lord's followers. So he went to the high priest. He requested letters addressed to the synagogues in Damascus, asking for their cooperation in the arrest of any followers of the Way he found there. He wanted to bring them—both men and women—back to Jerusalem in chains" (Acts 9:1–2 NLT). Here's a guy whose twisted worldview allowed him to claim strict obedience to Jewish Law in every respect, and yet he totally destroyed those who truly loved the one true God.

In the end, what did all of Paul's book learning net him? Well as Paul continues, "The very credentials these people are waving around as something special, I'm tearing up and throwing out with the trash—along with everything else I used to take credit for. And why? Because of Christ. Yes, all the things I once thought were so important are gone from my life. Compared to the high privilege of knowing Christ Jesus as my Master, firsthand, everything I once thought I had going for me is insignificant—dog dung. I've dumped it all in the trash so that I could embrace Christ and be embraced by him. I didn't want some petty, inferior brand of righteousness that comes from keeping a list of rules when I could get the robust kind that comes from trusting Christ—God's righteousness" (Philippians 3:7–9 MSG).

Isn't Paul making the same confession in 1 Corinthians 1:20–21? Who exactly did he have in mind when he wrote: "Where is the wise? Where is the scribe? Where is the disputer of this age? Has not God made foolish the wisdom of this world? For since, in the wisdom of God, the world through wisdom did not know God, it pleased God through the foolishness of the message preached to save those who believe" (NKJV).

Paul knew firsthand the folly of worldly wisdom.

## Full-Serve Salvation

Students often ask me, "With so many religions in the world, how do you know that yours is right?" On the surface, this question may seen too daunting to answer. Unless one understands that the premise of the question is flawed. In reality, there are not "so many religions in the world." There are really only two. For simplicity's sake, I'll call them Self-Serve and Full-Serve.

Self-Serve religion basically states that you and I can save ourselves—from everything from hell to the "human dilemma," or from whatever someone thinks he needs to be saved from. By keeping a list of rules, by doing good things to help other people, by not doing bad things that harm other people, followers of a self-serve religion believe they can put themselves in the driver's seat of their destinies, both temporal and eternal. Of this type of do-it-yourself salvation system there are too many varieties to count. Every false religion the world over falls into this all-too-common category.

Then there is Full-Serve religion. Only biblical Christianity fits into this category. Not a religion really, but a relationship with Christ in which one readily admits, "There is nothing I can do to save myself. Only God can save me. And I trust Him to do just that."

Paul divided the human race accordingly. On the one hand, unbelieving Jews and Greeks who, through their religious practices or philosophical pursuits, tried in vain to save themselves. And on the other hand, the genuine followers of Jesus, who threw themselves on God's mercy and received as a free gift the salvation that only He in His love, wisdom, and power can provide.

**what others say**

**John Stott**

Christianity is Christ. The person and work of Christ are the rock upon which the Christian religion is built. . . . Take Christ from Christianity and you disembowel it; there is practically nothing left. Christ is the center of Christianity; all else is circumference.[4]

## A Word to the Wise

1 CORINTHIANS 1:22–25 *For Jews request a sign, and Greeks seek after wisdom; but we preach Christ crucified, to the Jews a stumbling block and to the Greeks foolishness, but to those who are called, both Jews and Greeks, Christ the power of God and the wisdom of God. Because the foolishness of God is wiser than men, and the weakness of God is stronger than men. (NKJV)*

**the big picture**

**Could We Have a Sign, Please?**

The "sign" to which Paul referred is a flashback to multiple incidents in the life of Jesus, when the Jewish leaders demanded just such a sign. As but one example, Matthew 16:1 comes to mind where we read of Jesus's perennial enemies: "The Pharisees [note: who no doubt dutifully reported to fellow Pharisee Paul about this heated exchange] and Sadducees came, and testing Him asked that He would show them a sign from heaven" (NKJV). Understandably, Jesus got a bit miffed at their continual campaign of harassment. So, in His frustration, He offered them the mother of all signs, His resurrection from the dead. (In this context, it's interesting to note that Paul will make a big deal, a very big deal, of the Resurrection at the beginning of 1 Corinthians 15.)

As far as the "Greeks" were concerned, Paul was surrounded by them in Corinth. And I used the word *Greeks* not as a designation of nationality (although it also applied in that sense), but as a reference to a mind-set, a worldview, a way of thinking that, as we have seen, elevated worldly wisdom high above divine revelation. By now we know what Paul thought of that.

As far as the "Jews" were concerned, a crucified Christ was a "stumbling block" of mammoth proportions. In order to understand why, we need a crash course in Jewish Messiahship 101.

key point

Let's try a little classroom participation. If you have a Bible handy, put your right thumb in front of Matthew 1 and your right index finger behind John 21. Between your thumb and index finger are the four Gospels, the four biblical accounts of the life of Jesus (whose name means "<u>Savior</u>") Christ (a title that means "<u>Anointed</u> One" or "<u>Messiah</u>"). Flip through the pages of the four Gospels while squinting your eyes in their direction. Did you see it? There is an ominous shadow cast across these precious pages, a shadow that colors every event that happened during Jesus's life and ministry. For every word of the four Gospel accounts was written in the shadow of the imperial power of Rome—arguably the single most barbaric regime to terrorize the ancient world. It was the Romans, after all, who introduced crucifixion to the world as a way of not only killing, but also of torturing their victims in an excruciatingly painful act of sheer barbarism.

I cannot overstate the case that the Jews of Jesus's day hated the Romans. Burning in the guts of every Jew, like a seething volcano about to erupt at any moment, was the dream, the longing, the passionate desire that one day they would finally be freed from this menacing military occupation. You must understand that the Jewish concept of a promised Messiah had nothing to do with spiritual salvation; it had everything to do with a military deliverance from these Roman barbarians. As Jesus rode into Jerusalem on the back of a donkey, the people in their thousands blanketed the Mount of Olives and filled the air with their heartfelt cries, "Hosanna to the Son of David! . . . Hosanna in the highest" (Matthew 21:9 NKJV). "Hosanna" literally means "Save us now," not in the "Save-us-from-our-sins, save-us-from-hell" sense, but in the "Save us from Rome NOW and set us free from this political oppression" type of meaning.

Well, one can only imagine what must have gone through the minds of the multitudes, not to mention the minds of the disciples, when only five days later, this same Jesus was nailed to a Roman cross. The crowd as one turned against Him, shouting at the tops of their lungs, "We have no king but Caesar!" (John 19:15 NKJV). With that one statement, these religious leaders (Was Paul among them?) sold their souls to Rome. The disciples scattered. And Peter, who just a few hours before vowed to Jesus, "Even if I have to die with You, I will not deny You!" (Matthew 26:35 NKJV), did exactly the latter. He <u>swore</u> with an oath that he did not even know this Man.

**Savior**
Matthew 1:21

**Anointed**
Luke 4:18

**Messiah**
John 4:25

**swore**
Matthew 26:74

So yes, Jesus was a stumbling block to the Jews who regarded Him as just another in a long line of failed Messiahs. And to the Greek-thinkers? We have already discussed how "foolish" and how "moronic," the message of the cross of Christ was to *them*.

## Characteristics of the Called

1 CORINTHIANS 1:26–29 *For you see your calling, brethren, that not many wise according to the flesh, not many mighty, not many noble, are called. But God has chosen the foolish things of the world to put to shame the wise, and God has chosen the weak things of the world to put to shame the things which are mighty; and the base things of the world and the things which are despised God has chosen, and the things which are not, to bring to nothing the things that are, that no flesh should glory in His presence. (NKJV)*

It seems as if Paul was quite enamored with the fact that God chose him, and well he (and we!) should be. As a significantly flawed human being, Paul reconciled himself to the fact that there was nothing he could do to save himself. He readily admitted to his beloved church in Ephesus, in words that apply equally to every true follower of Jesus including us:

> How blessed is God! And what a blessing he is! He's the Father of our Master, Jesus Christ, and takes us to the high places of blessing in him. Long before he laid down earth's foundations, he had us in mind, had settled on us as the focus of his love, to be made whole and holy by his love. Long, long ago he decided to adopt us into his family through Jesus Christ. (What pleasure he took in planning this!) He wanted us to enter into the celebration of his lavish gift-giving by the hand of his beloved Son. (Ephesians 1:3–6 MSG)

Or, if you prefer the words of the New King James Version, God the Father chose us in Christ "before the foundation of the world" (Ephesians 1:4). Which begs the question, "Just what kind of people does God choose?"

Here's Paul's answer, and it's a very encouraging one: "The base things of the world and the things which are despised God has chosen, and the things which are not, to bring to nothing the things that are, that no flesh should glory in His presence. But of Him you are in Christ Jesus, who became for us wisdom from God—and

righteousness and sanctification and redemption—that, as it is written, 'He who glories, let him glory in the LORD'" (1 Corinthians 1:28–31 NKJV).

*key point*

The fact is, there are no superstars in Christ's kingdom. You and I don't have to be "somebodies" in the eyes of the world in order to be somebody to God. He delights in choosing people whom the world considers "nobodies." Because in choosing us "nobodies," He exposes "the hollow pretensions of the 'somebodies'" (1 Corinthians 1:29 MSG), who spend their lives desperately trying to be "somebody" in the eyes of anybody. Anybody except the One whose eyes really matter.

what others say

**C. S. Lewis**

No good work is done anywhere without aid from the Father of Lights.[5]

## The Wonder of It All

> 1 CORINTHIANS 1:30–31 *But of Him you are in Christ Jesus, who became for us wisdom from God—and righteousness and sanctification and redemption—that, as it is written, "He who glories, let him glory in the LORD." (NKJV)*

One thing about Paul—he never lost the wonder of it all. The wonder of how God could love him, save him, and use him as He did. Paul saw in himself, and in the Christians of Corinth, the wisdom of the God who planned his salvation; the righteousness of the God who made him righteous; the sanctification of the God who began the sanctifying process whereby Paul was being daily transformed into the likeness of Christ; and the redemption of the God who saw in Paul a soul worth redeeming.

*something to ponder*

What a way to end the first chapter of this great letter! With this reminder: "God has united you with Christ Jesus. For our benefit God made him to be [the embodiment of] wisdom itself. Christ made us right with God; he made us pure and holy, and he freed us from sin. Therefore, as the Scriptures say, 'If you want to boast, boast only about the LORD'" (1 Corinthians 1:30–31 NLT).

With Jesus as our focus, let the boasting begin!

# Chapter Wrap-Up

- Both the Corinthians and the Athenians loved philosophy more than they loved God.

- Paul addressed this by admitting that the message of the Cross truly is "foolishness" to those who love themselves more than God.

- However, he also made it clear that these two groups of people actually consist of those who are saved and those who are perishing—and it should be obvious which is which!

- Another way to look at the same reality is to think of only two major classifications of "religion" in the world—those that offer self-serve and those that offer full-serve salvation. And, of course, Christianity is the only one offering the latter.

- Jesus Himself was not recognized as the Jewish Messiah because He failed to fulfill one of the Jews' main expectations—He did not free them from Roman oppression.

- Whether God chose US for salvation—or whether WE chose HIM instead—is a question that's far too big and broad for this book. Besides, what really matters is that we are among His chosen ones, however God has arranged for us to be in that wonderful position.

# Study Questions

1. In what ways was the Athens of Paul's time a true sister city to Corinth?

2. Why does the message of the Cross appear to be foolishness to so many people?

3. Do you believe using the "Self-Serve" and "Full-Serve" designations is a helpful way to differentiate between other religions and Christianity? Why, or why not?

4. Why do you or why do you not believe that God literally "chose" us for salvation?

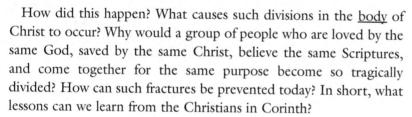

**Chapter Highlights:**
- Family Meeting
- The Third Member
- His Revelation
- His Inspiration
- His Illumination

# 1 Corinthians 2
# Reveling in Revelation

## Let's Get Started

We have a saying to describe people who share a unity of purpose grounded in a shared belief—they are "on the same page." One chapter into Paul's first letter to the congregation in Corinth, the incredulous apostle made his case that the Corinthian Christians were *not* on the same page. The sweet fellowship that should have characterized this body of believers fractured it into splinter groups to a degree that threatened the very existence, not to mention the mission, of the church.

How did this happen? What causes such divisions in the <u>body</u> of Christ to occur? Why would a group of people who are loved by the same God, saved by the same Christ, believe the same Scriptures, and come together for the same purpose become so tragically divided? How can such fractures be prevented today? In short, what lessons can we learn from the Christians in Corinth?

Like so many facets of the Christian life, the disunity in the Corinthian community was doctrinal at its core. In other words, in terms of their core beliefs, the Christians at Corinth were not on the same page. The page they should have been on is described in some detail in 1 Corinthians 2.

**body**
1 Corinthians 12:27

## Family Meeting

> 1 CORINTHIANS 2:1 *And I, brethren, when I came to you, did not come with excellence of speech or of wisdom declaring to you the testimony of God.* (NKJV)

Whenever my family and I need to discuss some matter of importance in our home, we have what we call a "family meeting." Whenever my dear wife or children call for a "family meeting," it's a sure sign that it's time to drop everything else and come together to discuss some serious issue that affects each of us in the Bertolini household. In 1 Corinthians 2:1, Paul called for a "family meeting."

strengthen your family

That's the significance of the word *brethren*, a term of endearment that underscores the familial feel with which Paul infused this letter, notwithstanding the confrontational tone Paul used in dealing with the serious sin-issues plaguing this church family that he so deeply loved. So—let's explore that word *brethren* for a bit.

Used about 190 times in the New Testament (depending on your translation), *brethren* emphasizes the intimate connection that the followers of Christ have with each other. Christians are kin, blood brothers if you like, related to one another by the blood of Christ. So important was this familial relationship to the apostle John that he chose to link it with the thematic statement of his Gospel. His two-sentence summary of the life of Christ goes like this: "He came to His own, and His own did not receive Him. But as many as received Him, to them He gave the right to become children of God, to those who believe in His name" (John 1:11–12 NKJV).

**key point**

what others say

### Charles Hodge

The Church is everywhere represented as one. It is one body, one family, one fold, one kingdom. It is one because pervaded by one Spirit. We are all baptized into one Spirit so as to become, says the apostle, one body.[1]

When you and I received Christ, we became God's children, a part of His family. As His blood-bought children we are brothers and sisters, related to one another by blood. Is there not the unmistakable implication in Paul's usage of the word *brethren* that the divisions in the church were estrangements within God's family? You can almost hear Paul pleading: "Brothers and sisters, you're members of God's family. Act like it!"

Paul then spoke to his motive, method, and message when he reminded his *brethren* that he came to them in absolute sincerity and simplicity of message. Paul did not attempt to dazzle the Corinthians with his oratory skill. He used no tricks. He did not manipulate. He steered clear of any type of technique that could have resulted in the Corinthians' receiving Christ solely on the basis of Paul's persuasions as a skillful public speaker. He was not pushing a product.

Ironically, some would argue (correctly, I believe) that Paul's abilities as a speaker were sadly lacking. He certainly did not have the reputation of a captivating communicator. Paul himself admitted

**apply it**

that the word on the streets of Corinth was that "his letters . . . are weighty and powerful, but his bodily presence is weak, and his speech contemptible" (2 Corinthians 10:10 NKJV). You might remember when Paul was speaking to the church at Troas. If you think your pastor is long-winded, get a load of this: Paul "continued speaking" (Acts 20:9 NKJV) until past midnight! Eutychus, a young man who happened to be sitting in the window, eventually fell into a deep sleep, fell out of the window, and fell to the street three stories below. You talk about someone dying to get out of church. Of course, Paul being Paul, he merely paused mid-sentence in his sermon, ran downstairs, raised Eutychus from the dead, and presumably picked up where he left off. To be sure, raise-'em-from-the-dead power doesn't necessarily translate into sermonic supremacy.

Nor did Paul engage in the kinds of philosophical discussions that they craved in Corinth. Unlike the philosophers of the day, Paul did not speculate on matters of a philosophical nature; his opinions simply did not matter. As he reminded the church in Thessalonica, "As we have been approved by God to be entrusted with the gospel, even so we speak, not as pleasing men, but God who tests our hearts. For neither at any time did we use flattering words, as you know, nor a cloak for covetousness—God is witness. Nor did we seek glory from men, either from you or from others, when we might have made demands as apostles of Christ" (1 Thessalonians 2:4–6 NKJV).

A model of consistency, Paul's sole purpose—in Thessalonica, in Corinth, and in every city to which he traveled—was to explain to his listeners who Jesus was and what Jesus did. He clearly respected the fact that their responses to the "Good News" about Jesus—to receive Him or reject Him—was a personal transaction between each individual and his or her God. Paul refused to interfere with that. Those in Corinth who received Christ did so by the power of God, not the manipulations of man.

## And Him Crucified

1 CORINTHIANS 2:2 *For I determined not to know anything among you except Jesus Christ and Him crucified.* (NKJV)

One of the mysteries of the gospel message is that it's comprehensive enough to satisfy the justice of God, to lavish upon us the love of God, and to save us by the grace of God. Yet, it's simple

**go to**

child
Mark 10:15

enough that a little <u>child</u> can understand it, believe it, and receive it. The heart and soul of Paul's message was this: Jesus Christ and Him crucified.

How elegantly simple. As Paul would later remind these same Corinthians, "God made Christ, who never sinned, to be the offering for our sin, so that we could be made right with God through Christ" (2 Corinthians 5:21 NLT). *Right with God.* The Cross was the sum and substance of Paul's message, and telling that story was what he lived for.

## The Paul You Never Knew

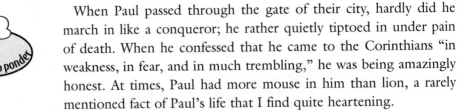

1 CORINTHIANS 2:3–5 *I was with you in weakness, in fear, and in much trembling. And my speech and my preaching were not with persuasive words of human wisdom, but in demonstration of the Spirit and of power, that your faith should not be in the wisdom of men but in the power of God. (NKJV)*

Paul was a fairly private person. We don't get many glimpses into the inner workings of his heart and mind. Only once in a great while does Paul drop his guard and let us look inside his rather complex persona. The above three verses afford us one of those rare looksees. And what we see might come as a bit of a shocker.

If your sense of Paul was that of a fearless crusader, a sure-footed man of boldness, utterly confident, strident-as-needed, unmovable, unshakable, you *are* in for a surprise. Fact is, he had his own set of insecurities. In that regard he wasn't much different from most of us. We are treated here to a very real, earthly, human Paul—a Paul not talked about in very many sermons, a Paul not ballyhooed in very many Sunday school quarterlies, a Paul some of us have never known.

When Paul passed through the gate of their city, hardly did he march in like a conqueror; he rather quietly tiptoed in under pain of death. When he confessed that he came to the Corinthians "in weakness, in fear, and in much trembling," he was being amazingly honest. At times, Paul had more mouse in him than lion, a rarely mentioned fact of Paul's life that I find quite heartening.

In fact, walking into the hostile climate of Corinth, Paul had good reason to be quaking in his sandals. Prior to setting foot in the wicked wasteland called Corinth, Paul was <u>beaten</u> to within an inch of his life and imprisoned in Philippi. They ran him out of town in <u>Berea</u>. And they laughed him to scorn in Athens. If Kermit the Frog could sing, "It isn't easy being green," Paul could croon his own chorus: "It isn't easy being an apostle." As was true throughout Paul's ministry, whatever he accomplished—from leading people to faith in Christ, to starting and establishing new churches, to mentoring men like Timothy and Titus, to writing much of the New Testament—he did so *not* in his own human power, but *solely* in the power of God, a power beyond the natural.

The next four verses sound confusing. They really aren't that hard to understand, though. And once we do, we are in for some mind-numbing surprises. Let's take a look.

**beaten**
Acts 16:22

**Berea**
Acts 17:10–14

## A Message to the Mature

*1 Corinthians 2:6–7 However, we speak wisdom among those who are mature, yet not the wisdom of this age, nor of the rulers of this age, who are coming to nothing. But we speak the wisdom of God in a mystery, the hidden wisdom which God ordained before the ages for our glory, (NKJV)*

the big picture

### Keeping it Simple—Again!

If the above two verses sound a bit convoluted, don't despair. Paul made a rather simple point, if you'll permit me to paraphrase: "Through His apostles, God is revealing new truth—call it 'the wisdom of God'—to those who are mature enough to understand it and obey it. That's what I am teaching you now. That's what this letter (1 Corinthians), and all of my letters, are all about—God's written revelation to you."

This true wisdom stands in stark contrast to the false "wisdom of the age," the kind of stuff the Athenian and Corinthian philosophers loved to discuss. In fact, to go a bit further, perhaps these two verses can be best explained in this way:

There have been periods in history during which God revealed His truth to His select servants, whom we'll call the biblical writers. These "revelatory periods" have been rare, and the circumstances surrounding them have been unique. For example, one such period

**go to**

inspired
2 Timothy 3:16

**inspired**
superintended the
writing process so
that each writer
committed God's
revelation to paper
and did so without
error

occurred when Moses walked the earth. The first five books of our
Bibles—Genesis through Deuteronomy—are the result of his hard
work. God revealed hitherto unknown truth to Moses, who then
dutifully wrote it all down in the "Five Books of Moses," also known
as the "Pentateuch," the "Torah," or the "Law."

God likewise **inspired** the writers of Old Testament History to do
the same, producing such masterpieces as Joshua, Judges, Ruth,
Ezra, and Nehemiah, to name but a few. The prophets spoke for
God, their banner cry being, "Thus says the Lord." In their writings
they often foretold future events, some of which happened within a
relatively short period of time while other prophecies have yet to be
fulfilled. God did the same during the apostolic period, with each
New Testament book being written by an apostle or a close associate of an apostle (such as Luke).

This is the doctrine of "Progressive Revelation," the notion that
the Bible did not drop out of the sky as a fully formed document.
Rather, during rare periods of history, God progressively revealed
His truth to His chosen writers, who then recorded without error
His written revelation to us.

One might ask, Is God still revealing truth today? In my opinion the
answer is a resounding "No," for this reason. In the closing verses of the
final chapter of the last book written—the book of Revelation—God
made clear the notion that once the final "t" was crossed, the final "i"
was dotted, and the final period was put in place, His written revelation
to us was complete. He said, "I testify to everyone who hears the words
of the prophecy of this book: If anyone adds to these things, God will
add to him the plagues that are written in this book; and if anyone takes
away from the words of the book of this prophecy, God shall take away
his part from the Book of Life, from the holy city, and from the things
which are written in this book" (Revelation 22:18–19 NKJV). It's a serious thing to play fast and loose with the Bible!

**what others say**

**William Barclay**

The revelation of the prophets had a variegated grandeur that
made it a tremendous thing. . . . It was never out-of-date. . . .
It was adapted to the need of every age. But, at the same
time, that revelation was fragmentary, and had to be presented in such a way that the limitations of the time would
understand.[2]

Therefore it was pretty bold of Paul to take on those who boasted of their hidden knowledge. He basically told them to take all that so-called "worldly wisdom" and chuck it. God is not into "hidden wisdom." He doesn't make His truth available only to a select few. The "hidden wisdom" to which Paul referred was hidden only until such time as God chose, through Progressive Revelation, to reveal it to the world. Here's the key: When the biblical writers wrote it down, they wrote it down for *everyone* to read and study. There is no secret truth with God, no hidden wisdom given only for the benefit of the initiated or spiritually elite.

**key point**

> ### what others say
>
> ### William Barclay
>
> Each prophet, out of his own experience of life, and out of the experience of Israel, had grasped and expressed a fragment, a part of the truth of God. No prophet had grasped the whole round orb of truth; but with Jesus it was different. Jesus was not a part of the truth; He was the whole truth. He was not a fragmentary revelation of God: He was the full revelation of God. In Him God displayed not some facet of the truth; God displayed Himself fully revealed to men.[3]

Every time we pick up our Bibles we hold in our hands the totality of God's written revelation. As Paul himself testified, "All Scripture is given by inspiration of God, and is profitable for doctrine, for reproof, for correction, for instruction in righteousness" (2 Timothy 3:16 NKJV). Note that the Bible is useful to everyone who will study and obey it. We don't need to join some secret society to get it. All we need do is pick up a Bible and read.

**something to ponder**

See that word *mature?* When we get to 1 Corinthians 3, Paul will contrast "those who are mature" with their opposite number, those who are "carnal . . . babes in Christ." He'll make the point that those who study God's Word to learn and obey it will grow up or mature in their faith. Those who neglect the study of God's Word will stagnate in their faith and their spiritual growth will become stunted.

## The Blind Leading the Blind

1 CORINTHIANS 2:8 *which none of the rulers of this age knew; for had they known, they would not have crucified the Lord of glory.* (NKJV)

John 19:15 may well be the saddest verse in the entire Bible. It reads, "They cried out, 'Away with Him, away with Him! Crucify Him!' **Pilate** said to them, 'Shall I crucify your King?' The chief priests answered, 'We have no king but Caesar!'" (NKJV).

Pilate and the chief priests are the "rulers of this age" to whom Paul here referred. Neither the spiritual leaders of the Jews (chief priests) nor the political rulers from Rome understood who Jesus was. At any point up until that fateful moment, the religious leaders could have embraced their Messiah. The Roman leaders could have refused to participate in this atrocity committed against an innocent man. Instead, the Jewish religious leaders demanded, and the Roman political leaders granted, that Jesus be executed for the one "crime" for which He was guilty—claiming to be exactly who He was, <u>God</u> in the <u>flesh</u>, the <u>King</u> of the Jews. Talk about the blind leading the blind.

Had these leaders known who Jesus was, they never would have crucified Him. But they didn't. Why didn't they? Because they did what so many people do today. In spite of His many miracles, in blatant disregard of His teaching, in denial of His <u>virgin</u> birth and sinless lifestyle, Pilate and the chief priests chose to reject the truth about Jesus.

go to

**God**
John 10:33

**flesh**
John 1:14

**King**
John 19:19

**virgin**
Matthew 1:23

**commanded**
Psalm 148:5

**spirit**
Hebrews 1:14

**speechless**
Matthew 22:46

**words**
2 Corinthians 12:4

**Pilate**
the Roman Governor responsible for ordering Jesus's execution

# Wonders to Behold

**1 CORINTHIANS 2:9** *But as it is written: "Eye has not seen, nor ear heard, nor have entered into the heart of man the things which God has prepared for those who love Him."* (NKJV)

For those whose eyes, ears, and hearts are open to the truth, what wonders we behold in the pages of Scripture, as indicated by Paul's paraphrase of Isaiah 64:4. For in the Bible we read of our God, who merely <u>commanded</u> the heavens and the earth into being, and the universe with all of its majestic mysteries exploded into existence. Of angels—countless numbers of these curious <u>spirit</u> beings—who flit here and fly there ministering tirelessly on our behalf. Of miracles and messages that dazzled the crowds and left Jesus's detractors <u>speechless</u>. Of a place called heaven, so awesome, so amazing, so incredible, that a man as prolific as Paul could not come up with the <u>words</u> to describe it. We who love God are in for an eternity of surprises—glorious scenes and sensations the likes of which we have never before seen, heard, or imagined—"things" that the worldly-wise among us have never even considered.

# The Third Member of the Trinity

The Holy Spirit is the unsung hero of our faith. Some might say that He's the silent member of the **Triune** Godhead. Though in reality, He's had a lot to say. Sixty-six books of the Bible worth of words to say. Whose words we live our lives by, whose words (as read in 1 and 2 Corinthians) we are now studying in this commentary.

He's humble enough to remain in the background, sight unseen, yet active in our lives to a degree few of us can readily recognize. As we become acquainted with Him, we'll briefly revisit two important terms we have previously discussed (*revelation* and *inspiration*), and throw in a third (*illumination*) which holds particular significance for our lives today.

**Triune**
three distinct personalities united in one singular essence

# The Holy Spirit's Revelation

> 1 CORINTHIANS 2:10–11 *But God has revealed them to us through His Spirit. For the Spirit searches all things, yes, the deep things of God. For what man knows the things of a man except the spirit of the man which is in him? Even so no one knows the things of God except the Spirit of God.* (NKJV)

Though He may be behind the scenes, the Holy Spirit's fingerprints are all over the Bible. The Holy Spirit revealed the Bible's truth, inspired its writing, and illuminates the minds of those of us who study it. Let's first consider the Holy Spirit's revelation of biblical truth, as revealed in 1 Corinthians 2:10–11.

In these verses, God the Holy Spirit revealed to Paul and to the other biblical writers exactly what truth He wanted them to know, at precisely the time He wanted them to know it. Apart from this ministry of revelation, we would never know these things. These thoughts are just too deep for us to discover on our own, since they are buried deep within the mind of God. The Holy Spirit was the perfect Person to reveal these things to Paul, because He knows God inside and out as no one else ever could. Just as your own human spirit knows who you are—what you think, what you choose, and what you feel at every moment of every day—so God's divine Spirit, the Holy Spirit, knows and understands the mind, will, and emotions of God. The Holy Spirit knows these things because He is God.

Such is the Holy Spirit's ministry of *Revelation*.

# The Holy Spirit's Inspiration

> 1 CORINTHIANS 2:12–13 *Now we have received, not the spirit of the world, but the Spirit who is from God, that we might know the things that have been freely given to us by God. These things we also speak, not in words which man's wisdom teaches but which the Holy Spirit teaches, comparing spiritual things with spiritual.* (NKJV)

It's one of those conundrums of Scripture that has kept theologians and Bible students awake at night ever since the first words of Holy Writ were penned. Phrased as a question, it might sound something like this: Who wrote 1 Corinthians? To which there are two possible answers: (a) Paul wrote 1 Corinthians; (b) God wrote 1 Corinthians. Which answer is correct? Both.

Now slow down and read this next section carefully, because here is where things get a bit dicey. Yes, it is absolutely proper to refer to the first epistle of *Paul* to the Corinthians because *he* wrote it. It is equally proper to refer to 1 Corinthians as "the Word of *God*," because *He* wrote it. That being said, this does *not* mean to imply that Paul and the Holy Spirit alternated verses. They did not confer with one another about how to compose each paragraph. Nor did the Holy Spirit dictate to Paul what to write, reducing Paul to a glorified stenographer.

The miracle of *inspiration* is that Paul wrote down precisely what the Holy Spirit wanted him to write down, and did so without committing any errors or making any mistakes. Yet throughout the process, Paul retained his own unique writing style, so much so that 1 Corinthians sounds distinctly different from, say, the Psalms or Proverbs. The *what* of inspiration is easy to define; the *how* of inspiration is truly miraculous and defies human explanation.

That's what Paul was saying in 1 Corinthians 2:12–13. To paraphrase the passage:

> As I just explained, we have received truth revealed to us by the Holy Spirit, via the ministry of the Holy Spirit called *revelation*. God gave us this truth freely, simply because He yearned to reveal Himself to us. As He revealed His truth to me, and to the other biblical writers, I wrote it down. I did so *not* using human reasoning, *not* using the terminology of worldly wisdom (like the philosophers you used to revere), *not* offering my meaningless opinions. No. I wrote exactly

what the Holy Spirit wanted me to write as He led me from one spiritual truth to the next. These truths that the Holy Spirit taught me I am now privileged as an apostle to teach you. The result of this teaching is this letter that you are now reading. You can trust it, because it did not originate in my mind, but rather in the mind of the Holy Spirit. He is the One who guided me as I wrote.

Such is the Holy Spirit's ministry of *Inspiration*.

key point

## The Holy Spirit's Illumination

1 CORINTHIANS 2:14–16 *But the natural man does not receive the things of the Spirit of God, for they are foolishness to him; nor can he know them, because they are spiritually discerned. But he who is spiritual judges all things, yet he himself is rightly judged by no one. For "who has known the mind of the LORD that he may instruct Him?" But we have the mind of Christ.* (NKJV)

**what others say**

**Blaise Pascal**

Instead of complaining that God had hidden Himself, you will give Him thanks for having revealed so much of Himself.[4]

We'll round out our trilogy of terms by considering the Holy Spirit's ministry of *Illumination*. Think of the metaphor of a light-bulb turning on in someone's mind. We often use the expression "He (or she) gets it." When you and I read Scripture, and a light suddenly turns on in our heads, at that moment "we get it." Our minds and hearts have in that moment been illuminated by the Holy Spirit. That's the ministry to which Paul was alluding when he said the following (again, my paraphrase):

Anyone who relies solely upon his own natural, human ability to figure spiritual things out will never understand the truths that the Holy Spirit has revealed to us. Spiritual truth simply sounds foolish to an unspiritual person. He or she can never discover these spiritual truths on his own because they must be revealed and explained by the Holy Spirit. I am sure that the psalmist had this in mind when he prayed, "Open my eyes, that I may see wondrous things from Your law" (Psalm 119:18 NKJV). The One who answers this prayer is

something to ponder

the Holy Spirit. He is the One who opens our eyes to His truth. Because of this, it is sheer folly for an unspiritual person to sit in judgment of a Christian's spiritual beliefs. He or she cannot know what we know since they have rejected biblical truth—truth that would have enabled them to understand who Jesus is, what Jesus taught, and how Jesus saved us from our sins. We understand these things because we love God and continuously rely on the Holy Spirit to open our eyes to His truth.

Such is the Holy Spirit's ministry of *Illumination*.

## Chapter Wrap-Up

- The Corinthians were absolutely not on the same page when Paul wrote his first letter to them. Therefore he started out as though he were conducting a family meeting, concentrating first on bringing them together, mentally and spiritually, so they could then deal with the important issues that were tearing the congregation apart.

- Paul emphasized their unity as brothers and sisters in Christ, which designation also includes you and me, and anyone else who accepts Jesus Christ as their Savior.

- Paul was truly a humble man, with many "human" failings. For one thing, he really wasn't much of a public speaker in his own right! But God enabled him to accomplish things for His own kingdom that transcended Paul's human limitations and made him a true instrument of God, able to accomplish things he could never bring about under his own power.

- Paul called the Corinthians to spiritual maturity and reminded them that only as mature Christians could they truly understand the things of God.

- Through the work of the Holy Spirit, God gives His servants (such as Paul) *revelation, inspiration,* and *illumination.* All these were essential to the writing of the Scriptures, but they are also essential to even a partial understanding of the mind of God, as revealed in His Word. This understanding is freely available to anyone who truly desires it, but it does *not* come about through our *human faculties* alone. God's truth requires God's help; it simply is not made for scoffers.

## Study Questions

**1.** What does Paul say about himself, at the opening of this chapter, that reveals his own humility?

**2.** What is the basic challenge that Paul extends to the Corinthians, after he has established his own dependence on God?

**3.** On what person of the Trinity does Paul seem to depend most, for his work as an apostle of God—and especially as one commissioned to speak for Him?

**4.** By what three "mechanisms" (if we can use that word!) does God enable His servants to do His work—and us to understand it?

# 1 Corinthians 3
# Floundering in the Flesh

**Chapter Highlights:**
• A Spade Is a Spade
• A Case in Point
• Laying the Foundation
• Tested by Fire
• Not Made with Hands

## Let's Get Started

Growth is a hallmark of health. If you have any doubts about that, take a gander at my wife's garden. I don't know how she does it, but somehow, every spring and summer, we are deluged with a delightful assortment of fruits and vegetables, all the handiwork of my wife's talent. Of course, it doesn't hurt that the soil is rich, the rainwater is plentiful, and the sunshine is just right to make for extremely healthy conditions. Healthy things grow.

While this simple axiom applies to plants and their physical growth, this health = growth principle is equally pertinent to a Christian's spiritual growth. The hallmark of a healthy Christian is that we grow in our faith. Using this same metaphor, Scripture says, "[Be] rooted and built up in Him and established in the faith, as you have been taught, abounding in it with thanksgiving" (Colossians 2:7 NKJV). That's the kind of Christians we want to be—healthy, people whose roots are deep and whose growth is evident to those around them. Unfortunately, as we are about to learn, the Corinthians were anything but healthy as far as their spiritual lives were concerned.

apply it

The opposite of our health = growth equation is also, sadly, true. The hallmark of an unhealthy Christian is what we might call "stunted growth." The Bible has a word for Christians in this sad state of spiritual immaturity. They are called "carnal." As you might expect, the Corinthian congregation included many who found themselves in this unfortunate "carnal" category. Paul addresses them in this section of Scripture.

## Calling a Spade a Spade

1 CORINTHIANS 3:1–3a *And I, brethren, could not speak to you as to spiritual people but as to carnal, as to babes in Christ. I fed you with milk and not with solid food; for until now you were not able to receive it, and even now you are still not able; for you are still carnal. (NKJV)*

**go to**

**third**
Acts 18:23

**Melchizedek**
Genesis 14:18

**apostolic**
writing with the
authority of an
apostle

**apply it**

Paul, never one to mince words, laid his cards on the table by telling the congregation at Corinth exactly what he thought of their spiritual condition. From Paul's **apostolic** vantage point, it was not a pretty picture. However, to understand Paul's level of frustration and angst over the church's level of spiritual immaturity, we need to consider the time line. Our best estimate of the year in which Paul wrote 1 Corinthians comes in at around AD 57, toward the end of his ministry in Ephesus, during his <u>third</u> missionary journey.[1] Considering that Paul spent a year and a half in Corinth, we're looking at a church at least approaching its fifth birthday. Paul had every reason to expect the Christians in Corinth to display some evidence of spiritual maturity. Instead, if you can believe it, they were acting like spiritual infants.

One of the many characteristics of little children is their inability to eat and digest solid food. Paul used this as a metaphor of their spiritual immaturity. The man who had invested eighteen months— under dire circumstances, at the risk of his life no less—teaching them the basics of what it means to live a victorious Christian life now had to remind them of the basics in this letter.

The Corinthians were not alone. The writer of Hebrews vented some measure of frustration when he indicted his readers in a similar way. As he attempted to engage his readers in a discussion of the mysterious man known as <u>Melchizedek</u>, certainly *not* a topic of Basic Christianity 101, he realized much to his chagrin that most of his readership was not ready for such topics. He rather bluntly stated, "Though by this time you ought to be teachers, you need someone to teach you again the first principles of the oracles of God; and you have come to need milk and not solid food. For everyone who partakes only of milk is unskilled in the word of righteousness, for he is a babe. But solid food belongs to those who are of full age, that is, those who by reason of use have their senses exercised to discern both good and evil" (Hebrews 5:12–14 NKJV).

Quite an indictment, wouldn't you say? The writer accurately identified the overriding issue plaguing both the Hebrews and the Corinthians. Five years or so into their Christian lives, many in the church at Corinth should have been teaching younger believers. But they weren't ready for meat—the deeper truths of Scripture. They had failed to grow beyond the basics—milk, baby formula, "the simplest things about what God has said."

what others say

**St. John of the Cross**

God perceives the imperfections within us, and because of his love for us, urges us to grow up. His love is not content to leave us in our weakness, and for this reason he takes us into a dark night. He weans us from all of the pleasures by giving us dry times and inward darkness. In doing so he is able to take away all these vices and create virtues within us. . . . Pride becomes simplicity, wrath becomes contentment, luxury becomes peace, gluttony becomes moderation, envy becomes joy, and sloth becomes strength.[2]

key point

Peter's situation differed from those of the Hebrews and Corinthians in that he wrote 1 Peter to brand-new baby believers who actually were young in their newly found faith. His encouragement to them was quite ironic when juxtaposed against the spiritual condition of those in Corinth. He encouraged them, "Laying aside all malice, all deceit, hypocrisy, envy, and all evil speaking, as newborn babes, desire the pure milk of the word, that you may grow thereby, if indeed you have tasted that the Lord is gracious" (1 Peter 2:1–3 NKJV).

Does anything in that passage grab you as relevant to the spiritual condition of the Corinthians? Peter's readers were just starting out in their faith. Because of their understandable lack of maturity, they were full of malice (intending ill will toward others), deceit (trying to trick people into believing that something false was true), hypocrisy (purposely appearing to be different than they really were), envy (jealously wanting something that rightfully belonged to another), and slander (seeking to destroy the reputation of another).

We'll talk more about this in 1 Corinthians 6:19, where we'll read, "Do you not know that your body is the temple of the Holy Spirit who is in you, whom you have from God, and you are not your own?" (1 Corinthians 6:19 NKJV). For now, we only need to understand that just as the Holy Spirit took up residence in Roman believers and in us, He did the same in the lives of the Corinthian Christians. The Spirit's presence in their lives should have made an obvious difference visible to all who knew them. But alas, to look at their lives, you'd never know that they were followers of Jesus and that He was their Lord. Their actions and attitudes were *no different* from the actions and attitudes of those who didn't know Christ. As such, Paul calls them "carnal," the polar opposite of "spiritual."

something to ponder

**go to**

**devour**
Galatians 5:15

**unsaved**
2 Corinthians 13:5

**world**
those who have no
relationship with
Jesus Christ

# A Case in Point

**1 CORINTHIANS 3:3b–4** *For where there are envy, strife, and divisions among you, are you not carnal and behaving like mere men? For when one says, "I am of Paul," and another, "I am of Apollos," are you not carnal?* (NKJV)

We might ask, "In what ways were they acting like unspiritual, *carnal* people?" Paul answered the question with a question when he asked, "For where there are envy, strife, and divisions among you, are you not carnal and behaving like mere men?" Ouch! Let's look beneath the surface to see what was really going on.

You've no doubt heard the cliché "It's not about you." The banner hanging in the foyer of the First Church in Corinth might have read "It's all about *me*." May I be blunt? The Corinthian congregation was infected with a hideous disease, a spiritual malady that caused the church members to selfishly bite and <u>devour</u> one another. Their worship services had degenerated into feeding frenzies as the brothers and sisters chewed up and spit out each other. Their self-centered, self-absorbed, self-focused envy led to "strife," a severe term that encompasses several meanings including such synonyms as *enmity, hostility, antagonism, animosity, rancor,* and *animus,* all of which, taken together, suggest a "mean, deep-seated dislike or ill will toward one another."

That's what their Sunday potlucks had become. They were acting just like the **world** acts. There was no difference between their worship services and some mean-spirited city council or contentious town hall meeting. As we saw in 1 Corinthians 1, factions fractured this family's fellowship. "I am of Paul," some cried. "Well—sniff, sniff—I am of Apollos," boasted another. Paul couldn't believe it. It was as if his year and a half of ministry to this church meant nothing. Paul could only address the Corinthians as immature, unspiritual, and perhaps even <u>unsaved</u> sinners because that's exactly how they were acting.

### what others say

**Ravi Zacharias**

Sin is not the violation of an abstract law. It is an action against a person—the person of God.[3]

# Keeping the Main Thing the Main Thing

1 CORINTHIANS 3:5–7 *Who then is Paul, and who is Apollos, but ministers through whom you believed, as the Lord gave to each one? I planted, Apollos watered, but God gave the increase. So then neither he who plants is anything, nor he who waters, but God who gives the increase.* (NKJV)

**power**
Acts 1:8

This is how it works: The Bible is taught, people hear the Word and choose to obey it, and over time their lives change. Now, we might ask, okay, when it does work the way it should, who gets the credit? Well, consider this: We didn't write the Bible; it's *His* Word, not ours. We cannot reach in and touch the heart of another person; only *God* can. We cannot compel an individual to obey Scripture; that's what the *Holy Spirit* does. We are not able to do anything in our own power; we depend upon *His* <u>power</u> to work through us to effect His will in the lives of others.

Do you get the idea? From start to finish the life-changing process in which we are but a tool, an instrument, is God's doing—He wrote the Book; He touches lives; He motivates people to obey; He empowers His servants; He does it all.

Paul was nothing more than a saved sinner-turned-servant of the Most High God. Apollos was nothing more than a saved sinner-turned-servant of the Most High God. *We* are nothing more than saved sinners-turned-servants of the Most High God. No one should be followers of us; they should only be followers of Jesus Christ. And we should not be followers of anyone else; we should only be followers of Jesus Christ. And all this simply reflects the raw reality that we can plant a garden, and we can water it to our hearts' delight, but only God can give life and cause that life to grow. This is something that those in Corinth apparently forgot.

**key point**

Yet, God graciously chooses to reward His faithful servants for their faithful service. The segue from the previous section into this one hinges on the word *Now*. It's as if God is saying, "*Now*, while it is utterly inappropriate for people to place My servants on pedestals and to pledge their allegiances to them, it is most appropriate for *Me* to honor my servants by graciously acknowledging My gratitude for their faithful service to Me."

**go to**

**labor**
1 Timothy 4:10

**teaching**
Acts 18:25

Think of it as a glorious graduation day when we shall each stand before Jesus Christ and receive from His gracious hands rewards for our <u>labor</u> and toil on His behalf.

## Laying the Foundation

1 CORINTHIANS 3:8–11 *Now he who plants and he who waters are one, and each one will receive his own reward according to his own labor. For we are God's fellow workers; you are God's field, you are God's building. According to the grace of God which was given to me, as a wise master builder I have laid the foundation, and another builds on it. But let each one take heed how he builds on it. For no other foundation can anyone lay than that which is laid, which is Jesus Christ. (NKJV)*

Literary purists generally stay away from mixed metaphors, but Paul uses them to great effect in this section of Scripture. Here he likened the church in Corinth both to a plant and to a building.

If you picture the church as a plant, then Corinth represented the field into which God called Paul to labor. If you'll permit me to use a metaphor of my own, Paul found in Corinth a corrupt culture of darkness desperately in need of the light of the gospel. The gospel is the seed of eternal life, which Paul planted in what had become a moral wasteland. As we read in the last section, Paul metaphorically planted the seed as the pioneer missionary who first brought the gospel message to Corinth. His fellow-laborer Apollos watered the seed with his <u>teaching</u> ministry.

**key point**

If we conceive of the church as a building, Paul thought of himself as the "master builder," someone who both designed the building and did some of the work of construction. He described his role as laying the foundation, a year-and-a-half-long process during which he systematically taught the people about Jesus Christ, the true foundation of the church. As he penned this portion of Scripture, Paul might have had in mind Jesus's words to Peter in Matthew 16:18: "I also say to you that you are Peter [a name that means "a small stone"], and on this rock [a huge Rock-of-Gibraltar-type rock, a reference to Peter's exclamation that Jesus is "the Christ, the Son of the living God"], I will build My church" (NKJV). This bit of a play on words was meant to underscore the fact that the church rests securely, unshakably, upon Jesus, *not* on any human being, even one as notable as Peter. The church of Jesus Christ is not built on fallible men—not Paul, not Apollos, not Peter, nor anyone else. The church of Jesus Christ is built on the firm foundation of Jesus.

The imagery that Paul used in these verses would have been abundantly familiar to his Corinthian readers. It was the custom during the Isthmian games for winning athletes to receive their crowns on an elevated platform in the middle of the city, much as Olympic athletes today receive their medals on just such a platform. Called the *bema* in 2 Corinthians 5:10—"We must all appear before the *judgment seat* of Christ, that each one may receive the things done in the body, according to what he has done, whether good or bad" (NKJV, emphasis added)—we will each mount the steps of the *bema* and stand before our Lord to give an account for the way in which we discharged our God-given duties, a judgment seat in which we will be given our rewards, not punishment. (Because, there is no punishment for us to receive since Christ received our punishment, in our place, on the cross.)

We'll comment further on this when we get to 2 Corinthians 5. Here we'll simply note that there was indeed such a *bema* seat in Corinth. Paul himself stood on the *bema* in Acts 18:12–13 where we read, "When Gallio was proconsul of Achaia, the Jews with one accord rose up against Paul and brought him to the judgment [*bema*] seat, saying, 'This fellow persuades men to worship God contrary to the law'" (NKJV). On that sad occasion, Paul was on trial for his life with punishment, not reward, as the aim. Years later, as Paul penned 1 Corinthians 3, he envisioned a coming day when he would stand on a similar seat, this time before his Lord, to receive not punishment but reward.

At the end of his life, Paul looked forward to mounting the steps of the *bema*. With absolute confidence he wrote, "I am already being poured out as a drink offering, and the time of my departure [death] is at hand. I have fought the good fight, I have finished the race, I have kept the faith. Finally, there is laid up for me the crown of righteousness, which the Lord, the righteous Judge, will give to me on that Day, and not to me only but also to all who have loved His appearing" (2 Timothy 4:6–8 NKJV). To *all* who have longed for His appearing. That includes me and that includes *you*. May we face death with the same confidence with which the apostle faced his as we anticipate receiving our rewards.

# Tested by Fire

*1 CORINTHIANS 3:12–15 Now if anyone builds on this foundation with gold, silver, precious stones, wood, hay, straw, each one's work will become clear; for the Day will declare it, because it will be revealed by fire; and the fire will test each one's work, of what sort it is. If anyone's work which he has built on it endures, he will receive a reward. If anyone's work is burned, he will suffer loss; but he himself will be saved, yet so as through fire. (NKJV)*

The "Day" to which Paul refers is a coming day of judgment for every Christian. Once again let me stress that this judgment is *not* for the purpose of God's meting out punishment, but rather for graciously conferring upon His servants our rewards. You might think of it this way: On Graduation Day, every high school or college grad receives his or her diploma. Each graduate will enjoy the privileges that accompany his or her diploma or degree.

But, there are always those who receive extra honors conferred upon them for outstanding academic achievement. While everyone else in a graduation ceremony might wear a black tassel, the honored graduates get to wear a gold one. They might wear gold ropes around their necks. In looking back to my own graduation, I recall that we doctoral graduates got to wear fancy hoods with our gowns. Some of the guys really thought that was something, and strutted around the auditorium looking like a flock of peacocks showing off their feathers. The lowly master's grads had hoods too, but not nearly as grand as the doctoral candidates.

The difference in this case is that there will be no reason for us to strut our stuff on the *bema*, because any rewards that we may receive are granted to us only by God's grace. Much like the scene in Revelation 4:9–11: "Whenever the living creatures give glory and honor and thanks to Him who sits on the throne, who lives forever and ever, the twenty-four elders fall down before Him who sits on the throne and worship Him who lives forever and ever, and *cast their crowns before the throne*, saying: 'You are worthy, O Lord, to receive glory and honor and power; for You created all things, and by Your will they exist and were created'" (NKJV, emphasis added). If holy angels respond with such humility, how much more will we? I have no doubt that we will look upon what God accomplished through such significantly flawed individuals as ourselves with equal

key point

wonder and humility! Perhaps we too will cast our rewards before His throne in humble recognition that He alone deserves the praise for any achievements He may graciously reward.

what others say

### F. F. Bruce

The wisdom which created the worlds and maintains them in their due order may well beget in us a sense of wondering awe, but the grace which has provided a remedy for the defilement of sin by a life freely offered up to God on our behalf calls forth a sense of personal indebtedness, which the contemplation of divine activity on the cosmic scale could never evoke.[4]

**go to**

**judgment**
Matthew 25:41

**refiner's**
Revelation 3:18

**judgment**
1 Peter 1:17–18

**world**
1 John 2:15

Paul continued to milk the building metaphor when he compared our "work" to two categories of building materials—those of durable quality (gold, silver, precious stones) and those that easily decay (wood, hay, straw). Fire is a common biblical metaphor used to symbolize God's <u>judgment</u>, a <u>refiner's</u> fire, and here God's discerning <u>judgment</u>. Again, this is judgment for the sake of rewards, not punishment.

While Paul does not specifically detail the differences between works that are rewarded and those that are "burned" up, we can certainly surmise what he most likely intended to convey. For instance, Christ's servants who are motivated to do what they do by a lust for power, popularity, or prosperity will most likely see their works incinerated right before their eyes. Though they may have done good things and helped people, the errant motives may disqualify them from receiving any rewards because, in the words of Jesus, "Assuredly, I say to you, they have their reward" (Matthew 6:5 NKJV). This Jesus spoke in reference to the power-hungry, applause-driven "hypocrites [who] love to pray standing in the synagogues and on the street corners to be seen by men. I tell you the truth, they have received their reward in full" (6:5 NIV). Their rewards came in the form they sought—their power over, and recognition of, the people they led.

Did Paul include in this passage a not-so-gentle jab at the Corinthians? As a congregation, they were strategically placed in a world of hurt, a city whose spiritual needs cried out to the heavens. Yet, they were so busy fighting among themselves that they were completely oblivious as to whom the real enemies were—the <u>world</u>,

**go to**

**flesh**
Romans 7:18

**devil**
1 Peter 5:8

**immorality**
1 Corinthians 6:18

**drunk**
1 Corinthians 11:21

the <u>flesh</u>, and the <u>devil</u>. Instead of standing against the decadence of downtown Corinth, they had become just like Corinth. Rather than resisting the pull of their flesh, they gave into their flesh even to the point of committing open <u>immorality</u> and even getting <u>drunk</u> on the Communion wine. Forget about striving against the devil; these Christians played right into his hands by allowing him to tear their fellowship apart at the seams. Their works would surely be burned to a crisp. How about ours?

## A Dwelling Not Made with Hands

*1 CORINTHIANS 3:16–17 Do you not know that you are the temple of God and that the Spirit of God dwells in you? If anyone defiles the temple of God, God will destroy him. For the temple of God is holy, which temple you are. (NKJV)*

Stephen got it right when he declared, in the shadow of the temple no less, "The Most High does not dwell in temples made with hands" (Acts 7:48 NKJV). God has chosen to dwell both within us and within the collective gathering of His people, which He calls "the church." When we get to 1 Corinthians 6, Paul will make the case that God dwells *within* us since our bodies are "the temple of the Holy Spirit who is in you" (1 Corinthians 6:19 NKJV). Here, he states emphatically that God similarly dwells *among* us when we come together in corporate worship. In that sense, a church—be it the church in Corinth or the church you faithfully attend each week—*is* God's temple.

**what others say**

**Lawrence O. Richards**
Only Christ's active support enables the universe and all processes in it to continue operation.[5]

The Christians in Corinth were engaged in behaviors that were being used by the enemy to destroy Christ's witness in that desperately needy city. In the eyes of God, theirs was not some minor infraction deserving a simple slap on the hand. This was a spiritual assault focused precisely on the one place of hope in an otherwise hopeless city. Those whose actions weakened and eventually destroyed the church will stand before God one day and give an account to Him for what they did. And when they do, He will not be pleased.

## People Are People

1 CORINTHIANS 3:18–21a *Let no one deceive himself. If anyone among you seems to be wise in this age, let him become a fool that he may become wise. For the wisdom of this world is foolishness with God. For it is written, "He catches the wise in their own craftiness"; and again, "The LORD knows the thoughts of the wise, that they are futile." Therefore let no one boast in men.* (NKJV)

While it may seem strange that Paul would revisit a topic he addressed two chapters ago, let us remember that Paul was not writing a book in the standard chapter-by-chapter format to which we are accustomed. He wrote a letter, an intensely practical, sometimes pointed, and in some places personal letter to a church he founded and loved. In reality, despite the arbitrary chapter divisions in our Bibles, he never actually left the topic of worldly wisdom and its devastating and divisive impact on a church.

key point

Paul warns those in Corinth that they ought not to allow themselves to be deceived into thinking that just because certain individuals hold positions of influence in a community they automatically have the spiritual qualifications to lead the church.

First and foremost, God looks for teachable humility in those who would lead His work. That's the essence of what Paul meant when he told the "wise in this age" to "become a fool that he may become [truly] wise" (1 Corinthians 3:18 NKJV).

To punctuate his point, Paul quoted Job 5:13 and Psalm 94:11. In both cases, God made clear that He is not impressed by a person's résumé. What often impresses us means nothing to God. It's the old story: "The LORD said to Samuel, 'Do not look at his appearance or at his physical stature, because I have refused him. For the LORD does not see as man sees; for man looks at the outward appearance, but the LORD looks at the heart'" (1 Samuel 16:7 NKJV).

**go to**

preached
Acts 2:14

# Only God Is God

1 CORINTHIANS 3:21b–23 *For all things are yours: whether Paul or Apollos or Cephas, or the world or life or death, or things present or things to come—all are yours. And you are Christ's, and Christ is God's.* (NKJV)

If Paul's final statement in 1 Corinthians 3 leaves you scratching your head as to its meaning, you are not alone. This is Paul's passionate appeal for the church in Corinth to come back together in unity. Don't see it there? Let's take it phrase by phrase and attempt to arrive at exactly what Paul was saying. Paul's final appeal can be paraphrased in the following "Big Picture."

## the big picture

### Paraphrasing Paul . . .

Dear Christians in Corinth, Please! Stop bragging about your achievements, or those of the men you follow. We are not in competition with one another. Everything you have has been given to you by God as His special blessing to enrich your life. I, Paul, am just a humble servant whom God sent to you as a gift to bring the gospel message to your city. Apollos was a gift from God to teach you and establish you in your faith. Peter was a gift from God who <u>preached</u> the first gospel message ever and got the whole thing going. All of the beautiful sights and sounds this world has to offer are gifts from God for you to enjoy. Life itself is a gift from God for you to experience to the full. Even death is a blessing since it is a doorway to heaven where you will live with Jesus forever. Think about the many things you can be thankful for right now, right here in the present. Look to the future and all of the blessings that God will shower upon you tomorrow. You are blessed people who are joined together as one with Christ, just as Christ is one with God. Now, put your petty little differences aside and start acting like it.

# Chapter Wrap-Up

- Most living things tend to grow throughout most of their life-times—if not in physical size, then into greater physical, mental, and (ideally!) spiritual maturity. But the Corinthians were behaving like spiritual infants.

- In particular, the members of the church at Corinth were behaving in very petty ways, with lots of envy and strife between them. They were also proclaiming their loyalty to various leaders, including both Paul and Apollos, when they should have been loyal only to Christ Himself.

- Paul used two basic analogies to make a fundamental point. Workers like himself are only "planters" and "waterers" who do not cause the plants to grow—they simply do their job while God Himself brings about the increase.

- Likewise, no one with any sense tries to build a building without first establishing a solid foundation. But any such spiritual foundation, undergirding our own growth as Christians, cannot be made of false "works" of our own hands.

- Only when we build our foundations on God's Word, and on the example of Jesus Christ Himself, will the Holy Spirit come to dwell within. We are not in competition with one another; we all have access to the same eternal truths, and the same limitless spiritual resources that God the Father, Christ the Son, and the Holy Spirit—together—provide.

## Study Questions

1. Who were two of the people that some of the Corinthians were claiming to follow, rather than Jesus Christ?

2. What are the two main metaphors that Paul uses in this chapter, to illustrate how Christians must grow in their individual walks with God?

3. Do the plaudits of the world carry any weight with God—that is, if you win every contest you enter, will God be impressed?

4. What do you think might be the most important qualification for a leadership position in God's church?

# 1 Corinthians 4
# Corinthians at a Crossroad

## Let's Get Started

I recently had a flashback to my elementary school days. Out on the playground during recess, I once got into a fight with a friend over my less-than-discreet declaration, "My dad is better than your dad." "Nah-uh," he promptly replied. "*My* dad is better than *your* dad." Of course, it never once occurred to us, nor would it have mattered, that neither of us had ever met the other's dad. We were just a couple of kids getting into a childlike fight over nothing of any substance.

It's one thing when children boast and brag about their natural fathers. In fact, on some level, there's a bit of a heartwarming side to the story, isn't there? But it's quite another thing, a pathetic thing, when grown-ups act like kids—in the case of the Corinthian Christians, boasting and bragging about their spiritual fathers. This congregation of Christ's followers was engaged in the first-century equivalent to a playground brawl, over nothing.

## A Storm a-Brewin'

By this point in Paul's letter we have become acutely aware of the divisions that split the congregation in Corinth. We have discussed in some detail how one group boasted to another that they followed Paul, or Apollos, or Peter, or Christ. On the surface, the Christians in Corinth seemed to compare the achievements of one leader to another, and accordingly align themselves behind their chosen patron saint. But there was something even more sinister afoot, something that's all-too-common in churches today.

**what others say**

**Earl Radmacher**

Don't become preoccupied with the agents God uses to accomplish his work.[1]

**Potiphar**
Genesis 39:1

Storm clouds had gathered over the seaport city. A tempest was raging just beneath the surface, one that was about to break forth with hurricane strength. It had nothing to do with Peter or Apollos, but it had everything to do with Paul. We get just the first inklings of it in this section of Scripture. It portended difficult days for Paul, as we'll discover more and more throughout the remainder of 1 and 2 Corinthians.

## A Matter of Trust

*1 CORINTHIANS 4:1–2 Let a man so consider us, as servants of Christ and stewards of the mysteries of God. Moreover it is required in stewards that one be found faithful. (NKJV)*

key point

Paul states his case: Whether we be apostles or ministers, we are servants, nothing more. The type of servant that Paul humbly called to mind was that of a galley slave, the lowliest and most dreaded type of slavery known throughout the Roman Empire. Galley slaves were consigned to the bowels of a ship, chained there to oars, and assigned the ignoble duty of rowing to the relentless cadence set by their overseer. These slaves served in squalid conditions, hidden from sight yet essential to the security of the ship. If speed was needed, they provided it. If a call to arms was sounded, they propelled the ship into battle. If cut-and-run became essential to the ship's survival, these men put their shoulders to their oars and rowed the ship to safety.

That's how Paul viewed himself—not as the "super apostle," not as the author second only to Luke for the sheer volume of his written revelations, not as the founder of many churches that spanned several cities, not as the first foreign missionary, and not as the leader of Christ's cause, but as a slave; as the lowliest of slaves.

Yet he was also a steward, a slave whom his master places in charge of his entire operation, even including his household in some cases. You might remember that the Egyptian military officer <u>Potiphar</u> placed Joseph in exactly this kind of a position over his household. Potiphar's military obligations required him to be away from home for extended amounts of time, so he entrusted the oversight of his household to Joseph.

The one virtue demanded by such a position was that the steward be found faithful. That is, that he conduct himself in such a trustworthy manner that the master need not give a thought or have a concern about how his affairs were being handled. These two images—galley slave and steward—form a beautiful duet of descriptions. Paul regarded himself as no more than the lowliest of slaves, yet one whom his Master elevated to a position of great trust. His one ambition in life was to faithfully discharge his duty in a manner that pleased his Master.

**polemic**
a refutation of another's principles or practice

However, Paul wasn't entrusted merely with the oversight of someone's home. His responsibility was infinitely greater. God entrusted to Paul "the mysteries of God." We encountered this word *mysteries* back in 1 Corinthian 2:7. Simply stated, God entrusted to His servant the written revelation of God that Paul, as an apostle, was writing even as he composed this first letter to the church in Corinth. As one of God's messengers, Paul devoted himself to making absolutely sure that he discharged his duty faithfully, so that what he wrote accurately reflected exactly what God was revealing to the world through him. Paul rightly saw his obligation as a sacred trust, one that he longed to fulfill in a way that pleased his Master. Once again, we see evidence of Paul's humility in that he directed all attention away from himself and placed it where it belonged, with his Master, Jesus Christ.

## A Handbook on How to Handle Criticism

1 CORINTHIANS 4:3–5 *But with me it is a very small thing that I should be judged by you or by a human court. In fact, I do not even judge myself. For I know of nothing against myself, yet I am not justified by this; but He who judges me is the Lord. Therefore judge nothing before the time, until the Lord comes, who will both bring to light the hidden things of darkness and reveal the counsels of the hearts. Then each one's praise will come from God.* (NKJV)

Okay, Paul, what's the deal? What's with all the talk about "a very small thing that I should be judged by you," or "judge nothing before the time"?

To answer these questions I must introduce you to a type—or genre—of literature, called a "polemic." As explained in the definition in the margin (because it bears repeating), a **polemic** is a refutation of someone else's principles or practice, which certainly can include that person's behavior. So, when an author writes in a polemical style, he is defining and correcting on paper the errant views or behaviors of the one to whom he is writing.

It should come as no surprise that Paul wrote often in just such a style. Specifically, Paul wrote the first six chapters of 1 Corinthians as a polemic in which he identified, confronted, and corrected the Corinthian Christians' errant behaviors and beliefs. (In chapters 7–16, Paul appropriately changed his style as he answered a series of questions that the church had sent him.) Thus, when Paul confronted the divisions in the church, he identified the problem and attempted to correct it. That's an absolutely classic polemic.

Here, in chapter 4, Paul addressed something intensely and painfully personal, and did so as a polemic. A significant number of the Christians in Corinth had turned against Paul and had become critical of him as a leader. In a word, they were *judging* him. Paul doesn't say so specifically, but we can infer that this was the case because he alludes to it in his characteristically confrontational fashion. Apparently, many in the Apollos and Cephas (Peter) camps were calling Paul's authority as an apostle into question. I say apparently because Paul did not lay out the specifics of the problem in any detail. But on the other hand, he didn't need to. It was widely known throughout the church that a segment of the congregation was highly critical of Paul, something all-too-common in churches today. Just ask anyone who's ever been a pastor. For Paul, and for pastors today, this kind of criticism went with the territory.

apply it

Now, two thousand years later, we can only surmise the specifics of the situation based upon Paul's refutation of the congregation's errant beliefs and behavior. But what Paul taught while confronting their criticisms becomes quite instructive to any of us who have been unfairly or wrongly attacked by another Christian. We could look upon this section of Scripture as a handbook on how to handle undeserved criticism.

Paul's basic approach to his critics? He essentially told the church, "I don't care if you judge me." He told them, "Look—it doesn't matter to me if I am judged by you, or even if I am judged by a court of law," thus adding a dash of hyperbole to the mix as well.

He then asserted that he knew of no proper basis for anyone to criticize him; his conscience was clear. He even (and this I truly admire) refused to beat himself up—"I do not even judge myself." The reason he was able to respond to harsh criticism in this way was that he wasn't accountable to the Corinthians. He was accountable to his Lord. He was content to let Jesus Christ "bring to light the hidden things of darkness and reveal" those things buried in his heart.

**God-given**
1 Corinthians 1:1

## Gifts from God

> 1 CORINTHIANS 4:6–7 *Now these things, brethren, I have figuratively transferred to myself and Apollos for your sakes, that you may learn in us not to think beyond what is written, that none of you may be puffed up on behalf of one against the other. For who makes you differ from another? And what do you have that you did not receive? Now if you did indeed receive it, why do you boast as if you had not received it? (NKJV)*

The situation had become personal. One faction puffed itself up by boasting that their patron pastor was superior to all others, while lowering themselves at the same time to committing a reprehensible form of character assassination by sullying the reputations of competing spiritual leaders. Paul found himself squarely in the crosshairs, as every faction except the "I am of Paul" group tried to discredit their church's founding apostle.

With what must have been an agonizing combination of disbelief and personal pain, Paul conceded that he used himself and Apollos as examples of this hideous form of class warfare that had infiltrated the church. He urged the church to take to heart his written words, knowing that he wrote the written revelation of God buttressed by his God-given authority as an apostle. He did all of this in 1 Corinthians 4:6.

Then in verse 7, he came right back at them with this well-deserved rebuke: "What gives you the right to make such a judgment? What do you have that God hasn't given you? And if everything you have is from God, why boast as though it were not a gift?" (NLT). They had no right to pit one pastor against another. They were outright sinful to boast about the one while judging another.

Of what did they have to boast? They had done nothing to earn the ministry of these men; their godly leaders did what they did because God called them to do it. Of what did they have to judge their leaders? The Christians in Corinth failed to understand a fundamental fact that applies as much to pastors and Christian leaders today as it did back then: Our pastors and other Christian leaders are gifts given to us by God. For as Paul taught the believers in Ephesus, "He Himself gave some to be apostles, some prophets, some evangelists, and some pastors and teachers, for the equipping of the saints for the work of ministry, for the edifying of the body of Christ, till we all come to the unity of the faith and of the knowledge of the Son of God, to a perfect man, to the measure of the stature of the fullness of Christ" (Ephesians 4:11–13 NKJV).

key point

**what others say**

**Dietrich Bonhoeffer**

I have community with others and I shall continue to have it only through Jesus Christ. The more genuine and the deeper our community becomes, the more will everything else between us recede, the more clearly and purely will Jesus Christ and his work become the one and only thing that is vital between us. We have one another only through Christ, but through Christ we do have one another, wholly, and for all eternity.[2]

## A Selfless Service

1 CORINTHIANS 4:8–13 *You are already full! You are already rich! You have reigned as kings without us—and indeed I could wish you did reign, that we also might reign with you! For I think that God has displayed us, the apostles, last, as men condemned to death; for we have been made a spectacle to the world, both to angels and to men. We are fools for Christ's sake, but you are wise in Christ! We are weak, but you are strong! You are distinguished, but we are dishonored! To the present hour we both hunger and thirst, and we are poorly clothed, and beaten, and homeless. And we labor, working with our own hands. Being reviled, we bless; being persecuted, we endure; being defamed, we entreat. We have been made as the filth of the world, the offscouring of all things until now. (NKJV)*

**Incarnation**
God in human flesh; the Son of God took upon Himself true humanity in Jesus and became "Immanuel"—"God with us."

## the big picture

### Let's Get Real!

For Paul, Apollos, Peter, et al., serving Christ was hard enough, without seeing the fruit of their selfless service going up in flames because of the carnality that characterized the Christians at Corinth. On the one hand, Paul was absolutely mystified that any group in the church would place any of them on a pedestal; they just didn't understand how difficult it already was to be Christ's servant. They were suffering enough at the hands of Christ's opponents outside the church; the last thing they needed was to suffer at the hands of Christ's so-called followers inside the church. The time had come for the Corinthian Christians to get a reality check.

The sarcasm that poured forth from Paul's pen is nothing short of breathtaking. These so-called followers of Christ thought they were spiritually full, when in reality they were only full of themselves; they thought they were rich, when in reality they were spiritually impoverished; they thought they were wise, when all the while they acted like spiritual simpletons. Self-righteous, self-satisfied, filled with a misplaced sense of their own self-importance. Paul's rebuke dripped with sarcasm.

One can't help but link Paul's rebuke of the Corinthian church to Jesus's rebuke of the Laodicean church, arguably the single most stinging rebuke in all of Scripture. Jesus addressed this equally self-focused, self-satisfied, self-righteous congregation by saying, "I know your works, that you are neither cold nor hot. I could wish you were cold or hot. So then, because you are lukewarm, and neither cold nor hot, I will vomit you out of My mouth. Because you say, 'I am rich, have become wealthy, and have need of nothing'— and do not know that you are wretched, miserable, poor, blind, and naked" (Revelation 3:15–17 NKJV). That was what life had become in Laodicea, and that was what life had become in Corinth.

something to ponder

## what others say

### Ravi Zacharias

When man lives apart from God, chaos is the norm. When man lives with God, as revealed in the **Incarnation** of Jesus Christ, the hungers of the mind and heart find their fulfillment. For in Christ we find coherence and consolation as he reveals to us, in the most verifiable terms of truth and experience, the nature of man, the nature of reality, the nature of history, the nature of our destiny, and the nature of suffering.[3]

These immature Christians needed to learn a lesson from the apostles as to what it really meant to follow Jesus. Far from thinking that they were full, rich, and self-satisfied, the apostles were reminded every day of the cost of following Christ, a price the Christians in Corinth were unwilling to pay. For if the members of that congregation got serious about making an impact in their morally bankrupt community, they too would have put their lives at risk just like the apostles, who regarded themselves "as men condemned to death." They too would have stood out as a spectacle to that sin-crazed city. They too would have been regarded as fools, rather than proclaiming themselves to be so wise. They too would have been weakened by the spiritual warfare they would have encountered, instead of boasting about how spiritually superior they were.

Does Paul's sarcasm begin to make some sense? The people to whom he wrote didn't have a clue about what it meant to be true disciples of Christ. Do you think that they were willing to "both hunger and thirst," to be "poorly clothed, beaten, and homeless," if that was the price they had to pay for taking a godly stand in the midst of their sinful city? Were they willing to be reviled, persecuted, or defamed for their faith?

If the previous section saw Paul's words dripping with sarcasm, he totally changed his approach in the remainder of chapter 4. Here, Paul became paternal in tone, writing as a loving father offering gentle correction to his disobedient children.

## Paul's Heartfelt Plea

> 1 CORINTHIANS 4:14–16 *I do not write these things to shame you, but as my beloved children I warn you. For though you might have ten thousand instructors in Christ, yet you do not have many fathers; for in Christ Jesus I have begotten you through the gospel. Therefore I urge you, imitate me.* (NKJV)

Paul realized that his words were harsh. He knew that if his original readers took them to heart, they would feel ashamed of their behavior. He assured them that he did not write to shame them. He loved them as a dad loves his kids, even though they were behaving as disobedient children. He sincerely wanted the best for them.

But to receive God's best, they had to correct their behavior. Like a responsible parent, he could not allow his children to continue to make sinful choices. The divisions in the church represented just the first of many areas of compromise that Paul had to correct. He knew there was more to come, much more, twelve chapters more, and that much of it would be painfully confrontational. So he offered a respite in his rebuke to assure his readers of his love, and to reinforce in their minds his genuine motive—"As my beloved children I [write to] warn you."

Paul then played his trump card. In a manner of speaking, he pulled rank on them. Despite their various allegiances to the other Christian leaders who instructed them in God's Word, they had only one father—Paul, the founding father of their church.

**Aquila**
Acts 18:2

Paul was the first to bring the gospel to Corinth. He led the first believers to Christ, <u>Aquila</u> and Priscilla. He labored there for eighteen months, systematically grounding them in the basic truths of their newfound faith. Spiritually speaking, everything they were and everything they had they owed to Paul. Yet in their arrogance, some had placed him on a pedestal, to the ridicule and rejection of their other leaders, while others had turned against him and in defense of their patron saints were casting aspersions, assassinating his character, and demeaning his apostolic authority. Both extremes were equally reprehensible to Paul, because both were equally damaging to the witness of Christ in their corrupt community.

Paul drew a line in the sand with his bold command: "Imitate me." Imitate him in what? Imitate him in becoming a humble servant of Christ. Imitate him in looking upon their leaders as gifts given to them by God and humbly submitting to their spiritual oversight. Imitate him in standing firm against the sin in their city, even if it meant that they would become reviled, persecuted, or defamed for their faith. Or to put it more simply, Paul wanted the Corinthian Christians to imitate him by stopping their sinful behavior and starting to obey God's Word.

**key point**

## <u>Help Is on the Way</u>

1 CORINTHIANS 4:17 *For this reason I have sent Timothy to you, who is my beloved and faithful son in the Lord, who will remind you of my ways in Christ, as I teach everywhere in every church.* (NKJV)

**Ephesus**
1 Timothy 1:3

As we'll see in a bit, Paul desperately wanted to travel to Corinth in order to set things in order in what had become a very disorderly church. But he was tied up in Ephesus, ministering to the believers there. Yet, so perilous had the situation become that he dispatched his number one deputy, Timothy (who would one day pastor the church in <u>Ephesus</u>), to implement much of the corrective contents of this letter.

Timothy and Paul were extremely close. He referred to Timothy as his son, not in the physical sense but in the spiritual sense. Paul devoted much time and personal attention to Timothy, discipling or mentoring his young protégé to the point where Paul could entrust to him such a vital and difficult mission. Timothy's mandate was to remind the Christians in Corinth of Paul's teaching.

The truth he embraced he taught "everywhere in every church." In other words, the biblical principles penned by Paul are transferable. They are as authoritative and relevant today as they were the day Paul signed, sealed, and delivered his many epistles. The same can be said for the entire corpus of biblical truth. The sixty-six books of the Bible are not dusty, outdated, obsolete books of ancient history that have absolutely no bearing on our lives today. Quite the contrary. "The word of God is living and powerful, and sharper than any two-edged sword, piercing even to the division of soul and spirit, and of joints and marrow, and is a discerner of the thoughts and intents of the heart" (Hebrews 4:12 NKJV). Just like the original recipients of Paul's Corinthian correspondence, we must choose to obey or reject his sound teaching.

## <u>Christians at a Crossroad</u>

1 CORINTHIANS 4:18–21 *Now some are puffed up, as though I were not coming to you. But I will come to you shortly, if the Lord wills, and I will know, not the word of those who are puffed up, but the power. For the kingdom of God is not in word but in power. What do you want? Shall I come to you with a rod, or in love and a spirit of gentleness? (NKJV)*

When I was growing up, if my mom wanted to strike terror in my heart, all she'd have to say was, "Wait until your father comes home." Nothing she could do or say would cause me to knock off the nonsense and get my act together quicker than that. From Paul's point of view, what worked for me he hoped would work for the Corinthian Christians. For their spiritual father, Paul, was planning on coming home to Corinth. And when he did, depending upon what he saw with his own eyes, he might or might not be happy.

I'll tell you this. From my own personal perspective, despite Paul's assurances that he did not intend to <u>shame</u> his readers, if I had been a member of that troubled church, I would have been feeling quite ashamed. Paul wrote to them as if they were little kids, because that's exactly how they were behaving.

Once again, his words oozed sarcasm, essentially telling them, "You guys are acting so proud, so high and mighty, as if when the cat's away you mice will play. Well, I've got some news for you. I'm on my way home. That's right. And when I get there, I'd better not see any evidence of your sinful pride. I am interested in only one thing—spiritual power, the Holy Spirit's power that comes only to a person who lives to please his Master, rather than to one who lives to please himself."

**go to**

**shame**
1 Corinthians 4:14

**power**
1 Corinthians 2:4–5

**image**
Romans 8:29

> ## what others say
>
> ### D. A. Carson
>
> All the correct theology in the world will not make a spanking sting less, or make a brutal round of toughening-up exercises fun. Yet it does help to know that there is light at the end of the tunnel, even if you cannot yet see it; to know that God is in control and is committed to His people's good, even though it still does not look like that to you.[4]

This was tough love at its best, coming from a loving daddy who now needed to be a firm father. Once he set foot in Corinth, once he "came home," he would know firsthand how these Christians were actually behaving. He was not interested in their talk-is-cheap excuses or rationalizations of their bad behavior. He wanted to witness for himself whether they displayed evidence of the Holy Spirit's <u>power</u> in their midst. For when it comes right down to it, God is not interested in cheap talk; His kingdom is all about the Holy Spirit's transforming power at work in our lives, molding us into the <u>image</u> of His Son. *That's* what Paul wanted to see.

But from every indication, the Christians at Corinth were not acting like anything even closely resembling Jesus Christ. So the choice was theirs: "What do you want? Shall I come to you with a rod, or

**cross**
1 Corinthians 1:18

in love and a spirit of gentleness?" If they wanted their spiritual father to "come home" brandishing a rod of discipline, so be it; they didn't have to change a thing. But if they wanted their loving daddy to come in a spirit of gentleness, and to experience a joyful reunion with the one who first brought the message of Christ's <u>cross</u> to them, wholesale changes in both their beliefs and behavior would have to be made. No one could make that choice for them. The Corinthian Christians were clearly at a crossroad.

## Chapter Wrap-Up

- Paul viewed himself—and all others who served God—as servants only. This stood in stark contrast to the way many people ruled in that era, as though they had some kind of a "divine right" to be in their positions of power. Paul looked at his own situation entirely differently. He was a servant, and he was a servant *only*; nothing more, but also nothing less.

- Paul insisted that he didn't even judge himself, let alone judge anyone else. For this was God's function and God's "right" only. No one else was qualified to judge any part of mankind.

- Paul responded to the problems in Corinth by writing a "polemic," which was essentially a carefully crafted, very specific correction of the Corinthians' behavior. Paul left nothing to the imagination and did not talk in circles—he confronted them directly!

- Paul explained that he knew of nothing he himself had done wrong, and therefore his own conscience was clear. He then took the opportunity to warn them against judging others, even as they were judging him.

- Paul used a lot of sarcasm in some portions of 1 Corinthians, but this was absolutely necessary to make his points. In a word, Paul knew how to speak the language of the people, and he used that understanding to teach them in terms they could understand.

- Paul then went one step farther by promising to send Timothy, his young protégé, to help straighten the Corinthians out.

# Study Questions

**1.** There is an old expression about what some church members often do to others, when they've managed to wound them. Paul was not referring to this, of course, because it undoubtedly did not come along until many years later. But do you know what this expression is? And if you know, do you think it would apply here?

**2.** Do you feel it was appropriate for Paul to use sarcasm in dealing with the Christians at Corinth? Why, or why not?

**3.** Even as he used sarcasm, in what spirit was Paul writing this letter? What was the additional metaphor that might apply here—in other words, Paul was acting like what?

**4.** Why would Paul consider sending Timothy, who was so much younger and less experienced than himself?

# 1 Corinthians 5
# An Unpleasant Business

## Let's Get Started

Church discipline. Not a pleasant topic. But a necessary one.

Fortunately, full-blown church discipline, in which an unrepentant sinning member must be removed from church membership, occurs rarely. In my thirty-four years of church ministry, I have seen church discipline reach the level of removing an unrepentant member only twice. But in both instances it was a gut-wrenching experience for everyone involved—for me and the other members of the leadership team, for the individuals who were being disciplined, and especially for the congregation. Divorce is never easy. Yet, in some ways church discipline is not unlike a divorce in the family.

The situation in the church in Corinth had deteriorated to the point where extreme church discipline needed to be exercised. But as we will soon see, the leadership refused to fulfill their God-given, Christ-commanded duty to remove the unrepentant sinning member. Paul's response to their unwillingness amplifies the seriousness of this unpleasant responsibility that Christ placed on churches today. The leaders of every congregation must exercise vigilance in protecting the churches they lead from ongoing, unrepentant, willfully defiant sin among its members. The dereliction of duty demonstrated by the leaders of the Corinthian congregation must not characterize our churches today. There is just too much at stake.

## A Scandal in the Making

In the above introduction, you might have noticed my repetition of the key adjective *unrepentant*. I repeated this term, and will continue to do so, for a very good reason. The individual in question in Corinth repeatedly chose to sin with a hard-hearted, defiant, stubbornly unrepentant attitude. He refused to change his behavior. Extreme action was needed to preserve the purity of this body of believers. You might be surprised to discover just how extreme the disciplinary action needed to be.

key point

**pagans**
irreligious
individuals

what others say

### J. I. Packer and Carolyn Nystrom

The Bible gives us life stories of many persons whom God chose and called to his service. Again and again it takes time out to tell us of the weaknesses, moral lapses and spiritual failures in their lives. God's way with these folk is to change them as he uses them and to use them while he's remaking them.[1]

*1 CORINTHIANS 5:1–2 It is actually reported that there is sexual immorality among you, and such sexual immorality as is not even named among the Gentiles—that a man has his father's wife! And you are puffed up, and have not rather mourned, that he who has done this deed might be taken away from among you. (NKJV)*

In the above passage of Scripture, you just read a barebones account of a tawdry tale. A man in the church was sleeping with his stepmother. Given the climate in Corinth at the time, Paul's assessment that this incestuous relationship represented a type of immorality "that does not occur even among **pagans**" (1 Corinthians 5:1 NIV) might have been something of a stretch. But it is no stretch to say that such behavior, known throughout the membership of the church and possibly throughout the community, needed to be confronted and corrected. Immediately. Decisively. That the leadership did absolutely nothing about it created an intolerable situation that cried out for correction.

Please note that the ongoing sin itself, as bad as it was, was not the scandal. The scandal rested squarely on the shoulders of the leaders of the church who regarded the situation with an appalling indifference.

Worse than that, the church was *proud* that they were so progressive in their thinking. They *boasted* about the sin. Was it that they didn't want to offend the sinning individual, so they justified their inaction by patting themselves on the back for being so gracious and forgiving? Did they fail to recognize the seriousness of open, defiant, *unrepentant* immorality? Did they market themselves to their sin-crazed city as a safe haven where sinners of every stripe could come and feel loved and accepted while defiantly continuing in their sin?

We don't know for sure. What we do know is that the church should have mourned the fact that the sanctity of a man's marriage was being violated, that a son betrayed his father by taking his father's wife, and that a wife violated her wedding vow. Also, that the reputation of Christ was being sullied by the reports of this sin that were no doubt circulating throughout the community, and that the members of a church for whom Christ died were encouraged to wallow in their sin without fear of consequence.

The situation demanded immediate action in the extreme. Consequently, Paul did not mince his words or pull his punches when he confronted this church.

**head**
Colossians 1:18

## <u>The Required Remedy</u>

> 1 CORINTHIANS 5:3–4 *For I indeed, as absent in body but present in spirit, have already judged (as though I were present) him who has so done this deed. In the name of our Lord Jesus Christ, when you are gathered together, along with my spirit, with the power of our Lord Jesus Christ,* (NKJV)

Removing someone from membership is an extreme measure, the final step in a church's disciplinary action against an unrepentant sinning member. Paul clearly advocated the removal of the sinning man from the church (1 Corinthians 5:2). Evidently the woman was not a part of the Corinthian congregation.

It might interest you to know that Paul was not the first person to advocate church discipline. This unpleasant topic comes right from the top. Jesus Christ, the <u>head</u> of the church, taught His disciples (and us) the steps involved in church discipline. We would do well to review what Jesus taught about this crucial subject:

"If your brother sins against you, go and tell him his fault between you and him alone. If he hears you, you have gained your brother. But if he will not hear, take with you one or two more, that 'by the mouth of two or three witnesses every word may be established.' And if he refuses to hear them, tell it to the church. But if he refuses even to hear the church, let him be to you like a heathen and a tax collector" (Matthew 18:15–17 NKJV).

If you count them, there are four separate steps involved in the church disciplinary process. The removal from membership is the fourth and final step.

what others say

**Billy Graham**

For some people guilt is an excuse. They won't accept the forgiveness that is offered to them; it is so hard to believe. It seems too good to be true that God should let us go eternally scot-free from our sins—and yet that is the message that the gospel brings to us.[2]

**key point**

Note that this four-step process immediately follows Jesus's parable of the lost sheep, in which the shepherd leaves the ninety-nine sheep to look for and rescue the one lost sheep. We must remember that kicking someone out of the church is not an end in itself. It is a means to a much greater end. The goal of every one of the four steps of church discipline is to restore a sinning member to a place of forgiveness, healing, wholeness, usefulness to the kingdom, and fellowship with God and His children. The desire for restoration is the context within which church discipline is exercised. With that in mind, let's consider each of the four steps.

*Step 1: Go to the sinning brother (or sister) privately.* I cannot emphasize enough that we are talking about a Christian brother or sister who is *sinning*. We are *not* talking here about someone who is violating some of our personal preferences. For example, someone who prefers a different style of music or dress than we do is not necessarily sinning.

So . . . before we get in someone's face about his or her behavior, we must first ask ourselves, "Where's the verse?" What is the biblical absolute that they are violating? In the case of Corinth, the man in question willfully, defiantly, stubbornly, and incestuously broke the clear and unambiguous biblical absolute, "You shall not commit adultery" (Exodus 20:14 NKJV). His actions clearly fell into the category of unrepentant sinful behavior.

When we have firsthand knowledge that one of our brothers or sisters in Christ is sinning, we are biblically obligated to go to the individual in the spirit of a shepherd lovingly seeking a lost little lamb, the same spirit Paul described in Galatians 6:1: "Brethren, if a man is overtaken in any trespass, you who are spiritual restore such a one in a spirit of gentleness, considering yourself lest you also be tempted" (NKJV). We do not confront by shaking a judgmental index finger in his or her face. We approach the sinning individual in a spirit of gentle humility, ever mindful that we are quite capable of sinning ourselves. We <u>speak</u> the truth in love, knowing that a person cannot enjoy the blessings of God in his or her life while defying Him.

Our hope, of course, is that the sinning brother (or sister) will *hear* us. That is, that he will respond to God's truth in <u>repentance</u>, evidenced by his changed behavior. If he does, we have "gained" a brother, meaning that we have restored him back to a lifestyle of obedience, one in which he receives God's forgiveness and enjoys His <u>cleansing</u>. If he refuses to hear us, we regretfully move to Step 2.

*Step 2: Return to the sinning brother with one or two witnesses.* By *witnesses,* Paul was referring to one or two other individuals who have firsthand knowledge of the same sin. He did not mean to imply that you or I should go to one or two people and gossip to them about the sin so that they can come with us to confront the sinning person. Jesus based this step on the principle established in Deuteronomy 19:15: "One witness is not enough to convict a man accused of any crime or offense he may have committed. A matter must be established by the testimony of two or three witnesses" (NIV).

Once again, if the sinning individual repents we have cause for a celebration. A lost little lamb has been found. But when faced with the fact that two or three people have independent, firsthand knowledge that this person is sinning, if he still stubbornly refuses to repent, we move to Step 3.

*Step 3: We "tell it to the church."* The church body is informed that a process of church discipline has begun with the goal of bringing the sinning member to a place of repentance and reconciliation with the body. Details of the sin ought not be shared. The church only needs to understand that the leadership is actively praying for the individual and seeking to bring him to a place of repentance. The entire assembly of believers can then unite around that goal by praying for the individual and encouraging him to stop making wrong choices and start making right choices. This is a time for the entire church membership to surround the individual with their loving care and concern for what is best for the person individually and the church collectively. This also prepares the congregation for the possibility that the fourth and final step is looming on the horizon, if the sinning brother or sister "refuses even to hear the church."

**speak**
Ephesians 4:15

**repentance**
2 Corinthians 7:10

**cleansing**
1 John 1:9

apply it

If the individual repents, then all is forgiven and forgotten. The church has cause for rejoicing that the lost lamb has been found and returned to the fold. But if the sinning brother or sister willfully, defiantly, and stubbornly refuses to repent, we sadly move to Step 4.

*Step 4: Treat him like an unbeliever.* Or as Jesus stated it, "Let him be to you like a heathen and a tax collector" (Matthew 18:17 NKJV). The individual is removed from the membership. That does not merely mean that they can no longer vote in church business meetings—it means that he is no longer permitted the privilege of attending the services, or in any other way of entering into the fellowship of the church. Treating a person like a heathen is to treat him like an unbeliever. We regard him as if he is not a Christian.

We do so because someone who reaches this fourth and final step and continues to stubbornly rebel against God is giving clear evidence that he may not be a true follower of Jesus. A person is removed from the life of the church for two reasons: (1) to remove his ungodly influence from the church; and (2) to give him over to the lifestyle that he has so defiantly chosen, with all of the consequences that will result from his sinful choices.

what others say

**Charles R. Swindoll**

It is in the church, week after week, where we learn faithfulness. It is in the church where discipleship is carried out. It is in the church where accountability is modeled. It is in the church of Jesus Christ where we find the doctrinal roots that establish us in our faith.[3]

key point

God Himself practices the principle of biblical discipline. Three times in Romans 1 we read that when individuals persisted in willful, defiant, rebellious behavior, "God gave them up," "God gave them up," and "God gave them over" (vv. 24, 26, 28) to their sin. He essentially abandoned them to the sinful choices that they insisted on making, and to the consequences that resulted from their choices.

# A Startling Statement

**Ephesus**
1 Timothy 1:3

**1 CORINTHIANS 5:5** *deliver such a one to Satan for the destruction of the flesh, that his spirit may be saved in the day of the Lord Jesus. (NKJV)*

We have already noted that the fourth and final step in the church disciplinary process means so much more than merely removing someone from church membership. Now we get a sense of how much more this action really entails.

This wouldn't be the last time Paul "delivered such a one to Satan." He did the same thing in Ephesus. Paul's young protégé, Pastor Timothy, was struggling as the pastor of the church in Ephesus. By this time, Paul was advanced in years and facing possible execution at the hands of the notorious Roman emperor Nero. He wrote two desperate letters to Timothy in a last-ditch attempt to bolster the courage of this struggling servant of God. In 1 Timothy 1, Paul urged his "son in the faith" (1:2 NKJV) to continue to fight the spiritual battle in which he was embroiled in Ephesus (1:18). He specifically warned Timothy about two men, "Hymenaeus and Alexander, whom I delivered to Satan that they may learn not to blaspheme" (1 Timothy 1:20 NKJV). Alexander especially was a thorn in Paul's side. He later spoke of Alexander, who "did me much harm" (2 Timothy 4:14 NKJV).

When Paul delivered these men over to Satan, he exercised his apostolic authority by pronouncing a judicial sentence upon them, "Guilty as charged." He then did what God did in Romans 1. He abandoned them to their chosen fate, the natural consequences of defying God and siding with Satan.

Church discipline is serious business, not to be taken lightly. Paul assured the church in Corinth that when they exercised biblical discipline on the sinning man, they did so with Paul's apostolic endorsement. More important, Jesus assured church leaders that when they exercise biblical discipline of sinning members, they do so with His blessing. In the context of church discipline, Jesus assured His disciples, and He likewise assures us, "I say to you, whatever you bind on earth will be bound in heaven, and whatever you loose on earth will be loosed in heaven. Again I say to you that if two of you agree on earth concerning anything that they ask, it will be done for them by My Father in heaven. For where two or three are gathered together in My name, I am there in the midst of them" (Matthew 18:18–20 NKJV). Jesus not only commanded churches to discipline unrepentant sinners; He assured them and us that we do so with His approval.

## Rising to the Occasion

1 CORINTHIANS 5:6–7a *Your glorying is not good. Do you not know that a little leaven leavens the whole lump? Therefore purge out the old leaven, that you may be a new lump, since you truly are unleavened. (NKJV)*

Lest the leaders in Corinth were to continue to shirk their responsibility and shrink from their God-given task, Paul underscored yet again the vital importance of removing a willfully defiant, unrepentant sinner from their midst.

By boasting of their church's tolerance of sin, the leaders and others effectively placed the church at risk to the spreading influence of such sin. Paul used a common biblical metaphor to illustrate the principle. When leaven or yeast is added to a lump of dough, over time the yeast permeates the entire loaf, causing the bread to rise.

what others say

**Ralph P. Martin**

Unity does not mean a monochrome, deadpan uniformity, which might be the case if the church were a thing, an inert and static object. Rather, the church is an organism, pulsating with life and made up of living persons who are responsible for growth of character and personal development, according as they use the gifts that Christ has bestowed.[4]

The remedy was clear, concise, and to the point: "Purge out the old leaven." In other words, stop bragging about the sin in your church and remove the sinner. Immediately.

## A Celebration of Freedom

1 CORINTHIANS 5:7b–8 *For indeed Christ, our Passover, was sacrificed for us. Therefore let us keep the feast, not with old leaven, nor with the leaven of malice and wickedness, but with the unleavened bread of sincerity and truth. (NKJV)*

Whenever you see the word *Passover* in the Scriptures, think "Freedom versus Bondage." Let's take a bit of a refresher course on the origins of Passover.

The Israelites suffered as slaves in Egypt for over <u>four hundred</u> years. God raised up Moses to deliver the Israelites from their bondage. But there was a problem. Pharaoh did not want to let the people go. God struck the land with ten plagues, each designed to demonstrate that the God of the Israelites—the God of Abraham, Isaac, and Jacob—was more powerful than the many gods worshipped in Egypt. The climactic tenth plague hit close to Pharaoh's home when every firstborn son in the land, including his own heir to the throne, would perish unless the people placed the blood of the "<u>Passover lamb</u>" on the sides of their doors and on the lintels above the doors. If they did so, the angel of death would "pass over" the house and the firstborn would be spared. In response to this tenth plague, Pharaoh finally agreed to let the people go, freeing them from four centuries of bondage.

The Passover lamb was an Old Testament picture of Jesus Christ, "the Lamb of God who takes away the sin of the world" (John 1:29 NKJV). Jesus not only saved us from our sins, but He <u>freed</u> us from our bondage to sin. Our Jewish friends celebrate their ancestors' freedom from bondage once each year at Passover. We have the privilege of celebrating our freedom from sin's bondage every day. Whenever the church family gathers together, it's as if we are celebrating a feast of freedom.

Can you see the hypocrisy of celebrating our freedom in Christ while at the same time condoning someone's bondage to unrepentant sin? Every time the church in Corinth met together, it was as if they were slapping God in the face, making a mockery of His Son's sacrifice on the cross, crucifying again for themselves the Son of God and putting Him to open <u>shame</u>. So Paul spoke sternly to them: Get rid of the leaven of malice (evil intent) and wickedness (sinful lifestyle choices), both in your lives and in the life of your church. Instead, celebrate your feast of freedom with sincerity (integrity, wholeness, genuineness, the opposite of hypocrisy) and truth (a commitment to obey the Scriptures).

The Christians in Corinth needed to purify their church body by ridding their church of its unrepentant sinful member. They then needed to be vigilant in preserving the purity of the body by not tol-

**four hundred**
Acts 7:6

**Passover lamb**
Exodus 12:21

**freed**
Romans 8:2

**shame**
Hebrews 6:6

erating such unrepentant sinful behavior ever again. Paul instructs them in how to do so in the final section of this chapter.

## The Company We Keep

1 CORINTHIANS 5:9–11 *I wrote to you in my epistle not to keep company with sexually immoral people. Yet I certainly did not mean with the sexually immoral people of this world, or with the covetous, or extortioners, or idolaters, since then you would need to go out of the world. But now I have written to you not to keep company with anyone named a brother, who is sexually immoral, or covetous, or an idolater, or a reviler, or a drunkard, or an extortioner—not even to eat with such a person. (NKJV)*

Leave it to the Corinthian Christians to get things 100 percent wrong. The people they should have been trying to influence with the message of the Cross—those in their community who had no relationship with God—they were avoiding like the proverbial plague. Yet they welcomed into their assembly compromising Christians whose lives were characterized by ongoing, unrepentant sin. Go figure.

In response to this reversal of responsibilities, Paul clarified his position as stated in a previous letter. In that letter, not preserved as a part of the New Testament canon, Paul evidently told the believers in Corinth not to associate with those who were "sexually immoral . . . covetous, or extortioners, or idolaters." He was *not* referring to "people of this world"—the unsaved, non-Christians, those who had no relationship with Christ—because short of moving to a monastery, it is impossible not to interact with non-Christians. However, he specifically instructed them "not to keep company with anyone named a brother"—Christians—whose lives were characterized by the above-listed categories of sin.

And so it was in Corinth. The Christians there prided themselves on not getting their hands dirty by reaching out to the "heathen" outside of their church; yet all the while they were equally proud of their tolerance of the unrepentant sinners they enthusiastically welcomed inside their church.

Paul established an ethic in the Corinthian church that, quite frankly, is hard to achieve. He stated categorically that the true followers of Christ are not to associate with those who call themselves Christians if their lives are characterized by unrepentant sin in six clearly defined categories. This is because their unrepentant behavior demonstrates that in truth they may not be Christians at all.[5]

The six categories are as follows:

1. **Sexually immoral:** from the Greek word *pornos*, from which we get our word *pornography*, someone engaged in some form of pornographic behavior.

2. **Covetous:** someone driven to have what belongs to others, and the willingness to do whatever it takes to get what he wants at the expense of others.

3. **Idolater:** someone who worships something or someone other than the true God; includes someone who worships himself.

4. **Reviler:** a verbally abusive person who rails against or attacks others with malicious words either to their faces or behind their backs; one who regularly traffics in malicious gossip that damages or destroys another's character or reputation.

key point

5. **Drunkard:** someone who regularly consumes alcoholic beverages to the point of intoxication.

6. **Extortioner:** predatory behavior in which someone regularly pillages, plunders, robs, or in any other way takes by force that which is not his.

For someone to fit into one or more of these categories, these definitions must describe the ongoing behavior pattern of the individual. For example, if someone goes to a friend's birthday party and drinks too much, that does not necessarily fit into the category of a drunkard. But, if drinking too much becomes a pattern of his life then his conduct does fit the category. However, if he then becomes genuinely repentant, seeks help for his alcohol addiction, becomes accountable to godly men, etc., he would not be a candidate for church discipline. Someone who defiantly demands his right to get drunk whenever or wherever he chooses, and responds to the steps of discipline in a belligerent, hard-hearted way, certainly would be in line for discipline.

go to

fellowship
Acts 2:42

Paul equated each of these broad categories of sin by mandating the same consequence. We are not to associate ourselves in any way with these individuals. We ought not even to eat with them, not individually nor as a part of a <u>fellowship</u> meal with the church as a whole. To borrow the imagery of the apostle John, it basically comes down to this: "If we say that we have fellowship with Him, and walk in darkness, we lie and do not practice the truth. But if we walk in the light as He is in the light, we have fellowship with one another, and the blood of Jesus Christ His Son cleanses us from all sin" (1 John 1:6–7 NKJV).

## A Timeless Truth

> 1 CORINTHIANS 5:12–13 *For what have I to do with judging those also who are outside? Do you not judge those who are inside? But those who are outside God judges. Therefore "put away from yourselves the evil person."* (NKJV)

Bottom line: We have no business judging those outside the church. We should expect unbelievers to act like unbelievers. We should have no expectation that they will obey Christ as Lord, because they have not named Him as their Lord. Dogs bark. The sun shines. Sinners sin. That's to be expected. So Paul did not judge them. He left that to God, and so should we.

Inside our churches it's a totally different matter. One of the reasons we attend them is to "consider how we may spur one another on toward love and good deeds" (Hebrews 10:24 NIV). Consequently, we should "not give up meeting together, as some are in the habit of doing, but let us encourage one another—and all the more as you see the Day [of our Lord's return] approaching" (10:25 NIV). A healthy church life should include a built-in accountability framework in which we motivate each other to love more and to obey Christ more. When a member of the community of faith that makes up a church belligerently, stubbornly, and repeatedly defies Scriptures by his or her ongoing sin, he must be dealt with according to the four steps of church discipline as outlined above. If the sinning member will not allow himself to be spurred on toward "love and good deeds," Paul makes the final course of action all too clear with words from the Old Testamewnt: "Put away the evil from among you" (Deuteronomy 17:7 NKJV).

key point

Under Old Testament Law, the guilty person was to be put to death. That's how seriously God treats ongoing unrepentant sin among His people. That's how passionate God is about preserving the purity of His people. Thankfully, churches operate under New Testament grace; stoning is no longer required. However, God makes this mandatory: unrepentant sinning members *must* be removed from the church. The implication of Paul's Old Testament quotation couldn't be clearer: Removing a sinning member from his or her community of faith is non-optional. The command to do so is unequivocal.

# Chapter Wrap-Up

- This chapter concerns itself with the need for discipline of the members within the church at Corinth. By extension, of course, all that Paul said on this subject applies to the churches of today.
- The key condition of the heart of the sinner who needed to be disciplined, said Paul, was a refusal to repent.
- Paul gives us four steps to take when dealing with an unrepentant sinner within the church. These include talking to the sinner privately, returning to the sinner with one or two witnesses, telling the situation "to the church," and finally asking the person to leave the church, while also asking the other members not to associate with him anymore.
- Everything Paul taught, with respect to the above, has ample precedent both in the Old Testament Scriptures and in the New Testament words of Jesus Christ Himself.
- Paul also gave us six categories of sin, any of which could lead to the disciplining of an unrepentant member of the church.

# Study Questions

1. Why was it so important to discipline an unrepentant, sinning member of the church of Corinth? Would it be equally important today?

2. Does any of the above mean that we should not associate with known sinners?

3. How do you feel about the four steps Paul laid out for dealing with an unrepentant, sinning member of the church?

4. What are the six categories of sin that Paul defined in 1 Corinthians 5?

**Chapter Highlights:**
- How Dare You?
- Split Decision
- Should Be Ashamed
- Dangerous Disconnect
- Pushing the Envelope

# 1 Corinthians 6
# Who and Whose We Are

## Let's Get Started

The problems in Corinth continued to mount. Things were getting uglier by the minute. The man who "has his father's wife" (1 Corinthians 5:1 NKJV) aside, it seems that rampant immorality infected the entire church. In addition, people were at each other's throats, suing one another over matters that could have and should have been resolved within the framework of the church. The Christians in that congregation had totally lost perspective. They evidently forgot *who* they were, and (more important) *whose* they were.

Paul couldn't believe his ears when he heard that members of the Corinthian congregation were suing each other in court. So frustrated was the apostle that he wrote to say, "How dare you do this?" Given the fact that we live in a litigious society today, perhaps we would do well to consider Paul's instructions to the Christians in Corinth.

## How Dare You?

> 1 CORINTHIANS 6:1 *Dare any of you, having a matter against another, go to law before the unrighteous, and not before the saints? (NKJV)*

Interesting word, *dare*. It comes from the same word that can be translated *bold*. Paul's use of this term conveys the question, "How can you be so boldly defiant as to dare to do something as utterly reprehensible in the sight of God as suing one another in full view of a watching world?" I'd have hated to be on the receiving end of *that* rebuke.

But truth to tell, the Corinthians *were* acting in a daredevil manner by airing their petty differences in open court, entrusting their fate to *unrighteous* judges rather than allowing godly *saints* to mediate their disputes. This sad story helps chronicle the heights from which this church had fallen and the depths to which it had sunk. We

key point

**Holy Spirit's Fullness**
Galatians 5:22

**apologetic**
defense of, or proof
that, our faith is the
real deal

have already documented the desperate need for a beacon of truth to shine in the darkened city of Corinth. The actions and attitudes of the Christians there should have been governed by this one overarching concern: How will my actions affect my witness for Christ in this city? But it never occurred to them that they were compromising their witness by putting their deep divisions on public display.

**what others say**

**Pam Farrel**

God's power, ability, creativity and strength are there to help us walk the walk we are called to. God doesn't point to His place for us and say, "Good luck, hope you can pull it off!" No, God leads us to be usable by living the calling through us by His Spirit, and that pulls the pieces together. My life falls into place with more clarity, and less frustration, when I am relying on His power rather than my own.[1]

Just before He went to the cross, Jesus left His disciples with this mandate: "By this all will know that you are My disciples, if you have love for one another" (John 13:35 NKJV). Jesus clearly intended for our love for one another—something utterly impossible for those outside of God's love to duplicate—to be the singular mark of authenticity for a Christian. God designed our love for each other to be the principal **apologetic** of our faith. When Christians truly love one another, not just in word but in deed, the world will look up and take notice that we have something everyone craves, but that no one else can achieve. The love of which Jesus spoke is beyond the natural, an evidence of the <u>Holy Spirit's fullness</u> in our lives. The unmistakable fact that the Corinthian Christians failed miserably in their love for each other, evidenced by their suing one another in court, totally invalidated their witness in their community. They were acting just like the non-Christians. Christ made no observable difference in their minds or hearts, causing the townspeople to conclude that the Christians had nothing that they needed or wanted in their lives.

## Split Decision

1 CORINTHIANS 6:2–3 *Do you not know that the saints will judge the world? And if the world will be judged by you, are you*

*unworthy to judge the smallest matters? Do you not know that we shall judge angels? How much more, things that pertain to this life?* (NKJV)

"We shall judge angels." A curious comment, no? What could Paul have possibly meant by *that* statement? Add to that the fact that we will likewise "judge the world."

As you might imagine, among many respected Bible teachers, opinions are split as to the significance of that phrase. For instance, "Aquinas, Meyer, Alford, Hodge (notable Bible scholars all) think the reference is to good angels. But, as there is no hint in Scripture that they will come to judgment," Thomas Edwards holds the view that we will participate in God's judgment of the evil angels.[2] Gordon Fee, a biblical scholar in his own right, categorically states, "This possibly reflects an apocalyptic as to the judgment of fallen angels. . . . So inclusive will be our participation in God's eschatological judgment that not only the world but even the angels will be judged by the newly formed eschatological people of God."[3] If you read that and went, "Huh?" you are not alone.

Let's cut to the chase. Paul's main point is quite simple: Since we Christians are going to judge the world and the angels, we don't need to sue each other and catalog our conflicts before some unrighteous judge. What Paul meant by our judging the world and the angels is anybody's guess since he did not explain it. So I will give you my best guess. In order to do so, we'll utilize a tried-and-true principle of biblical interpretation: We'll let clear biblical statements shed light on the unclear.

Regarding the world, Jesus said, "He who overcomes, and keeps My works until the end, to him I will give power over the nations" (Revelation 2:26 NKJV). During the **Millennium**, Christ will rule the earth during a time of unprecedented bliss and blessing. And we will reign with Him. As such, we will "judge"—*krino*, a word that means "to administer affairs, to govern"[4]—or exercise authority over the nations of the world.

Think of it: During that blessed period in our future, we will be a part of Jesus's administration on earth. *That's* a humbling point to ponder. But even more, we will be given some measure of authority over His holy angels. The primary function of these angels today is to "to minister for those who will inherit salvation" (Hebrews 1:14

**go to**

**Millennium**
Revelation 20:1–3

**reign**
Revelation 20:6

**holy angels**
Matthew 25:31

**Millennium**
the future thousand-year reign of Christ on the earth

**go to**

evil angels
Matthew 25:41

NKJV). In the coming Millennium, these angels will evidently assist us as we assist Jesus in His rule over the earth. Any notion that we will sit in judgment of the <u>evil angels</u>, doling out God's punishment in some judicial sense, I find biblically problematic since the Scriptures clearly teach that God Himself will judge the devil and his angels (2 Peter 2:4; Jude 6).

Back on point: Given the fact that we will one day assist Jesus in His rule over the earth, and that we will even have some limited authority over the angels, we are abundantly qualified to mediate our petty differences without resorting to lawsuits.

---

**what others say**

**Wellington Boone**

The Lord is the Creator of race. There is no reason for whites in America, or any other culture anywhere in the world, to feel superior. None of us had anything to do with our coming into this world. It was God's idea.[5]

---

## You Should Be Ashamed

*1 CORINTHIANS 6:4–7 If then you have judgments concerning things pertaining to this life, do you appoint those who are least esteemed by the church to judge? I say this to your shame. Is it so, that there is not a wise man among you, not even one, who will be able to judge between his brethren? But brother goes to law against brother, and that before unbelievers! Now therefore, it is already an utter failure for you that you go to law against one another. Why do you not rather accept wrong? Why do you not rather let yourselves be cheated? (NKJV)*

It wasn't that long ago (1992 to be exact) that the haunting refrain, "Can we all get along?" echoed throughout our collective consciousness. Sadly, before and after Rodney King asked the question of the riot-torn city of Los Angeles, people did not and cannot "get along." James, our Lord's half brother, tells us why. "Where do wars and fights come from among you? Do they not come from your desires for pleasure that war in your members? You lust and do not have. You murder and covet and cannot obtain. You fight and war. Yet you do not have because you do not ask" (James 4:1–2 NKJV). It's one thing when such *quarrels* and *fights* happen on the streets and in the dark alleys outside of the church; it's quite another when they happen inside the church.

So Paul made this impassioned plea: "Stop it! It would be far better for a Christian to *accept wrong* and be *cheated* than to go before an unbelieving judge to resolve your differences."

Jesus set the same standard of behavior for His followers when He taught, "I tell you not to resist an evil person. But whoever slaps you on your right cheek, turn the other to him also. If anyone wants to sue you and take away your tunic, let him have your cloak also" (Matthew 5:39–40 NKJV).

Paul reaffirmed this ethic when he told the believers in the church at Rome, "Repay no one evil for evil. Have regard for good things in the sight of all men. If it is possible, as much as depends on you, live peaceably with all men. Beloved, do not avenge yourselves, but rather give place to wrath; for it is written, 'Vengeance is Mine, I will repay,' says the Lord. Therefore 'If your enemy is hungry, feed him; if he is thirsty, give him a drink; for in so doing you will heap coals of fire on his head.' Do not be overcome by evil, but overcome evil with good" (Romans 12:17–21 NKJV).

Note in particular the phrase, "Be careful to do what is right in the eyes of everybody." Like it or not, people do watch us. Once we named Christ as our Lord and identified ourselves as His followers, many people put us under a microscope. They look to see if our actions back up our words, if there is a genuine quality of goodness to our lives. The Christians in Corinth lost this perspective. They publicly humiliated themselves in full view of the citizens in their sin-filled city. They acted shamefully when they should have acted nobly. As a consequence they violated their calling and compromised their mission. Better to be wronged than to risk all of that; so said Jesus, and so said Paul.

Given the seriousness of their situation and the sky-high stakes, Paul didn't pull any punches when he confronted the Corinthians. Their reprehensible behavior was motivated by greed, pure and simple. Their concern was not their higher calling, which should have been their God-given mandate to reach their city for Christ. They cared only about their losses, and about getting even with those who hurt them. It was James all over again: "You want something . . . you kill and covet . . . you quarrel and fight."

Paul was astounded that there was no one in the church who had enough credibility among the people to step in and mediate the conflicts. They instead turned to the courts, in full view of a watching and mocking world. God regarded their behavior as *shameful*, evidence of their total *failure* to take the high road and to make morally righteous choices.

## A Dangerous Disconnect

1 CORINTHIANS 6:8–11 *No, you yourselves do wrong and cheat, and you do these things to your brethren! Do you not know that the unrighteous will not inherit the kingdom of God? Do not be deceived. Neither fornicators, nor idolaters, nor adulterers, nor homosexuals, nor sodomites, nor thieves, nor covetous, nor drunkards, nor revilers, nor extortioners will inherit the kingdom of God. And such were some of you. But you were washed, but you were sanctified, but you were justified in the name of the Lord Jesus and by the Spirit of our God. (NKJV)*

There is an undercurrent that runs throughout both 1 and 2 Corinthians. It's a sub-theme of these letters that appears almost as a shadow cast across their pages until it emerges into the bright sunlight for all to read and consider at the very end of 2 Corinthians. There Paul posed to his readers the challenge that defines the context within which Paul wrote to this troubled church. He ordered the so-called Christians there to "examine yourselves as to whether you are in the faith. Test yourselves. Do you not know yourselves, that Jesus Christ is in you?—unless indeed you are disqualified" (2 Corinthians 13:5 NKJV). From where Paul sat, there were several in that church who "failed the test," placing the genuineness of their salvation in question.

key point

We tend to place great value in a person's verbal claim that he is a Christian. The Bible does no such thing. To the biblical writer, if you'll pardon the cliché, talk is cheap. A person's words do not validate his salvation. A person demonstrates his salvation by his life. "Faith without works is dead," cried James (2:20 NKJV). The so-called Christians in Corinth claimed to be followers of Christ with their words, but their talk was contradicted by their walk. Their lives displayed no evidence that Christ had made any difference in the way they lived. They were living exactly like the unbelievers surrounding them. So Paul offered his challenge: From where I am standing I see no evidence that you are truly saved. You'd better take a long, hard

apply it

look at your lives. It's time to put up or shut up. If you claim to be a Christian, live like one. Or don't make the claim at all.

The Corinthian Christians wronged and cheated one another. They responded to each other not as *brethren*, but as the *unrighteous* who will "not inherit the kingdom of God." The question of their salvation hung in the balance.

Paul identified ten broad categories of sin that describe those who "will not inherit the kingdom of God." This is serious stuff. Paul is wielding his apostolic sword as he consigns these categories of sinners to the destiny of the damned. As we discuss them, make a mental note that Paul is describing individuals whose lives are so given over to one or more of these sins that they can be labeled by them. He is *not* talking about someone who occasionally sins; he *is* talking about someone whose lifestyle is characterized by one or more of these categories of sin.

The categories of sinful lifestyles as outlined by Paul are as follows:

- *Fornicators:* those who indulge themselves in ongoing, unrepentant, pornographic (from the Greek word *pornos* translated here as "fornicators"), immoral sex

- *Idolaters:* those who worship a false god or follow a false religion (Note that in Corinth, their particular form of idolatry centered upon the temple to Aphrodite and was inexorably linked to fornication.)

- *Adulterers:* those who have "intercourse with the spouse of another"[6]

- *Homosexuals:* In the original Greek, this term (*malakos*) literally means, "soft to the touch." It is also used in Matthew 11:8 and Luke 7:25, both times in reference to "soft garments." However, in the context of 1 Corinthians 6, Paul is clearly talking about those who violate the very words that came from God's own mouth: "You shall not lie with a male as with a woman. It is an abomination" (Leviticus 18:22 NKJV). Though many would like to make their own rules, with God's blessing, it's very difficult to argue convincingly against what He Himself said.

- *Sodomites:* an unfortunate translation that refers back to the people of Sodom, who were given over to homosexuality of the basest form. You might remember how the people of

**Judas**
John 12:6

**Barabbas**
John 18:40

**Zacchaeus**
Luke 19:8

Sodom were so enflamed by their lustful passions that God was forced to lament to Abraham, "The outcry against Sodom and Gomorrah is great . . . because their sin is very grave" (Genesis 18:20 NKJV). *Arsenokoites* would be better rendered exactly as the King James Version defines it— "abusers of themselves with mankind" (1 Corinthians 6:9 KJV). This term perfectly describes those in Rome of whom Paul wrote, "For this reason God gave them up to vile passions. For even their women exchanged the natural use for what is against nature. Likewise also the men, leaving the natural use of the woman, burned in their lust for one another, men with men committing what is shameful, and receiving in themselves the penalty of their error which was due" (Romans 1:26–27 NKJV). Political correctness notwithstanding, God designed sex as the physical union of a man and a woman, and that within the context of marriage. Any perversion of this by a same-sex union falls squarely within this category.

- *Thieves:* those who take from another that which is not theirs. The term in the original is *kleptes*, from which we get our word *kleptomaniac*, referring to someone who has a "neurotic impulse to steal." Judas was a thief, as was Barabbas, and (before his conversion to Christ) Zacchaeus.

- *Coveters:* those who, because of overpowering greed, regularly take advantage of others in their insatiable hunger to have more

- *Drunkards:* those who become habitually intoxicated with alcohol or high on illicit substances

- *Revilers:* those who destroy the reputations of others with their malicious words and slanderous gossip

- *Extortioners:* those who ravenously swindle or embezzle money from businesses or individuals, those who exhibit predatory behavior in their never-ending quest to devour the funds of another

You have no doubt heard, and even sung, the beloved hymn "Amazing Grace." Just how amazing is God's grace? Paul wrote of the Corinthians, "And such were some of you." Every one of the genuinely converted Corinthian Christians was saved from one or more of those categories of sin. Every one of them could say from his or her forgiven heart, "I'm not what I want to be. And I'm not what I'm gonna be. But thank God I'm not what I was." From the depths of that depraved and darkened pit God saved them. He _washed_ them (cleansed them completely in the same way a surgeon's scalpel is sanitized before surgery), _sanctified_ them (set them apart as holy people for a holy purpose), and _justified_ them (declared them "not guilty," just as if they had never sinned at all).

That's the good news. The bad news is that there was a disturbing disconnect between who they were and how some of them still lived. Peter was not thinking of the Corinthian Christians when he wrote the following passage, but it surely applies: "It would have been better for them not to have known the way of righteousness, than having known it, to turn from the holy commandment delivered to them. But it has happened to them according to the true proverb: 'A dog returns to his own vomit,' and, 'a sow, having washed, to her wallowing in the mire'" (2 Peter 2:21–22 NKJV). Clearly, like the people to whom Peter penned his letter, some of the Christians in Corinth forgot _who_ they were.

They were _washed_, _sanctified_, and _justified_ all right. If only they had lived like it.

**go to**

**washed**
Titus 3:5

**sanctified**
1 Thessalonians 4:3

**justified**
Romans 5:1

something to ponder

what others say

**Steve Farrar**

We need both the right diet and the right exercise. Prayer and Scripture go together, and we are most effective when we have a good balance of the two. The man who studies the Bible without praying will develop a good mind with a cold heart. The man who prays without knowing Scripture will consistently pray outside the will of God, for that is where his will is revealed. This balance is critical to standing firm in spiritual battle.[7]

## Pushing the Envelope

1 CORINTHIANS 6:12 _All things are lawful for me, but all things are not helpful. All things are lawful for me, but I will not be brought under the power of any._ (NKJV)

Just in case the Corinthian Christians wanted to hide behind the truth of Ephesians 1:7—"In Him we have redemption through His blood, the forgiveness of sins, according to the riches of His grace" (NKJV)—and other similar verses, Paul emphatically stated a foundational principle of victorious Christian living that should have been obvious to every one of Christ's followers, both inside and outside of Corinth. That principle is this: Just because something is forgivable, that does not make it beneficial; just because God is willing to forgive you of the *penalty* of your sins, woe to the Christian who willingly places himself under the *power* of that sin.

**key point**

Sin wields a seductive, self-destructive sword. When God draws a line in the sand and tells us not to cross it, it's not because He gets a kick out of depriving us of fun. While I appreciate the sentiment behind the literary blockbuster *You: The Owner's Manual*, the real owner's manual is the Bible. The perennial bestseller is the only book written about us by the manufacturer. God put us together. He knows best what will enhance the fulfillment of our lives, and what will ultimately destroy our lives.

In that context He says a definite "Yes" to those things that will benefit us—love, joy, peace, patience, etc.—and a resounding "No" to those things that will harm us—adultery, thievery, coveting, drunkenness, etc. Sure, those things are forgivable, but they are *not helpful or beneficial*. Even worse, if we excuse such behavior in ourselves, over time our sinful choices will come to hold a profound power over us. Sow a choice, reap an action; sow an action, reap a habit; sow a habit, reap a lifestyle; sow a lifestyle, reap a destiny.

Or in the words of our old friend James, "Each one is tempted when he is drawn away by his own desires and enticed. Then, when desire has conceived, it gives birth to sin; and sin, when it is full-grown, brings forth death. Do not be deceived, my beloved brethren" (James 1:14–16 NKJV).

## A Cliché of Catastrophic Consequences

1 CORINTHIANS 6:13–14 *Foods for the stomach and the stomach for foods, but God will destroy both it and them. Now the body is not for sexual immorality but for the Lord, and the Lord for the body. And God both raised up the Lord and will also raise us up by His power.* (NKJV)

As far as Paul's Corinthian readers were concerned, whatever they did with their bodies or put into their bodies was of no more consequence than eating. Satisfying their hunger for food was, in their warped reasoning, no different from satisfying their hunger for anything else. So if flooding their bodies with alcohol to the point of drunkenness was their thing, so what? If indulging their sensual appetites, be it with a prostitute, another man's wife, or someone of the same gender, who cared? The prevailing attitude in the First Church of Corinth was, "It's my body. It's my right to choose to do with my body whatever I want."

Using that flawed logic, the Corinthians were only too happy to sing, "Foods for the stomach and the stomach for foods; sex for the body and the body for sex." However, while sexual immorality, like every other sin, is certainly forgivable, becoming a slave to our sexual impulses is certainly not beneficial, not for the Christians in Corinth and certainly not for us. Yet, that's exactly what happened in Corinth. Just as Corinth had degenerated into a sex-crazed city, so had the church. The time had come for the spiritual father of the church to have "the talk" with his sons and daughters in the <u>faith</u>.

**faith**
1 Timothy 1:2

## <u>When One Plus One Equals One</u>

> 1 CORINTHIANS 6:15–18 *Do you not know that your bodies are members of Christ? Shall I then take the members of Christ and make them members of a harlot? Certainly not! Or do you not know that he who is joined to a harlot is one body with her? For "the two," He says, "shall become one flesh." But he who is joined to the Lord is one spirit with Him. Flee sexual immorality. Every sin that a man does is outside the body, but he who commits sexual immorality sins against his own body.* (NKJV)

Harking all the way back to the scene in the Garden of Eden, when God performed the first wedding ceremony between Adam and Eve, God defined marriage when He said, "A man shall leave his father and mother and be joined to his wife, and they shall become one flesh" (Genesis 2:24 NKJV). This definition has profound ramifications. When one man sexually joins himself to one woman they become *one flesh*. Where the sexual union of two people is concerned, one plus one equals one.

This is precisely why sexual intercourse between two people outside of marriage is such a devastating sin in the sight of God. A person who is joined to a harlot is *one body with her*. This is serious

apply it

**lives**
Galatians 2:20

enough. But add to that this bit of news that Paul told the Corinthian Christians: "Now you are the body of Christ" (1 Corinthians 12:27 NKJV). In other words, Christ <u>lives</u> in us. Consequently, when a person joins himself to another in an illicit sexual union, something quite rampant among the Corinthian Christian population, he essentially *takes the members of Christ and makes them members of a harlot.* Yes, you read that right. Just imagine forcing the holy Son of God to participate in such an unholy act. Yet that's exactly what the Corinthian Christians were doing. They were *feeding* their immoral impulses, when all the while they should have been *fleeing* them.

## God's Holy Temple

> 1 CORINTHIANS 6:19–20 *Or do you not know that your body is the temple of the Holy Spirit who is in you, whom you have from God, and you are not your own? For you were bought at a price; therefore glorify God in your body and in your spirit, which are God's.* (NKJV)

Apparently Paul's Corinthian readers did not know that their bodies were *the temple of the Holy Spirit who is in you.* They were acting as though their bodies were their own to do with as they pleased. Wrong! When they made the conscious decision to become followers of Jesus and named Him as their Lord, both the Son of God and the Holy Spirit of God took up residence right inside of them, just as He has with us. Our bodies are His temple. Just as God manifested His presence in the temple of old, so today He manifests Himself in us. We are the place where God touches the earth. That is *not* to say that we are God. That is to say that both God's Son and God's Holy Spirit dwell in us. We dare not do to or with our bodies whatever we like. We don't own them. He does. He paid a pretty hefty price to purchase our bodies. He paid the blood of His Son.

This is what sets sexual sin apart from every other sin. There is a sense in which the sexual union of two people outside of marriage has a destructive force unlike any other sin. As intimate and pleasurable as it may be, it possesses the power to destroy individuals (through unwanted diseases, pregnancies, guilt, shame, unreturned love), marriages (How many marriages hit the rocks the moment one partner illicitly joins himself or herself to another?), children (the innocent bystanders), societies, and even empires. (Case in point: the Roman Empire, seemingly indestructible at the time Paul wrote 1 Corinthians, eventually collapsed under the weight of its many perversions.)

Cleary, the Christians in Corinth forgot *who* they were (washed, sanctified, and justified). But they also forgot *whose* they were—His blood-bought temple. So are we. And as such, we have the singular responsibility to glorify God in our bodies. Unlike the Christians of Corinth, may we take our responsibility seriously.

what others say

**Charles R. Swindoll**

In any other earthly organization, when you draw together a number of human beings, you're going to have prejudice, emphasis on status, and a display of favoritism. But not in the body of Christ! This is one place that has no room for "preferred customers" or second-class citizens.[8]

## Chapter Wrap-Up

- Paul was outraged at the Corinthians for having so many disagreements among themselves. But he was even more upset at them for airing their disagreements in public and suing each other in court.

- As so often happens today, the conduct among the Corinthian believers that disturbed Paul so greatly included a great deal of envy, hypocrisy, and "backbiting."

- Paul reminded the members of the Corinthian church that—as Christians—they would one day be called upon to help judge even the angels. So, they desperately needed to get their lives in order to be ready, eventually, for such a grave responsibility.

- Paul listed ten separate categories of sin, and the Corinthians had members in every category.

- Paul took great pains to emphasize the holiness of marital sex. He made it clear that our bodies are the temple of the Holy Spirit, and that we should not do anything to profane those temples.

## Study Questions

1. Why is suing each other in open court such a counterproductive example of non-Christian behavior?

2. How do you feel about the possibility that you will one day be called upon to judge an angel? Would this be fair? Would you be up to the job?

3. List the ten categories of sinners corresponding to the sins that Paul mentioned in 1 Corinthians 6:8–11.

4. Why is sexual intercourse, outside of marriage, such a devastating sin?

# Part Two
# Six Intriguing Questions

# 1 Corinthians 7
# On Matters of Marriage

## Let's Get Started

We have now come to a major division in this great letter. In the first six chapters, Paul confronted the Corinthians about some of the many compromises in the church. He did this based upon the disturbing <u>report</u> that he received concerning their <u>carnality</u>.

So . . . at this point in our study, you might be thinking that there was little hope for the church in Corinth. Granted, the challenges faced by the members of that congregation might have seemed insurmountable. But all was not lost. They had some good things going for them. First, they had access to their founding apostle and all of the apostolic wisdom that Paul brought to the table. And second, they were teachable. To their credit, they sought Paul's advice about a wide-ranging assortment of subjects.

Beginning with chapter 7, Paul answered a series of questions they asked via a letter they had <u>written</u> to him, most likely delivered to Paul in Ephesus by Stephanas, Fortunatus, and Achaicus (1 Corinthians 16:17). Their questions dealt with many different topics—from relationships to proper behavior at the Lord's Supper, from so-called gray areas to spiritual gifts, from wearing head coverings to the Resurrection.

Paul did not repeat the questions in his letter back to the Corinthians, but we can deduce the nature of each question from the answers that he gave. Their questions and Paul's answers evidence the confusion that existed among the members of the church, and their desire to receive the apostle's instructions.

The first series of questions had to do with marriage, divorce, and remarriage. Marriages were a mess in Corinth. We now have enough background information from the first six chapters of 1 Corinthians to understand why. Given the cesspool from which these believers "were washed . . . sanctified . . . justified"—which included widespread fornication, adultery, and homosexuality—we should not be surprised to learn that trying to bring order to these out-of-order

**report**
1 Corinthians 1:11

**carnality**
1 Corinthians 3:1

**written**
1 Corinthians 7:1

lifestyles was like trying to unscramble an egg. Many, if not most, of these Christians had made omelets out of their personal lives, not unlike many dear people in our churches today.

what others say

**Beth Moore**

Can you think of any need you might have that would require more strength than God exercised to raise the dead? Me either. God can raise marriages from the dead, and He can restore life and purpose to those who have given up. He can forgive and purify the vilest sinner. You have no need that exceeds His power. Faith is God's favorite invitation to RSVP with proof.[1]

Some in the church had been married, divorced, and remarried multiple times. Sound familiar? Some were living together outside of marriage. Others concluded that the best way to be spiritual was to forfeit sexual pleasure altogether and to become celibate for the rest of their lives. They didn't know where the lines were drawn.

It's not surprising, then, that Paul devoted a full forty verses to the subjects of singleness, marriage, divorce, and remarriage, for obviously their questions came fast and furious. Is it better to be married or single? If I am divorced, can I remarry? If I am married to an unbeliever who is involved in adultery or homosexuality, should I stay married to him or leave him?

There isn't much to applaud the Corinthians for, but I'll give them this. They apparently wanted to do the right thing. They turned, therefore, to their father in the faith in order to find out what the right thing was.

Even so, we must keep in mind that Paul was writing a letter, not a handbook on how to have a happy marriage. As a result, Paul's epistle sounds much more conversational in tone than a tightly outlined book manuscript. In some places Paul went off on tangents. In others, he began a topic, set it aside while addressing another, and then returned to the earlier one. In other words, he wrote it as he might speak if we were meeting him for coffee at Starbucks. We'll discuss each section of this great chapter in chronological order, keeping in mind that we might find ourselves dancing to the drumbeat to which Paul wrote.

## A Touchy Topic

**sister**
Genesis 12:19

*1 CORINTHIANS 7:1 Now concerning the things of which you wrote to me: It is good for a man not to touch a woman. (NKJV)*

"It is good for a man not to touch a woman" may seem like a strange statement to us. After all, what does "touch a woman" mean exactly? But strange though it may sound, it had a familiar ring to anyone familiar with the Old Testament.

We first encounter this phraseology in Genesis 20:6 where we read of Abimelech, the king of Gerar. Here, history repeated itself as far as Abraham was concerned. Twenty-five years earlier, while in Egypt, Abraham had lied to Pharaoh about his wife, Sarah, in a foolish attempt to save his skin while placing her at considerable risk by telling the monarch that Sarah was his <u>sister</u>. Even though Abraham left Egypt in disgrace because of this lie, twenty-five years later he once again told the same lie to Abimelech. In a dream, God commended Abimelech for acting with integrity toward Abraham's wife, instructed him to remove Sarah from his harem and to return her to Abraham, and pointed out that He protected Sarah when He "did not let [Abimelech] touch her" (Genesis 20:6 NKJV).

The same term is used in Ruth 2:9. When Boaz invited Ruth to glean in his field, he assured her of his protection when he said, "Have I not commanded the young men not to touch you?" (NKJV).

Proverbs 6:28–29 provides us with the clearest understanding of this phrase. Solomon asked, "Can one walk on hot coals, and his feet not be seared? So is he who goes in to his neighbor's wife; whoever touches her shall not be innocent" (NKJV).

Paul began chapter 7 right where he left off in chapter 6. He again called the Corinthian church to sexual purity, and commanded the men not to "touch a woman" in a sexually intimate manner outside of marriage.

## A Burning Issue

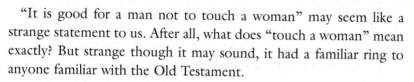

the big picture

**1 Corinthians 7:2–9**

Paul emphasized that sexual temptation is extremely difficult to resist. For this reason, he affirmed marriage as the one legiti-

**saved**
1 Corinthians 3:15

**duty**
1 Corinthians 7:3

mate man-woman relationship wherein sexual needs can and must be met. He gave his readers a number of guidelines regarding the role of sex in marriage, and the responsibilities of husbands and wives to one another regarding each other's sexual needs.

As we have noted, God <u>saved</u> a good number of the Corinthian Christians out of a lifestyle of sexual impurity. Consequently, many in the church were confused about how to live a sexually pure life. Precisely because of the sheer power of sexual temptation, Paul placed his apostolic rubberstamp on marriage as a good thing, a needed thing. In a sense, he gave his pastoral permission to his unmarried readers to get married when he said, "I say to the unmarried and to the widows: It is good for them if they remain even as I am; but if they cannot exercise self-control, let them marry. For it is better to marry than to burn with passion" (1 Corinthians 7:8–9 NKJV).

But don't think for one minute that Paul reduced marriage to nothing more than an outlet for sexual desire. In other passages—Ephesians 5:22–23 comes to mind, where Paul used the love of a husband for his wife as a metaphor for God's love of the church—Paul extolled the virtues of marriage as so much more than a sexual relationship. But in Corinth, where immorality in all of its perverted forms ruled the day, Paul talked turkey with them about marriage in the context of sexual purity.

Sexual temptation goes beyond physical desire; there is a spiritual component to it. Satan understands how powerful the urge to impurity can be and exploits it as a human weakness. Therefore, Paul warned his readers that every husband has a <u>duty</u> to his wife, and every wife a duty to her husband. That duty is to satisfy the sexual desire of the other, lest Satan take advantage of their human weaknesses and tempt one or both marriage partners into making bad choices with disastrous consequences.

We should derive much comfort from the fact that Paul specifically, and the biblical writers generally, understood the nature of human weakness. The Bible clearly stipulates that we humans lack self-control in a variety of areas, not just the sexual. We err in our thinking when we wrongly conclude that a spiritual person should somehow be above fleshly desires, sexual or otherwise. When Jesus's disciples could not keep from falling asleep just prior to His arrest in the Garden of Gethsemane, He warned them, "Watch and pray, lest you enter into temptation. The spirit indeed is willing, but the flesh is weak" (Matthew 26:41 NKJV). Just as their flesh is weak, so our flesh is weak.

It may be shocking to some that Paul spoke in such frank terms about this—not the kind of stuff one might expect to come pouring out of an apostle's pen. But this is right where many of us live, as did the Christians in Corinth.

The sexual union between a husband and his wife is the most beautiful, intimate, pleasurable, bond-building expression of love between two people. But on a purely pragmatic level, different people have different degrees of sexual needs. One aspect of selfless love that makes for a good marriage involves one marriage partner giving more of himself or herself sexually to his or her mate in recognition of, and with a desire to meet, those needs. When a husband or a wife willingly deprives his or her spouse of having that need met, he opens the other up to a satanic temptation "because of your lack of self-control" (1 Corinthians 7:5 NKJV). The Bible can't get much more practical than that!

Let's summarize. There is value to being single for reasons that Paul will outline toward the end of this chapter. There is also value to being married, particularly given the immorality out of which many in the Corinthian community were saved. Those who are married must understand that each partner takes upon himself certain responsibilities vis-à-vis the sexual union of a husband and wife. If one marriage partner chooses to deprive the other of sexual satisfaction, he opens the other up to satanic temptation "because of your lack of self-control" (7:5 NKJV). Simply stated, Paul told his confused Corinthian believers, "If you can handle being single, be single. But if you're burning sexually, get married. And if you do get married, celebrate your sexuality. Have sex often, and enjoy it to the full!"

## <u>On Matters of Marriage</u>

Paul tackled two questions in this next section of Scripture: (1) What about divorce and remarriage between two Christians? (2) What about divorce and remarriage when a Christian is married to an unbeliever?

**leave**
Genesis 2:24

Before we consider Paul's answer to each of these questions, allow me to offer this one caveat: In giving his answers, Paul is stating God's will, God's best in each situation. Paul set a high standard for marriage, and rightly so, especially given the cavalier attitude that many of the Corinthians had toward marriage. Marriage as God defined it in Genesis 2:24 was in short supply in Corinth. Some of Paul's answers might have seemed unrealistic, given the deplorable state of marriage in that seaport city. Indeed, some of his answers might seem unrealistic to us at a time when we in our own country are debating the definition of marriage. Nevertheless, what we are about to read in the remainder of this chapter clearly expresses God's will concerning marriage, divorce, and remarriage.

## A Biblical View of Divorce

> 1 CORINTHIANS 7:10–11 *Now to the married I command, yet not I but the Lord: A wife is not to depart from her husband. But even if she does depart, let her remain unmarried or be reconciled to her husband. And a husband is not to divorce his wife.* (NKJV)

Paul reinforced a principle of marriage—a *command*—that Jesus had already addressed, namely that the word *divorce* has no place in a Christian's lexicon. Jesus put it this way: "Have you not read that He who made them at the beginning 'made them male and female,' and said, 'For this reason a man shall <u>leave</u> his father and mother and be joined to his wife, and the two shall become one flesh'? So then, they are no longer two but one flesh. Therefore what God has joined together, let not man separate" (Matthew 19:4–6 NKJV). By reaching all the way back to the Garden of Eden, Jesus affirmed that from the very beginnings of the human race God designed marriage to be a committed (*joined*), monogamous (*to his wife,* singular), heterosexual (*male and female*) union that lasts for "as long as they both shall live" (*let not man separate*). Paul reiterated this standard by categorically stating, "A husband is not to divorce his wife."

Note that in that culture, the husband initiated the divorce and not the wife. You might remember that when Joseph discovered that his betrothed, Mary, was pregnant, "not wanting to make her a public example, [Joseph] was minded to put her away secretly" (Matthew 1:19 NKJV).

If Paul wrote to a church in this culture, he would surely state the principle "A husband is not to divorce his wife, nor is the wife to divorce her husband."

According to Malachi 2:16, "The LORD God of Israel says that He hates divorce" (NKJV). You don't need a PhD in clinical psychology to understand why. No one comes through a divorce unscarred—not the husband, nor the wife, nor the children. The collateral damage from every divorce is incalculable. Divorce not only destroys families; divorce tears at the very fabric of society. When God designed marriage and created the family, He did so with the intention that marriages last a lifetime.

You might be thinking, "But didn't Jesus permit divorce when the husband or the wife committed <u>adultery</u>?" If so, doesn't that mean that it's okay for a Christian to get a divorce? Well, yes and no.

Yes, Jesus permitted divorce in the case of adultery. When someone joins himself sexually to another, he has by that adulterous act shattered the marriage vow. The divorce doesn't shatter the marriage vow, the adultery does.

But no, even though Jesus *permitted* divorce in that situation, He did not *command* divorce, and He certainly did not *approve* of divorce. There are many things that God *permits* to happen even though He does not *approve* of them. In that sense, there is no such thing as a "biblical divorce"—a divorce of which God approves—adultery notwithstanding. The disciples clearly understood the sky-high standard that Jesus set for marriage, and so replied, "If such is the case of the man with his wife, it is better not to marry" (Matthew 19:10 NKJV). In other words, at the very least, marriage is not to be entered into lightly.

**adultery**
Matthew 19:9

---

**what others say**

**Kevin Leman**

Wives, your relationship with your husband must be your greatest concern. In modern times, we are sold such a bill of goods by "experts" who tell us marriage is a 50–50 proposition. It has to be 100–100; we don't just go halfway but put our spouse's needs ahead of our own.[2]

---

As far as Paul was concerned, divorce is not an option. But separation is. If a wife chooses to "depart from her husband," or a husband depart from his wife, she is to "remain unmarried or be reconciled to her husband," and vice versa. They are to remain unmarried lest they commit adultery. The fact that we are talking here about separation and not divorce is indicated by Paul's use of a word translated "depart" that is different from the one he used for *divorce*. Paul also spoke of the separation as temporary in that he held out the hope that the husband and wife would eventually be "reconciled."

God designed marriage to be a committed, monogamous, lifelong union of a husband and a wife. That's the standard the church is to hold out to society. That's the standard most parents would like to hold out to their children. No reasonable parent would want a son or daughter to experience the pain or bear the scars of a divorce. That being said, divorces do happen. When they do, it is incumbent upon a church to become a redemptive community of caring Christians who lavish upon a *repentant* divorcee the love and support he needs in order to rebuild his life. Divorce is not a scarlet sin. Divorced individuals should not be ostracized, degraded, or made to feel as though they are second-class Christians. God forgives divorce. So should we.

*apply it*

**what others say**

**Bill and Lynne Hybels**

In the covenant of marriage, God asks two self-willed sinners to come together and become one flesh—not in body only, but in spirit, in attitude, in communication, in love. Think about the implications. Imagine two self-willed sinners trying to submit to one another as God calls them to do. That will take a decade. Or imagine two self-willed sinners trying to serve one another joyfully. Another decade. It is a lifetime challenge—perhaps the single greatest challenge there is.[3]

## Living with an Unbelieving Spouse

1 CORINTHIANS 7:12–16 *But to the rest I, not the Lord, say: If any brother has a wife who does not believe, and she is willing to live with him, let him not divorce her. And a woman who has a husband who does not believe, if he is willing to live with her, let her not divorce him. For the unbelieving husband is sanctified by the wife, and the*

*unbelieving wife is sanctified by the husband; otherwise your children would be unclean, but now they are holy. But if the unbeliever departs, let him depart; a brother or a sister is not under bondage in such cases. But God has called us to peace. For how do you know, O wife, whether you will save your husband? Or how do you know, O husband, whether you will save your wife?* (NKJV)

go to

**salvation**
1 Corinthians 6:11

**blessing**
Ephesians 1:3

Unlike the previous section, where Paul affirmed an earlier teaching of Jesus, here Paul charted some new territory that Jesus did not address. Hence his statement, "But to the rest I, not the Lord say . . ." Specifically he answers the question, What should a Christian do who is married to a non-Christian?

The question likely arose because as individuals heard the gospel and received Christ, they suddenly found themselves married to unsaved spouses. They did not know if they should divorce them and marry Christians, or if they should remain married to the unbelievers. Paul's answer is not as complicated as you might think. He basically said that if the unbelieving spouse is willing to remain married to the Christian, they should not divorce. If, however, the unbeliever chooses to leave, the Christian should let him leave. Let's look at these two scenarios in a bit more detail.

While Paul's answer—a Christian should not divorce an unbelieving spouse—is not complicated, the reason behind the answer is confusing to some. A Christian should not divorce an unbelieving spouse because "the unbelieving husband is sanctified by the wife, and the unbelieving wife is sanctified by the husband; otherwise your children would be unclean, but now they are holy." Where this gets confusing is Paul's use of the words *sanctified* and *unclean.*

key point

• *Sanctified:* the word basically means, "set apart." In some contexts *sanctified* is a salvation term, but not here. Here Paul meant that a Christian enjoys God's blessing upon his or her life. That blessing spills over onto his or her family. Just as a family will suffer collateral damage from the wrong choices of a sinful family member, so too a family will enjoy (to coin a phrase) the collateral blessings that God lavishes upon His children. Indeed, a believing spouse may be the only source of grace in the home.

One of the possible collateral blessings might be the eventual salvation of the unbelieving spouse. With that in mind, Paul asked, "How do you know, O wife, whether you will save your husband?

Or how do you know, O husband, whether you will save your wife?" (1 Corinthians 7:16 NKJV).

Peter held out this hope to his readers who were married to spouses who opposed the gospel. In 1 Peter 3:1–7, Peter outlined a blueprint of behavior for a Christian wife married to an unsaved husband (vv. 1–6), and for a Christian husband married to an unsaved wife (v. 7). The principles Peter outlined in this passage are good advice for every husband and wife to follow, regardless of the spiritual condition of their mates. Peter wrote: "Wives, likewise, be submissive to your own husbands, that even if some do not obey the word, they, without a word, may be won by the conduct of their wives, when they observe your chaste conduct accompanied by fear. Do not let your adornment be merely outward—arranging the hair, wearing gold, or putting on fine apparel—rather let it be the hidden person of the heart, with the incorruptible beauty of a gentle and quiet spirit, which is very precious in the sight of God. For in this manner, in former times, the holy women who trusted in God also adorned themselves, being submissive to their own husbands, as Sarah obeyed Abraham, calling him lord, whose daughters you are if you do good and are not afraid with any terror. Husbands, likewise, dwell with them with understanding, giving honor to the wife, as to the weaker vessel, and as being heirs together of the grace of life, that your prayers may not be hindered" (NKJV).

• *Unclean:* The opposite of *sanctified*. Children born to two unbelieving parents have no godly influence in their home. They are separated from the unique blessings that God lavishes upon His children. But if one of their parents is a believer, they are *sanctified*, or made *holy* (from the same root word as *sanctified*), or "set apart" to enjoy God's blessings that comes to their home through their one believing parent.

Please don't wrongly conclude that it's a good thing for a Christian to marry a non-Christian, since God's blessings can flow through the believing spouse to the unbeliever. God does not endorse "missionary marriages." In 2 Corinthians 6:14, God clearly states, "Do not be unequally yoked together with unbelievers. For what fellowship has righteousness with lawlessness? And what communion has light with darkness?" (NKJV). A Christian should only marry a Christian. But if two non-Christians get married, and one of them commits his or her life to Christ, he should not divorce the unbelieving spouse for the reasons cited above. The only exception is when the unbeliever chooses to leave. In that situation, the believing spouse "is not under bondage," or bound by his or her marriage vow. If the unbelieving spouse chooses to leave, the believing spouse is permitted to marry another believer.

## To Be, or Not to Be?

The Corinthian Christians also wanted to know: (1) Does a Jew need to renounce his or her Jewish heritage when he becomes a Christian? (2) Does a Gentile (non-Jew) first have to become a Jew before he can become a Christian? (3) If a Christian slave is given the opportunity to become free, should he do so or is he obligated to remain with his master? (4) Just how free is a free man when he becomes a Christian?

At first blush, each of these four questions seems culturally irrelevant to us. But on the contrary, Paul's answers are applicable even to some situations today.

## To Be, or Not to Be Jewish?

1 CORINTHIANS 7:17–20 *But as God has distributed to each one, as the Lord has called each one, so let him walk. And so I ordain in all the churches. Was anyone called while circumcised? Let him not become uncircumcised. Was anyone called while uncircumcised? Let him not be circumcised. Circumcision is nothing and uncircumcision is nothing, but keeping the commandments of God is what matters. Let each one remain in the same calling in which he was called. (NKJV)*

While answering the four questions mentioned above, Paul stated this overarching principle: "As the Lord has called each one, so let him walk" (1 Corinthians 7:17 NKJV). He then repeated the principle in verse 20: "Let each one remain in the same calling in which he was called" (NKJV). And he repeated it one more time in verse 24: "Brethren, let each one remain with God in that state in which he was called" (NKJV). I think the good apostle was trying to tell us something.

As it applies to the Jewish question, Paul assured his readers that a Jew does not need to stop being Jewish when he acknowledges Jesus as his or her Messiah. "Was anyone called while circumcised?" he asked. *Called* is a term Paul used to refer to a Christian, a person whom God has *called* to Himself as His child—just as he did in 1 Corinthians 1:24. *Circumcised* is synonymous with being Jewish.

Those in the church who were Jewish when they received Christ wondered if they needed to stop being Jewish in order to follow Jesus. No doubt some in the church believed that they did, and put pressure on these Jewish Christians to renounce their Jewish heritage. I have many Jewish friends who have been taught that in order to receive Christ, they must first renounce their religious upbringing, stop going to synagogue, cease and desist from observing Jewish practices, and turn their backs on all things Jewish. Nothing could be farther from the truth.

Paul could not have stated the case more clearly when he said, "Was anyone called while circumcised? Let him not become uncircumcised." In other words, "Let him not stop being Jewish."

We Gentile believers owe much to our Jewish friends. Were it not for the Jews, we would not have our Bibles—Old or New Testaments—and we wouldn't have our Savior who was Himself Jewish. We share a common heritage. I have often expressed to people how envious I am of my Jewish brothers and sisters who continue to celebrate Passover and devote the Sabbath to God and family with a deeper meaning than I will ever know. There is a sense in which acknowledging Jesus as their long-awaited, prophesied and promised Messiah makes them more Jewish, not less. We place an unbiblical, offensive stumbling block in front of our Jewish friends when we demand that they renounce their heritage to become a Christian. To any Jew who receives Jesus as his or her Messiah, Paul wrote, "As the Lord has called each one, so let him walk." If he was Jewish when called, Paul said, let him continue to walk as a Jew.

What about a Gentile? Does he first have to become a Jew before he can become a Christian? A number of people in the early church taught exactly that. If that seems far-fetched to you, check out Acts 15:1–2: "Certain men came down from Judea and taught the brethren, 'Unless you are circumcised according to the custom of Moses, you cannot be saved.' Therefore, when Paul and Barnabas had no small dissension and dispute with them, they determined that Paul and Barnabas and certain others of them should go up to Jerusalem, to the apostles and elders, about this question" (NKJV). This heresy became such a big deal that Paul devoted an entire letter—Galatians—to correcting this doctrinal error.

To answer the question, Paul repeated the same principle when he said, "Was anyone called while uncircumcised? Let him not be circumcised." No, Paul assured them, you do not need to become a Jew before you can become a Christian. What mattered most was not whether they were Jewish. What mattered most was whether they kept the commandments.

Obedience is always the central issue for a follower of Jesus. It is the height of hypocrisy for someone to claim to follow Christ as Lord while living in willful defiance against Him.

When we stand before God some day, He will not ask us, "Were you a Jew or a Gentile?" His only concern will be, "Did you walk in My ways? Did your life demonstrate a desire to obey Me?" Remember the words with which Jesus concluded the Sermon on the Mount where He warned, "Not everyone who says to Me, 'Lord, Lord,' shall enter the kingdom of heaven, but he who does the will of My Father in heaven" (Matthew 7:21 NKJV). It's always been about doing the will of God. As the apostle John wrote, "He who does the will of God abides forever" (1 John 2:17 NKJV). Which begs the question, How obedient are we?

## To Be or Not to Be a Slave?

**1 CORINTHIANS 7:21–24** *Were you called while a slave? Do not be concerned about it; but if you can be made free, rather use it. For he who is called in the Lord while a slave is the Lord's freedman. Likewise he who is called while free is Christ's slave. You were bought at a price; do not become slaves of men. Brethren, let each one remain with God in that state in which he was called.* (NKJV)

To make some sense of this section of Scripture, we need to consider Paul's little letter (25 verses total) to Philemon. At the time, slavery was widespread throughout the Roman Empire. Some estimates of the number of slaves run as high as one-third of the empire's population. Slavery was woven seamlessly into the fabric of the empire, with slaves holding down jobs as teachers, artists, librarians, physicians, musicians, accountants—most any job could have been held by a slave. That's the upside.

**key point**

The downside is that slaves were considered subhuman chattel, and as such could be bought and sold at the whim of their masters. By the time of the New Testament, the face of slavery was changing throughout the empire. In AD 20, for example, the Roman Senate granted slaves accused of crimes the right to a fair trial. Increasing numbers of slaves were granted or purchased their freedom. Treatment of slaves was becoming more human as slave owners recognized that improved treatment tended to result in increased productivity. Paul's letter to Philemon gives us much insight into the slavery of the New Testament era.

It's likely that Paul was instrumental in Philemon's coming to faith in Christ (Philemon 19). We know that the church in Colossi met in his house (v. 2), and that he owned at least one slave—Onesimus.

Onesimus stole some money from Philemon and escaped to Rome. There he met Paul and eventually became a Christian. Paul loved Onesimus and wanted to keep him in Rome since he provided a valuable service to Paul while Paul was in prison (v. 11). However, Paul knew that Onesimus had broken Roman law (by stealing) and defrauded his master (by running away). Paul persuaded Onesimus to return to Philemon and wrote Philemon the letter in order to prepare the way. In the letter, Paul assured Philemon that Onesimus was returning to him as a brother in Christ (v. 16), urged Philemon to forgive him, and pledged to Philemon that Paul would repay Onesimus's debt, lest that be a hindrance to Philemon's graciously receiving Onesimus (vv. 17–20).

With that as our backdrop, let's revisit Paul's words in 1 Corinthians 7:21–24. Paul wrote to the slaves in the Corinthian church that, if they were granted their freedom or could purchase their freedom, they were under no obligation to remain with their masters. However, if they must remain slaves, Paul said, "Don't be concerned about it."

That phrase sounds grossly insensitive unless placed in its proper context. It's a matter of perspective. What Paul meant was this: "Were you a slave when you were saved? Don't be concerned that your being a slave will interfere with your ability to live a dynamic Christian life." This is evidenced by Paul's statement in verse 22, "remember, if you were a slave when the Lord called you, you are now free in the Lord" (NLT).

**King**
Revelation 19:16

> what others say
>
> **James S. Jeffers**
>
> The traditional expectations were that masters would take advantage of their power over their slaves, and that slaves would respond with deceptiveness and lack of zeal for their work. Masters are told in the New Testament to deal with their slaves in justice and fairness, knowing that God is their master, and to give up threatening their slaves.[4]

On the other hand, those who were free when they became Christians were now willing slaves of Jesus Christ, not by force but by choice, bound to Him as a blessed taskmaster who called them to the privileged position of serving the <u>King</u> of kings.

Both those who were slaves and those who were free were once held hostage in sin's iron-fisted grasp. Jesus paid a huge ransom to save us all. How tragic, then, for a Christian, slave or free, to become a "slave to men" by doing the sinful things everyone else pressures him to do. So Paul implored his *brethren* to "let each one remain with God in that state in which he was called" (1 Corinthians 7:24 NKJV).

## Celebrating Singleness

Paul also answered questions concerning marriage, divorce, and remarriage. And, he diffused the confusion regarding Judaism as it relates to Christian conversion. For good measure, he hit head-on some questions regarding slavery. That left one more question to be answered in this chapter—"What about the *gift* of singleness?"

In many of our churches, those who are single are often viewed as having a stigma. Single men are often made to feel guilty that they are not married; single women are often made to feel somehow inadequate, as if marriage is the be all and end all of a fulfilling life.

In my first youth pastorate, our church had a Sunday school class for singles that they called the "Spares and Pairs" class. Can you imagine the shame some felt when they were invited to join that class?

Before we dissect this large section of Scripture, we should first define a vitally important term. In 1 Corinthians 7:7, Paul referred to the *gift* of singleness. I submit that of all the gifts that God gives, the gift of singleness is arguably the most misunderstood.

The gift of singleness is typically defined as the God-given ability for someone to live a fulfilling, celibate life. That's a tactful way of saying that a person who has this gift is able to handle living with an unfulfilled sex drive. Though that's how the gift of singleness is typically viewed, that's not at all what Paul meant when he referred to singleness as a *gift*.

The reality is this: Every single individual *has* the gift of singleness. Being single is a gifted state of being. When a person gets married, he voluntarily relinquishes the gift of singleness. Singleness is not a gift that God gives to some, but not to others. A person has the gift of singleness by virtue of the fact that he is single. And as such, the gift of singleness ought to be embraced with gratitude rather than rejected with contempt.

While many well-meaning Christians put the pressure on the single members of a church to get into a relationship, Paul elevated singleness to heights rarely discussed in our churches today. Paul offered six compelling reasons why singleness is a gift given by God to be embraced, rather than some societal stigma to be avoided at all costs. The six reasons are: (1) the stresses of life; (2) the potential pressures in a marriage; (3) the brevity of life; (4) divided devotion; (5) the conviction of a father; and (6) the nature of marriage.

## The Stresses of Life

1 CORINTHIANS 7:25–27 *Now concerning virgins: I have no commandment from the Lord; yet I give judgment as one whom the Lord in His mercy has made trustworthy. I suppose therefore that this is good because of the present distress—that it is good for a man to remain as he is: Are you bound to a wife? Do not seek to be loosed. Are you loosed from a wife? Do not seek a wife. (NKJV)*

Paul used the word *virgins* as a reference to those who were single by virtue of the fact that they had never been married. He acknowledged that he was about to embark upon a subject that Jesus never addressed. Thus Paul essentially said, "Concerning those who have never been married, there is no teaching of Christ that I can quote. So I will offer my opinion as one entrusted by Christ to be an apostle."

His advice was this: Whatever state you are in, be content. If you are married, be content in your marriage. If you are single, be content in your singleness.

**what others say**

**Jan Frank**

Most of us struggle with waiting. If we have stepped out and done what we believe God has led us to do, we feel cheated or tricked when we don't receive what we think will be secured by our obedience. Americans have been conditioned to expect immediate gratification. We want to see the results in a timely fashion.[5]

The principle of contentment is one of the most vital dynamics of joyful Christian living. An attitude of contentment acknowledges that God has provided me with everything I need for my present fulfillment. Contentment is the result of focusing on everything that we have with gratitude, rather than dwelling upon what we don't have with resentment. Contented people are thankful people; discontented people tend to be embittered, resentful, angry.

Paul underscored the principle of contentment in 1 Timothy 6:6–9 when he wrote concerning personal finances, "Godliness with contentment is great gain. For we brought nothing into this world, and it is certain we can carry nothing out. And having food and clothing, with these we shall be content. But those who desire to be rich fall into temptation and a snare, and into many foolish and harmful lusts which drown men in destruction and perdition" (NKJV). The same can be said of contentment regarding one's marital status. Those who are discontented in their marriages, and those who are discontented being single, are often likely to "fall into temptation and a trap and into many foolish and harmful desires that plunge men into ruin and destruction."

Paul then alluded to "the present distress." Life under the bondage of Rome was distressing in ways we cannot begin to imagine. The people to whom Paul wrote were not free. Their every move was monitored, their every word weighed against the paranoia

of Roman rulers, who had a zero tolerance policy toward anything that sounded even remotely treasonous. Heavy taxation broke the backs of those subject to Rome's whims, to the point of exerting enormous pressure on a family's finances. Given "the present distress," Paul encouraged his readers to seek contentment whatever their marital status, though those who only had themselves to worry about obviously had an easier situation during distressing times than those who had to worry about a spouse and their children.

## The Potential Pressures in a Marriage

1 CORINTHIANS 7:28 *But even if you do marry, you have not sinned; and if a virgin marries, she has not sinned. Nevertheless such will have trouble in the flesh, but I would spare you. (NKJV)*

By *trouble*, Paul used a term that refers to the pressure created when two things are pushed together. *In the flesh* refers to this earthly life. Put them together and Paul said this: If you do decide to get married, you have not sinned. Just understand that when two people are pushed together, there will be pressure in the relationship.

Marriage is the lifelong, unconditional commitment of two imperfect people to one another, with emphasis on the word *imperfect*. Even though we are Christians, we are each significantly flawed. Marriage often magnifies our flaws, bringing pressure to bear upon both husbands and wives. Paul wanted to *spare* his readers that pressure by advocating the virtues of singleness.

## The Brevity of Life

1 CORINTHIANS 7:29–31 *But this I say, brethren, the time is short, so that from now on even those who have wives should be as though they had none, those who weep as though they did not weep, those who rejoice as though they did not rejoice, those who buy as though they did not possess, and those who use this world as not misusing it. For the form of this world is passing away. (NKJV)*

You've perhaps heard the adage "The main thing is to keep the main thing the main thing." The main thing, as Paul saw it, was to serve the Lord in whatever capacity you can for as long as you can, because hell's too hot and life's too short. Paul's catalog of couplets—"those who have wives should be as though they had none, those who weep as though they did not weep," etc.—was Paul's lyrical way of saying, "Don't get caught up in, or distracted by, the cares and emotions of a world that is soon passing away." The busyness of life often intrudes upon "the main thing" and distracts us from investing our time wisely. Having a spouse and kids compounds this reality, as we find ourselves shuttling between soccer games, music lessons, and dentist appointments, not to mention our jobs. Those who are single can also live on a lot less money and can limit their distractions when the only schedule they must keep is their own.

## Divided Devotion

1 CORINTHIANS 7:32–35 *But I want you to be without care. He who is unmarried cares for the things of the Lord—how he may please the Lord. But he who is married cares about the things of the world—how he may please his wife. There is a difference between a wife and a virgin. The unmarried woman cares about the things of the Lord, that she may be holy both in body and in spirit. But she who is married cares about the things of the world—how she may please her husband. And this I say for your own profit, not that I may put a leash on you, but for what is proper, and that you may serve the Lord without distraction. (NKJV)*

This section is the heart and soul of Paul's reasoning. A single person can serve the Lord with single-minded devotion. Without a spouse and children to care for, one who is single enjoys a mobility that a married individual cannot have. Those who are single should enjoy to the full the freedom that comes from not having to meet the needs of an immediate family, and should use their freedom to serve the Lord without the distraction of family.

## The Conviction of a Father

1 CORINTHIANS 7:36–38 *But if any man thinks he is behaving improperly toward his virgin, if she is past the flower of youth, and thus it must be, let him do what he wishes. He does not sin; let them marry. Nevertheless he who stands steadfast in his*

*heart, having no necessity, but has power over his own will, and has so determined in his heart that he will keep his virgin, does well. So then he who gives her in marriage does well, but he who does not give her in marriage does better. (NKJV)*

This is arguably the most challenging passage in 1 Corinthians to translate. It's also culturally specific, which makes it difficult to understand and to apply to our culture. Without getting into the nitty-gritty of the reasons for the various interpretations and translations, I'll simply offer my best determination as to what Paul meant.

During biblical times, marriages were arranged, usually by the father of the bride. Apparently, there were some dads in the Corinthian congregation who, out of devotion to God, dedicated their daughters to the Lord's work as single servants. Their intentions were commendable. If their daughters agreed, so much the better. Each father, having "so determined in his heart that he will keep his virgin, does well."

key point

But what if a daughter did not agree to remain single for her entire life? What was a father to do? Having dedicated her to the Lord's work as a single servant, should he refuse her desire for marriage and keep her single? Or could he violate his commitment and give her away in marriage? Paul said, "But if any man (her father) thinks he is behaving improperly toward his virgin (unmarried daughter), if she is past the flower of youth (if she is now of marriageable age), and thus it must be (that she wants to get married), let him (her father) do what he wishes. He does not sin; let them marry."

## The Nature of Marriage

1 CORINTHIANS 7:39–40 *A wife is bound by law as long as her husband lives; but if her husband dies, she is at liberty to be married to whom she wishes, only in the Lord. But she is happier if she remains as she is, according to my judgment—and I think I also have the Spirit of God. (NKJV)*

As we have noted throughout this chapter, marriage is a monogamous commitment between a man and a woman for a lifetime. They are bound to one another for as long as they both shall live. For this reason, marriage ought not be entered into lightly. It is one of the few choices that we make for which there is no exit strategy except the death of a spouse, over which we have no control; or a divorce, which causes enormous heartache for everyone involved. Given that reality, singleness should be for some an attractive and viable option.

When these six reasons are taken together, we can understand why Paul said that from his vantage point, all things considered, a person will be happier if he remains single. Sound advice, but only advice. Ultimately, when it comes to matters of singleness and marriage, each believer is free before God to make his or her own decision as God leads them.

## Chapter Wrap-Up

- The members of the Corinthian church had apparently sent Paul a long list of questions, which he proceeded to answer.

- Paul began by saying that it was "good for a man not to touch a woman," but by that he did not mean that men and women should not marry and have normal marital relations. He was simply saying that devoting your entire life to Christ can sometimes be easier for those who are not married, providing they are able to resist their sexual impulses given their lack of a legitimate outlet.

- Paul also knew the incredible value of a spiritual relationship between a husband and a wife, and was not in any way denigrating it or denying its validity and importance.

- Paul answered several questions about divorce and remarriage. Basically, he was against it just as God is, but made exceptions for situations in which one partner might turn out to be unfaithful. But even so, the divorce itself would still be unfortunate and regrettable.

- Paul admonished the Corinthian believers not to marry unbelievers. But if an unbeliever becomes an unbeliever while his or her spouse does not, this is not cause for divorce.

- Paul made it clear that Jews were not required to renounce Judaism and quit practicing the faith of their fathers because they accepted Christ as their Messiah.

- Paul had much to say about how a slave should conduct himself as a believer, which seems a contradiction in terms to modern readers but, within the culture of the times during which 1 Corinthians was written, was not a contradiction at all.

## Study Questions

1. What are some of the undocumented questions that the members of the church at Corinth might have asked Paul, based on his responses?

2. Did Paul oppose marriage for those who became full-time servants of God?

3. Is divorce ever okay with God?

4. Is it ever necessary for a Jew to renounce Judaism, if he becomes a believer in Christ?

# 1 Corinthians 8–10
# What Is Christian Liberty?

**Chapter Highlights:**
• No Other Gods
• The Weaker Ones
• Rights/Responsibilities
• All Things to All
• Focus on the Finish

## Let's Get Started

This next series of questions posed to Paul by the Corinthian Christians revolves around the thorny issue of Christian liberty. As Christians we are people of liberty. We have a tremendous amount of freedom when it comes to making choices. Indeed, Jesus said, "You shall know the truth, and the truth shall make you free" (John 8:32 NKJV). We have been set free from sin's <u>penalty</u>, free from sin's <u>power</u>, and we ultimately will be set free from sin's curse and <u>corruption</u>. That's the good news. But we live in a world where we are bombarded by stimuli strategically aimed at our <u>flesh</u>, where the enticement to sin is ever-present, where we battle our fleshly urges to do what we know is wrong.

That's the bad news. In such a sin-crazed city as Corinth, the Christians wrote Paul to ask, Just how free are we? For example, are we free to sin, knowing that God is gracious and that all will ultimately be <u>forgiven</u> and <u>forgotten</u>? An even more basic question: What makes a sin a sin? Are sins limited to the <u>Ten Commandments</u>? Or are there other sins not mentioned in that list? What should we do about situations in which we don't think something is sinful, but other Christians do? Are we free to follow our own consciences, or are we bound by the consciences of others? You can see where this gets kind of messy.

I am fairly confident that most of us would agree that where God has drawn a clear, indelible, unmistakable line in the sand and said, "Don't cross that line," we must obey Him; we are not free to sin. For instance, God said, "You shall not steal" (Exodus 20:15 NKJV). So, can we agree that as Christ's followers, it would not be a good thing to walk out of Wal-Mart with a 46-inch LCD HDTV we didn't pay for?

That being said, what about so-called "gray" issues, matters of choice for which we have no clear command? Are we free to do whatever we want, and to have the confidence that we are not sin-

**penalty**
Romans 8:1

**power**
Romans 8:2

**corruption**
Romans 8:21

**flesh**
Romans 7:18

**forgiven**
1 John 1:9

**forgotten**
Isaiah 43:25

**Ten Commandments**
Exodus 20:1–17

**go to**

temple
1 Corinthians
6:19–20

ning by doing it? If so, what about Christians who believe that a certain behavior is sinful even though there is no verse declaring it to be so?

As but one example, smoking comes to mind. Many of us might feel quite strongly that smoking is a sin. Yet, there is no verse that says, "Thou shalt not smoke." "Oh," but someone will say, "we just learned that our bodies are the <u>temple</u> of the Holy Spirit. We should not pollute God's temple with smoke. Besides, smoking produces a health risk." But then someone else might say, "Well, have you checked out the ingredients of a Big Mac recently? If that's not polluting God's temple, I don't know what is! And you're talking health risk? Your arteries might have something to say about eating fast food."

Both sides of the smoking question have a good point. Smoking is not specifically forbidden in Scripture. Nowhere does the Bible tell us that we will go to hell if we smoke cigarettes. We might smell like we did, but there simply is no verse. Does the silence of Scripture mean we are free to smoke? But if we follow the arguments offered by the smoking-is-sin faction, then eating at McDonald's is equally sinful.

Where do we draw the line when God has not drawn one for us? That's the overarching question Paul will attempt to answer in 1 Corinthians 8–10.

something to ponder

what others say

**Anne Graham Lotz**

Resistance to His authority will block the "flow" of His life within us. If we do not deal with it, our spiritual lives become stagnant and we lose our attractiveness and usefulness to God. And we have nothing refreshing about us that would draw other people to Christ.[1]

Smoking and eating Big Macs were not matters of concern in the Corinthian church. They faced other pressing issues. Namely, as they asked Paul, "Are we free to eat meat offered to idols?"

This would be no big deal to us. After all, I can't remember the last time I was tempted to eat an Idol Burger. But make no mistake about it—this issue not only threatened to divide the church in Corinth even further (as if *that* was possible), but this issue placed at risk the fragile faith of many in that city who were saved out of a background steeped in idol worship. So they asked Paul about it. His answer, while being rather lengthy (three full chapters), lays out for us a number of practical principles that will help us to navigate our lives around the many "gray" areas that we face each and every day.

**polytheism**
the belief in many gods

## No Other Gods but One

the big picture

**1 Corinthians 8:1-8**

Paul made his case: "Food does not commend us to God; for neither if we eat are we the better, nor if we do not eat are we the worse" (1 Corinthians 8:8 NKJV). He based his answer on the fact that there is only one true God. Since idols are false gods, the meat offered to them is just meat, nothing more and nothing less.

While this dispute might seem silly to us, it was anything but silly to a young, struggling church trying to survive in a culture of paganism and **polytheism**. We get a glimpse of what life was like in downtown Corinth by Luke's cryptic description of Athens in Acts 17:16: "The city was given over to idols" (NKJV). As was Athens, so was Corinth. Statues of false gods lined the streets. Temples to these false gods filled the back alleys. Many, if not most, of the members of the church in Corinth were saved out of a background of idol worship. They were vexed by vivid memories of times spent in those temples, worshipping at the feet of pagan gods.

It should come as no surprise to us that superstitious beliefs became attached to these idols and their respective religious practices. Animal sacrifice was not uncommon in idol temples. Followers of this god or that would bring the best of their flocks, or the best animals that their money could buy, and sacrifice them on an altar to their god.

The priests ate portions of the meat, and the leftovers were sold on the open market. There was a commonly held belief that evil, demonic spirits associated with each false god somehow infiltrated the meat as it was offered to each idol. Eating the meat could therefore result in demon possession. Many of the Christians in Corinth could not stomach the possibility of consuming such contaminated meat.

There were others who didn't buy into the whole demon-contaminated meat superstition, but who nevertheless could not bring themselves to eat the meat; it reminded them of their past participation in pagan sacrifices and ritual feasts. They were now ashamed of how they used to live and wanted to remove any and all reminders of their past devotion to such false gods.

A third faction in the church saw nothing wrong with eating the meat. They looked at the situation from a purely logical point of view. Like Paul, they realized that "an idol is nothing in the world, and that there is no other God but one" (1 Corinthians 8:4 NKJV). They were right in their belief. An idol was nothing but a statue. The meat offered as a sacrifice to an idol was just meat; nothing mysterious happened to the meat just because it was placed over a fire that was burning at the base of a statue.

key point

Paul's verdict? There was nothing wrong with eating the meat sacrificed to false *gods* or phony *lords*. But like most things in Corinth, it wasn't that simple.

Paul was concerned that those who clearly understood this issue would become proud because of their *knowledge*, and would hold it over the heads of those whose consciences would not permit them to eat the meat. I can understand his concern. Those who allowed their children to eat Halloween candy were tempted, I'm sure, to react with some measure of scorn toward their superstitious brethren, a reaction just as damaging to the unity of the body as the superstition itself. So Paul warned them not to let their knowledge puff them up or make them proud of their spiritual insight. The most important concern was to show love to those with whom they disagreed, and to build them up in their faith. Love, Paul reminded them, never acts superior toward others, or ridicules those whose beliefs differ from our own.

## The Weaker Brother or Sister

*the big picture*

### 1 Corinthians 8:9–13

Paul drew a distinction between those whose knowledge gave them the freedom to eat the meat and those who abstained from eating the meat due to a weak conscience. He then pointed out that love trumps liberty.

The Smart Guide to the Bible

This section of Scripture is easy to understand but difficult to apply. Paul urged those who felt free to eat the meat offered to idols to make certain that their liberty did not cause "the weak brother" to sin. It would be better, Paul told them, for the stronger brother to limit his freedom and not eat the meat, than for the stronger to cause the weaker brother to *stumble*—to violate his conscience by eating the meat, an action that the weaker person truly believed to be sinful.

what others say

**Pam Farrel**

There are times when we can ponder, plan, and think out our actions and reactions, but this title of *children of the light* seems to lead us to the conclusion that when we are in Christ we *are* different. We have radically different reactions, even when there is no time to think, no time to wonder, no time to rationalize, and no time to write a flowchart or business chart.[2]

If you think about it, this is easy to do in the abstract but difficult to do in the specific. Here's a good example. Person A, one of the stronger people in the Corinth congregation, might respond by thinking, *Okay, I'll invite my weaker brother over for a barbecue, but I won't serve any idol burgers.* Problem solved. Or is it? What if next week that same "Person A" invites some *other* friends over for a meal and this time serves idol burgers? If the weaker brother hears about it, won't he be offended? Is there not the risk that the stronger brother's freedom to eat the idol burgers might confuse the weaker brother and even tempt him to violate his own conscience, via one of those all-too-familiar "If he can do it why can't I?" justifications? Where do we draw that line?

True, Paul did say, "If food makes my brother stumble, I will never again eat meat, lest I make my brother stumble" (1 Corinthians 8:13 NKJV). But here's another good example of how that can backfire in real, modern-day life. My wife and I have a lot of friends. They represent a variety of backgrounds, life experiences, and Christian convictions. One of our friends used to worship at the altar of the NFL. In fact, watching games took so much of his time it caused him to miss church for the entire football season, and cost him a lot of money because he couldn't resist betting on the games.

something to ponder

**go to**

**Lord's Day**
Revelation 1:10

Now, to his credit, after a lot of prayer and meditation (plus a lot of convicting by the Holy Spirit), our friend has given up watching football on Sunday because he knows that the temptation to pervert the <u>Lord's Day</u>, by gambling and avoiding worship services, is not what God wants for him. Football had become his lowercase "god," and he had to recognize that particular weakness and make some changes to put God Himself back into His rightful position within my friend's own life.

And yet, at the same time, to me a football game is just a football game. I can take it or leave it. But I enjoy it. Many of my other friends enjoy it. Watching football has never been a stumbling block to my faith. I applaud the lifestyle change that my friend has made. But—and here's where the rubber meets the road—am I therefore wrong to invite other people over to my home after church to watch a game as long as I don't invite this one particular friend? Might my liberty tempt him to violate his conscience and get sucked right back into a behavior pattern that was so spiritually destructive for him?

Before I answer that, let's consider what Paul meant by the stronger and weaker brother (or sister). Truth be told, we are all the weaker brother; we just have different areas of weakness. For instance, I have some friends who cannot enter a bar and live to tell the tale. Alcohol is their weakness. When they made the decision to follow Jesus, they vowed that they would never drink alcohol again. Regarding anything alcohol-related, they are the weaker brothers and sisters.

*Something to ponder*

I work with some college students for whom unfettered access to online pornography is their greatest weakness and pathway toward certain spiritual destruction. They will not permit themselves to get online without supervision. Regarding anything Internet-related, they are the weaker brothers and sisters.

Point is, you have your weaknesses and I have mine. In that sense, we are each the weaker brother or sister. We just each have different weaknesses.

*apply it*

So the question remains: To what degree do I allow myself to be held hostage to other people's weaknesses? Let's consider each of the above examples. My friend with the football weakness and I have talked this through. I have applauded his conviction against watching a football game on Sunday. He understands that I do not have the same weakness, though I have other weaknesses that he may not have. He accepts the fact that football does not present to me the potential conflict of conscience that it presents to him. He is totally supportive of my watching a game, and even of my inviting others to watch a game with me. It's amazing how easily some potential issues that could otherwise divide us are readily resolved just by having a conversation in the spirit of love and humility, one weaker brother to another.

**drunkenness**
Ephesians 5:18

Alcohol abuse is a big deal among the college students in my community. Add to that the fact that my own dad could not control his own alcohol consumption, and that his drinking contributed to the breakup of our family. For these reasons, even though I have the *knowledge* that the Bible forbids <u>drunkenness</u> but not drinking, I have established for myself a conviction that I will not drink. My attitude toward drinking is this: Others may, but I will not. I don't look down in judgment on those who have an occasional glass of wine with their meal. I have simply chosen not to—lest one of my students open my refrigerator, see a can of beer, decide that since the pastor drinks he too can drink, and eventually becomes a regrettable statistic, a casualty of college-age drinking.

I have counseled students that if they cannot handle unsupervised online access, place filters on their personal computers. If that doesn't work, use the computer lab at school. If that's not practical, make the commitment that they will not use a computer unless their roommate is home. In other words, do whatever it takes to ensure that you do not place yourself in a potentially compromising situation. That being said, I don't limit my computer use out of a fear that, if I go online unsupervised, they will be tempted to do the same. Like the situation with my football friend, a frank conversation in the spirit of love and humility will go a long way to resolving an otherwise messy situation.

If eating a piece of meat offered to an idol was a big deal to the Corinthian Christians, Paul completely trumped the issue by talking about his right to receive money in comparison to their right to receive meat. Paul had a right to be paid by the churches he served for the ministry he rendered on their behalf. But Paul willingly chose to limit that liberty in order to magnify the effectiveness of his ministry. As he developed this illustration, we gain some significant insight into the scriptural responsibility of a church to pay its pastors, and a tidbit of information about Peter's matrimonial arrangement. All in all, 1 Corinthians 9 is quite an interesting read.

# Rights Versus Responsibilities

**go to**

**Jerusalem-based**
Acts 22:3

**Pharisee**
Philippians 3:5

**Jesus**
Acts 9:5

**the big picture**

## 1 Corinthians 9:1–18

In the previous section of Scripture, Paul exhorted his readers to limit their freedom lest their *liberty* cause a *weaker* brother or sister to *stumble*. In this section, Paul illustrated from his own life how he voluntarily limited his liberties.

With a flurry of rhetorical questions, Paul reminded his readers that he wrote to them with apostolic authority, and as an apostle he was free to correct their flawed thinking regarding matters of liberty. He certainly had all the necessary credentials. He saw Jesus up close and personal. (Though Paul never mentioned a time when he heard Jesus teach, it is inconceivable to me that a Jerusalem-based Pharisee would not have gone to see Him out of curiosity, if nothing else. We do know that Paul saw the resurrected Jesus on the road to Damascus.) Of all people, the Christians in Corinth witnessed Paul's apostolic authority in action and should have been the first to affirm his role in their lives as an apostle.

Having reminded his readers of his authority, Paul next asserted his rights as a Christian. In rapid-fire, staccato-like questions, Paul affirmed his right to enjoy a meal (whether or not the meat had been offered to an idol), to be accompanied on his missionary journeys by a Christian wife, and to be supported by the churches for his ministry to them.

We know from Mark 1:29–31 that Peter was married. (You can't have a mother-in-law unless you've walked down the center aisle.) Though we never hear about her directly, it is evident from 1 Corinthians 9:5 that Peter and the other married apostles were accompanied in their travels by their wives.

Paul had a right to receive support from the churches for his ministry. He illustrated this right by a series of examples. Soldiers who go to war on behalf of their country are paid a salary by that country; no soldier is expected to be self-supporting. A person who plants a vineyard has the right to eat of the fruit of his labor. A person who tends a flock has the right to drink of the milk of his flock.

That a person has the right to be paid a fair wage for his labor is a principle that goes all the way back to the Law of Moses, who wrote,

something to ponder

"You shall not muzzle an ox while it treads out the grain" (Deuteronomy 25:4 NKJV), a directive commanding a farmer to allow his beast of burden to eat of the grain he is using his animal to thresh. Using this example as a metaphor for ministry, Paul planted spiritual seed and the church at Corinth was part of the fruit of his labor. He therefore had a right to be supported by the church. Indeed, even the priests who served in the temple in Jerusalem were supported in their ministries by the tithes and <u>offerings</u> presented at the temple.

offerings
Numbers 18:8–24

Jesus taught this same principle in Luke 10:7 when He *commanded* His disciples, "Stay in that house, eating and drinking whatever they give you, for the worker deserves his wages" (NIV).

Paul established beyond any reasonable doubt that as an apostle he had both the right and the liberty to receive support from those to whom he ministered. "I have used none of these things, nor have I written these things that it should be done so to me; for it would be better for me to die than that anyone should make my boasting void" (1 Corinthians 9:15 NKJV). Paul willingly relinquished his right to a paycheck. "What is my reward then?" he asked. "That when I preach the gospel, I may present the gospel of Christ without charge, that I may not abuse my authority in the gospel" (1 Corinthians 9:18 NKJV).

Paul expanded this thought a bit when he wrote to the church in Thessalonica, "Affectionately longing for you, we were well pleased to impart to you not only the gospel of God, but also our own lives, because you had become dear to us. For you remember, brethren, our labor and toil; for laboring night and day, that we might not be a burden to any of you, we preached to you the gospel of God" (1 Thessalonians 2:8–9 NKJV). While it would have been perfectly appropriate for Paul to receive regular paychecks for each of these churches—in Corinth and Thessalonica—he voluntarily relinquished his rights and limited his liberty in order to increase the effectiveness of his ministry. By implication, Paul was challenging the Christians in Corinth, "If I can lay aside my right to receive money from you, you can surely limit your liberty and choose not to serve up idol burgers if doing so would cause a weaker brother or sister to violate his or her conscience and sin."

key point

# Becoming All Things to All Men

*1 CORINTHIANS 9:19–23 For though I am free from all men, I have made myself a servant to all, that I might win the more; and to the Jews I became as a Jew, that I might win Jews; to those who are under the law, as under the law, that I might win those who are under the law; to those who are without law, as without law (not being without law toward God, but under law toward Christ), that I might win those who are without law; to the weak I became as weak, that I might win the weak. I have become all things to all men, that I might by all means save some. Now this I do for the gospel's sake, that I may be partaker of it with you. (NKJV)*

You might call this section of Scripture "Paul's Philosophy of Ministry." As the cliché goes, "The main thing is keeping the main thing the main thing." Paul summarized the main thing when he said in verse 22, "I have become all things to all men, that I might by all means save some" (NKJV).

**key point**

No matter to whom he was speaking, Paul never compromised his message. He presented the gospel truthfully and forcefully. By the same token, Paul never unnecessarily offended those to whom he spoke by behaving in an insensitive manner. For example, when Paul went to a Jewish community he purposely limited his freedom so as not to offend his Jewish audience.

For instance, in Acts 16:3, out of deference to the Jews in Derbe and Lystra, Paul circumcised Timothy, lest his uncircumcision be a stumbling block to those whom Paul was trying to reach. In Acts 18:18, Paul shaved his head and took a Nazirite vow. In Acts 21:20–26, Paul instructed those who were with him to act in such a way as not to offend the Jews in Jerusalem. They were told, "Concerning the Gentiles who believe, we have written and decided that they should observe no such thing, except that they should keep themselves from things offered to idols, from blood, from things strangled, and from sexual immorality" (Acts 21:25 NKJV). Paul told them to limit their freedom so that their behavior would not be a stumbling block to the Jews hearing the gospel. Paul consistently applied this principle whether he was trying to reach Jews or Gentiles.

So here were the Corinthian Christians, all worked up into a dither over whether they could eat meat offered to idols, even when such an exercise of freedom destroyed the fragile faith of those whose consciences were weak. Once again, by implication, if Paul could limit his freedom for the spiritual good of others, so could those in the church in Corinth.

How do we apply this principle today? I don't have a perfect answer to that question since at times I apply the "all things to all men" principle imperfectly. But I'll offer a few examples from my own life and ministry.

I am free to dye my hair some fluorescent color, but I choose to limit my freedom in this area because (1) I really don't want to walk around with a purple stripe through my hair, but more important because (2) I don't want my hair color to become a distraction from the message I am seeking to bring to the people God has called me to reach. However, I know of some very effective youth pastors who have died their hair precisely because, by doing so, they have been given an entrée to an entire population of street kids who hang out and in some cases live under the bridges of Portland. Those were the people God called them to reach, and they became all things to those young people in order to reach them.

There are individuals in our community who will not come to our church if invited, unless it's to attend a Super Bowl party. So we are having a Super Bowl party at our church.

I love to ride motorcycles. Guess what I discovered? There are guys in my town who would not come to my church to hear me preach until they discovered that I'm a biker. Once that bond was built, they were willing to give me their ear.

I love to play softball. By joining a softball team in town, I have been able to meet dozens of guys I wouldn't meet in any other way.

## what others say

### Carol Kent

When I pray about who God wants me to mentor intentionally, I ask that I would be able to look past the woman's current ministry position and past her education (or lack of it) and see her potential. Perhaps she doesn't look like it today, but she may be the next Henrietta Mears or Corrie ten Boom or Elisabeth Elliot. We need to ask God to give us lenses through which we can see the potential of the people around us, to quicken our mind and touch our spirits with discernment as we seek to invest time and training in helping someone else carry the message of Christ.[3]

You get the idea. Each of our hobbies and interests can provide open doorways of opportunity through which we can build relationships with the people we are seeking to reach with the gospel.

So Paul's "all things to all men" principle is a double-edged sword. On the one hand, we limit our freedom to do some things if those things would become a distraction to our message. But on the other hand, we capitalize on our freedom when such freedom enables us to build relationships with those whom we might not otherwise reach.

## Focusing on the Finish

*1 CORINTHIANS 9:24–27 Do you not know that those who run in a race all run, but one receives the prize? Run in such a way that you may obtain it. And everyone who competes for the prize is temperate in all things. Now they do it to obtain a perishable crown, but we for an imperishable crown. Therefore I run thus: not with uncertainty. Thus I fight: not as one who beats the air. But I discipline my body and bring it into subjection, lest, when I have preached to others, I myself should become disqualified. (NKJV)*

Paul was as committed to his mission as an Olympic athlete is to winning the gold. We are not striving for a medal or trophy to wear around our necks or to mount on our mantels. We are striving for something of infinitely greater value—the eternal souls of men and women, and an imperishable "crown of righteousness, which the Lord, the righteous Judge, will give to me on that Day, and not to me only but also to all who have loved His appearing" (2 Timothy 4:8 NKJV).

Just as athletes exercise strict discipline—regarding their diet, sleep schedule, workout regimen, etc.—so Christians who take their calling seriously exercise strict discipline, especially in matters of freedom. There are places they won't go, activities in which they won't participate, freedoms they won't allow themselves simply because to do so could lessen their effectiveness as Christ's servants. There may be certain activities that other Christians can enjoy, but they won't because they know that, given their weaknesses, they might not be able to handle it. The wise Christian knows his or her weaknesses. They know where their lines need to be drawn. Like Paul, they live in mortal fear of one day becoming *disqualified*. They don't want to fall during the race and forfeit their prize.

Paul knew too many people who did just that. For example, Paul warned Timothy to "wage the good warfare, having faith and a good conscience, which some having rejected, concerning the faith have suffered shipwreck, of whom are Hymenaeus and Alexander, whom I delivered to Satan that they may learn not to blaspheme" (1 Timothy 1:18–20 NKJV). By setting themselves in opposition to God, Hymenaeus and Alexander disqualified themselves and became casualties of war.

Paul wrote that his one-time fellow <u>laborer</u>, Demas, "has forsaken me, having loved this present world" (2 Timothy 4:10 NKJV). By renouncing his faith and embracing a <u>world</u> of wickedness, Demas disqualified himself.

Paul *disciplined* himself, <u>denied</u> himself, and limited his freedom in order to make sure that he didn't disqualify himself. We should do no less.

Paul ended this rather lengthy, three-chapter discussion of Christian liberty with this bottom-line statement: "Therefore, whether you eat or drink, or whatever you do, do all to the glory of God" (1 Corinthians 10:31 NKJV). And, of course, whenever we see the word *therefore*, we should ask ourselves, "Why is the *therefore* there for?" The answer can be found in 1 Corinthians 10.

**go to**

**laborer**
Philemon 24

**world**
1 John 2:15–17

**denied**
Luke 9:23

key point

## Wisdom from the Wilderness

the big picture

### 1 Corinthians 10:1–13

The example of the Israelites in the wilderness paints a vivid portrait of what can happen to God's people when they exercise freedom without self-control. In a word, that generation of disobedient and undisciplined Israelites became *disqualified* as far as entering the Promised Land was concerned.

The exercise of our freedoms, absent self-control, can lead to excess. And excess, if left unchecked, can result in disqualification. That's the point Paul wanted to hammer home. And he used a perfectly appropriate biblical illustration to do so.

**fire**
Exodus 13:21

**Red Sea**
Exodus 14:26–31

**food**
Exodus 16:15

**serpents**
Numbers 21:6

**destroyer**
Numbers 16:3–41

**hard-hearted**
Matthew 19:8

The Israelites suffered as slaves under the iron-fisted rule of the wicked pharaohs of Egypt. In rather dramatic fashion, God delivered His people and led them to the safety of their own land. You might recall our brief discussion of the Passover in 1 Corinthians 5. God led them by a cloud by day and a pillar of <u>fire</u> by night. He led them through the <u>Red Sea</u>. He supernaturally provided them with daily <u>food</u> and water. Yet, with all of those blessings and daily reminders of God's presence and provision, they lusted "after evil things" (1 Corinthians 10:6 NKJV) and became immoral *idolaters*. Consequently, some "were destroyed by <u>serpents</u>" (10:9 NKJV). Still others "were destroyed by the <u>destroyer</u>" (10:10 NKJV). At one point, "twenty-three thousand fell" (10:8 NKJV). And eventually that entire generation died in the wilderness. Their <u>hard-hearted</u> behavior disqualified them from entering the Promised Land.

I have often taught that the four deadliest words in the Christian life are "I can handle it." So many Christians, thinking they can handle it, enjoy their freedoms without self-control only to discover that they can't handle it. Paul warns us that the moment we think we can handle it, just when we think we can stand on our own two feet, is when we fall. For make no mistake about it. With every temptation, God will give us a way out. But when we refuse to take the way out, that's when disaster is looming.

What we're sensing from the pen of Paul is the tension that exists between liberty and legalism. Legalism involves a man-made list of rules that, by their very nature, tend to be arbitrary and will differ from person to person. Legalism is the mentality that says God gave us ten commandments, but He left out of a few. So we're going to help Him out by adding to the list. Invariably, when we add to the list, we come up with a litany of absolute statements for which we have no scriptural backing. The comforting thing about such a list is that we don't have to exercise any sort of discernment; we just keep the rules. Problem is, since there is no scriptural backing, many people rebel against the list and are viewed by others who are devoted to the list as sinful and unspiritual.

For example, it's a whole lot easier to say to someone, "Thou shalt not go to R-rated movies" than it is to teach someone to discern between movies that are helpful and those that are harmful. Yet I will tell you that I know of several PG-13 movies that are worse than some R-rated movies as far as some of the scenes, language, and themes are concerned.

That being said, if we opt for liberty versus legalism we quickly encounter the reality that "all things are lawful for me, but all things are not helpful. All things are lawful for me, but I will not be brought under the power of any" (1 Corinthians 6:12 NKJV). In other words, my exercise of my liberty, if left unchecked, might result in behaviors that are harmful rather than beneficial. I might even find myself mastered by, or addicted to, something that might ultimately lead to my disqualification. See the dilemma?

So Paul rightly opted for liberty over legalism, but with this one caveat: Don't let your liberty do to you what it did to the Israelites.

**legalism**
holding to the Law
precisely

> **what others say**
>
> **Charles Stanley**
>
> Freedom from **legalism** comes through accepting the truth about our favored position in the family of God. Those who have put their trust in Christ have been adopted into His family. There is no concept that speaks any clearer of acceptance than adoption. Whereas a pregnancy can come as a surprise, adoption is always something that is premeditated and planned.[4]

## All to the Glory of God

> **the big picture**
>
> **1 Corinthians 10:14–33**
>
> Paul wrapped up this discussion of Christian liberty by making a final appeal that "whether you eat or drink, or whatever you do, do all to the glory of God" (v. 31 NKJV).

Back to the meat offered to idols issue. Paul basically told them, "Look, when it comes to eating meat offered to idols, use discernment. If you are eating the meat as a part of a worship ritual dedicated to an idol—just like when you take Communion as a part of your worship of God—then do not eat the meat. You cannot worship the Lord through Communion and then turn around and worship a demon by eating meat offered to a false god. That's exactly what Israel did in the wilderness. They tried to have it both ways. They worshipped the true God, and then turned around and worshipped an idol. That's exactly what Gentile unbelievers do. By saying that they want to worship God, but then worshipping an idol, they provoke God to jealousy.

"However, when you just want to have a meal, and you look upon the meat as just meat, go ahead and eat it. You don't need to feel guilty just because it comes from the temple meat market. But if a Christian brother or sister is with you and says to you, 'Don't you know that that meat was offered to idols?' limit your liberty and refrain from eating the meat. It's just not worth tempting your brother or sister in Christ to violate his or her conscience by enticing them to eat the meat with you."

This is what Paul meant by eating to the "glory of God." Even in the mundane activities of life—like eating and drinking—we can give God glory, or rob Him of His glory. It really all comes down to this: "I don't just do what is best for me; I do what is best for others so that many may be saved" (1 Corinthians 10:33 NLT).

# Chapter Wrap-Up

- These chapters in 1 Corinthians deal with issues of "freedom and liberty," as faced by the Corinthian believers.

- Whether it was okay to eat meat that had been offered to pagan idols was a big issue for them in that time and place. Paul did not give a hard-and-fast answer, but admonished them to conduct themselves in ways that would not lead others astray. There was nothing intrinsically wrong in eating such meat, but would their doing so, in certain situations, suggest to others that they were still pagans?

- Paul examined all sides of the above question, explaining that "freedom to be me" (to use a modern expression!) is fine as long as we maintain our focus on God and do not allow our own actions to distract or influence others in negative ways. We are responsible to God for our inner spiritual condition, but also for how we behave in front of others on the so-called surface. Thus the parallels to today's situations become obvious.

- Through everything, Paul admonished the Corinthians to keep their eye on the "finish," meaning God Himself, to whom our respect, love, and obedience are all part of the same package.

# Study Questions

1. Have you ever been accused by a nonbeliever of doing something that "a Christian is not supposed to do"? If so, how did you handle the situation? What did you learn from it?

2. What parallels can you draw between the "eating meat offered to idols" controversy in 1 Corinthians and your own life?

3. What freedoms do you feel you have as a Christian that might be considered controversial to others?

4. What freedoms do you *not* have that other Christians believe they *do* have?

# 1 Corinthians 11
# Conduct in the Church

## Let's Get Started

Take a deep breath. We are about to set sail through some extremely turbulent waters of controversy.

The second half of 1 Corinthians 11 will raise nary an eyebrow. There we'll be discussing proper conduct when we partake of the Lord's Supper or Communion. As we'll soon learn, many of the Christians in Corinth were actually getting drunk on the Communion wine. And that was just the start of their problems. I'm sure we'll all agree that such a reckless disregard for the symbolism of the Lord's Supper was not kosher, and that Paul had to lower the boom on that kind of behavior.

But it's the first half of this chapter that will cause some wrinkles of concern. Paul made some pretty pointed statements about the roles of men and women in the church, many of which would draw catcalls from certain segments of our society if he dared to make them today. He included as a part of his discussion the need for women to wear head coverings or veils in church. I don't know if you've taken any sort of a survey lately. But last Sunday, as I scanned my own congregation, there wasn't a veil in the place, worn by either the men or the women. Paul wrote at some length about the length of men's and women's hair. And he even dared to suggest that women were subordinate to men. Imagine how that would play if Paul made such statements on *Larry King Live*.

So what gives? Are the women in my church sinning because they don't wear veils? Are some of the men who prefer longer hair, and some of the women who prefer shorter hair, violating an absolute teaching of Scripture? Are women truly subordinate to men?

Is the first half of 1 Corinthians 11 as absolutely binding upon us as the second half of the chapter? Or, if we regard Paul's words as culturally specific and therefore non-binding upon believers today, what about Paul's controversial statement in verse 3, "But I want you to know that the head of every man is Christ, the head of woman is man, and the head of Christ is God" (NKJV)? Is that statement relevant to our lives and in our culture today?

If these issues seem confusing to us, we're in good company. The Corinthian Christians wondered about them too. Apparently they asked Paul questions like, What is the role of men and women in the church? Should men and women wear head coverings? What constitutes appropriate and inappropriate behavior at the Communion table?

We might be tempted to think that these matters were Corinth-specific. On some level they were. However, as has been true up to this point in Paul's letter, the underlying principles in Paul's answers to the Corinthians say volumes to us today.

## A Cultural Consideration?

Before we get into the particulars regarding the issues of head coverings and women's roles within the church, we must first place ourselves in the context of Corinth. Confusion abounded regarding these sensitive issues. Two cultural practices were colliding in their church, and this collision created an enormous amount of confusion for the Christians who worshipped there.

**key point**

For example, most Jewish women customarily covered their heads when at a worship service. Naturally, these women who converted to Christianity brought their head-covering custom into the church. In truth, if some of these women went to church without covering their heads, some would have interpreted that cultural faux pas as a tacit admission on the part of these women to having loose morals. Some liberated Greek women, on the other hand, went to worship services without wearing head coverings. We can only imagine the tension that collision of cultures created for the Corinthian Christians.[1]

Add to this the additional confusion concerning male and female roles within the church. Paul found himself having to defuse yet another bomb that threatened to further blow apart the fragile fellowship of this troubled congregation.

## Exemplary Behavior

1 CORINTHIANS 11:1 *Imitate me, just as I also imitate Christ.* (*NKJV*)

Remember that the chapter and verse divisions that help us to locate specific passages quickly and effortlessly were not a part of the original text. When Paul wrote this letter, he did not include chapter and verse designations. Consequently, the editors who first added them to the text had to make certain editorial decisions as to where the biblical writers intended to make such breaks. For the most part, these editors did a good job. But once in a while, certain chapter breaks occur in questionable places. Such is the case with 1 Corinthians 11:1.

**go to**

**studying**
Acts 22:3

Some translators believe that 1 Corinthians 11:1 should have been included at the end of chapter 10 as the thirty-fourth verse, and that chapter 11 really begins at verse 2. Others believe that the original editor was correct in placing the chapter break after 1 Corinthians 10:33 as it appears in our Bibles. The truth of the matter is that it simply doesn't matter. The principle contained in 1 Corinthians 11:1 applies equally to Paul's discussion of meat in chapter 10, and to his treatment of men's and women's roles in the church in chapter 11.

On the face of it, Paul's statement—"Follow my example"—may strike some as arrogant. In reality, 1 Corinthians 11:1 drips with humility, as if Paul said, "Follow my example, but only do so to the degree that I follow Christ's."

You might remember a few years back when bracelets that had the four letters—WWJD—were all the rage. These letters, of course, asked the question, "What would Jesus do?" A good sentiment in the abstract, to be sure, but often difficult to apply in the specific. In our culture, we don't always know what Jesus would have done in any number of situations. What kind of car would Jesus drive today? What kind of clothing would Jesus wear? For whom would Jesus vote in one of our elections? It's like trying to nail Jell-O to the wall. We each have differing opinions about what Jesus would do if He were walking today in our Nikes.

**something to ponder**

The situation in Corinth was quite similar. Just as our world today is quite removed from life in first-century Galilee or Judea, so Corinth was culturally in a world of its own, one that was utterly unlike Capernaum or Jerusalem. It wasn't always clear what Jesus would do if He was walking the streets of Corinth. The believers there had no access to Him; by the time Paul wrote this letter, Jesus had been dead some twenty-two years. But they did have access to Paul, someone who was <u>studying</u> in Jerusalem at the same time Jesus

**go to**

**Damascus**
Acts 9:3

**love**
1 Corinthians 8:1

**die**
Philippians 2:8

**order**
1 Corinthians 14:40

taught and performed miracles in the Holy City. It's quite likely that Paul had seen and heard Him teach. Paul saw the resurrected Jesus on the road to <u>Damascus</u> and spoke with Him face-to-face. Since Paul saw Jesus up close and personal, he was in a position to say to his readers, *As you watch me strive to follow Christ's example, so you follow my example.*

**what others say**

**William Barclay**

When we are undergoing hardship, unpopularity, or material loss for the sake of Christian principles, we may regard ourselves either as victims or as the champions of Christ. Paul is our example; he regarded himself not as the prisoner of Nero but as the prisoner of Christ.[2]

One common thread that links 1 Corinthians 10 and 11 together is the idea of submission or subordination. Many people today view these words negatively, as if they imply some forced limitation of their freedom. How unfortunate. The biblical concept of submission conveys the idea of someone voluntarily giving up or yielding his or her rights to another.[3]

In 1 Corinthians 8–10, Paul elevated the ideal of submission/subordination to a place of virtue. He encouraged his readers to willingly yield, submit, and subordinate to others their rights to eat meat offered to idols if eating such meat spiritually harmed their weaker brothers or sisters. Such submission was, in his view, a supreme act of <u>love</u>, love for God and love for one another.

By voluntarily yielding his right to eat meat, Paul followed the example of Christ, who voluntarily yielded His rights as God when He chose to humble Himself and become a man. He further yielded His right when He allowed Himself to <u>die</u> on a cross to save us from our sins. Throughout those three chapters—1 Corinthians 8–10—Paul encouraged his readers to follow his example (of yielding his right to eat meat) just as Paul followed Christ's example (of yielding His rights as God).

Paul will do the same in this chapter. Just as Christ submitted Himself to His Father, so each of us, men and women alike, should voluntarily yield our rights according to a clearly prescribed biblical framework. The purpose of this God-ordained framework is to maintain <u>order</u> in a world of chaos and confusion. By so yielding our lives, we are following Paul's example as Paul followed Christ's.

# "I Want You to Know"

## the big picture

**1 Corinthians 11:2–16**

Paul answered the Corinthian Christians' questions concerning the respective roles of men and women.

Paul began this section by praising the Corinthians for keeping the "traditions" (1 Corinthians 11:2 NKJV) that he originally taught them. An interesting word, *traditions*. As used here and in 2 Thessalonians 2:15, *traditions* refer not to man-made ideas, but rather to the biblical principles that Paul passed on to his readers as a teacher to his students. Indeed, in both this and the Thessalonians passage, the NIV translators rendered the word *teachings*. There was a subtle bit of subliminal motivation going on here—Paul thanked his readers for those times that they obeyed his teachings, and by implication thanked them in advance for following his teaching now, especially regarding the roles of men and women in the church.

Then he dropped his bombshell when he wrote, "I want you to know that the head of every man is Christ, the head of woman is man, and the head of Christ is God" (1 Corinthians 11:3 NKJV). There. He said it. And I just repeated it. However, before anyone reacts to it we must delve more deeply into it to discover exactly what Paul was saying. But before we do that we need to consider some things about the Corinthians' mental frame of reference.

## what others say

**William Barclay**

The only thing which can keep the individual Christian solid in the faith and secure against persuasive arguments that lead people astray, the only thing which can keep the church healthy and efficient, is an intimate association with Jesus Christ, who is the head and the directing mind of the body.[4]

For starters, women in Greek culture received little respect and were treated as if they had no value. Many women were forced into prostitution as their only hope for survival in the harsh, cruel culture of Corinth. Those who were married were totally dominated by their husbands. They lived under the constant threat of divorce which would leave them to fend for themselves on the streets of Corinth.

Wives often lived in mortal fear of their husbands, who were free to brutalize them at will with little or no accountability.

Perhaps because they felt so dominated, so helpless, and so hopeless, many women rebelled and asserted their rights as equal to or superior to those of men. This ancient form of women's liberation crept into the church, as evidenced by Paul's words to Timothy, pastor of the church in Ephesus: "[I also desire] that the women adorn themselves in modest apparel, with propriety and moderation, not with braided hair or gold or pearls or costly clothing, but, which is proper for women professing godliness, with good works" (1 Timothy 2:9–10 NKJV).

When you read passages such as this, keep in mind that Paul never wrote in a vacuum. He only addressed real-time, real-life situations. Sadly, some of the women in Timothy's church dressed in such an immodest and over-the-top flamboyant manner that they looked and acted like prostitutes, unbecoming for a woman of God by anyone's standards. The same held true in Corinth.

Please consider that in a culture in which women were not valued very highly, Paul elevated the status of women by ascribing to them equality with men, and repeatedly taught that women should be treated with the honor and dignity that they deserve. Consider such statements as, "There is neither male nor female; for you are all one in Christ Jesus" (Galatians 3:28 NKJV), or Paul's teaching that husbands must "love your wives, just as Christ also loved the church and gave Himself for her" (Ephesians 5:25 NKJV). I cannot overemphasize how revolutionary such statements were in that male-dominated culture. Any thought that Paul put down women or was some kind of first-century misogynist simply fails to acknowledge or understand the totality of Paul's teaching.

Case in point: Before stating, "The head of woman is man," Paul first said, "The head of every man is Christ." Paul is emphatic when he basically says, "Men, you need to understand something. Do you want your wives to show you the proper respect that you deserve as husbands? Then you must first align yourselves under your head, who is Christ, and submit to His authority. Subordinate yourself to Him. Show Him the proper respect that He deserves as the Lord of the universe and the Lord of your lives. That means you must strive every moment of every day to lay aside your rights and to choose to live the way Jesus wants you to live."

As we learned earlier in our study, a godly man is a Holy Spirit-filled man. A Spirit-filled man manifests the characteristics of a Spirit-filled life as found in Galatians 5:22–23. Was all of this included in Paul's statement, "I want you to know that the head of every man is Christ"? Absolutely. A man who is totally yielded to the lordship of Christ will, by definition, be a loving, joyful, peaceful, patient, kind, faithful, gentle, and self-controlled man—a Spirit-filled man, a godly man. I guarantee you that most women would not hesitate to place themselves under the protective care of a genuinely Spirit-controlled man.

**what others say**

**Elisabeth Elliot**

What an assignment. What an honor—for him to love her so, for her to be so loved. The husband is to pay honor to the wife's body specifically *because* it is weaker and because they are heirs together of (they share) the grace of life. Thus honor is understood to mean not only respect for superiority, but reverence under God for the inferior, which means "the one placed under." There is no room for tyranny here, no such thing as bullying, lording over, bossing. It is a gracious humility that honors the weak one.[5]

I know that some Christian women chafe when reading Ephesians 5:22: "Wives, submit to your own husbands, as to the Lord" (NKJV). But that's only because they fail to read, and their pastors fail to preach, verse 25, in which Paul also said, "Husbands, love your wives, just as Christ also loved the church and gave Himself for her" (NKJV). But verse 25 puts an entirely different spin on the passage. Most wives would not hesitate to submit to, or voluntarily yield their rights to, their husbands if they genuinely loved their wives in the same self-sacrificing way that Christ loves the church.

I mention Ephesians 5:22–25 because it is clearly a parallel passage to 1 Corinthians 11:1–16. Put the two passages side by side, and you'll see that they both articulate the same principle.

Let me remind you that this passage has nothing to do with the respective values or personal worth that God places on men versus women. God established this pattern only as a means of restoring order in an otherwise disorderly, chaotic world.

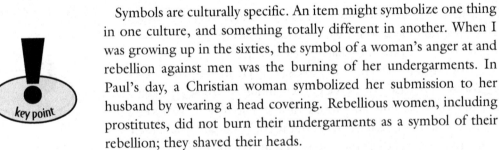

what others say

**Life Application Bible**

God calls for a submission among *equals*. He did not make the man superior; he made a way for the man and woman to work together. Jesus Christ, although equal with God the Father, submitted to him to carry out the plan of salvation. Likewise, although equal to man under God, the wife should submit to her husband for the sake of their marriage and family. Submission between equals is submission by choice, not force.[6]

Let's move on to Paul's discussion of head coverings. The interpretive key that unlocks Paul's meaning is found in the fact that when he stated his opening premise—"I want you to know that the head of every man is Christ, the head of woman is man, and the head of Christ is God"—he stated it as an absolute, timeless principle. However, when he moved into the discussion of women wearing veils, he stated, "For this reason the woman ought to have a symbol of authority on her head, because of the angels" (1 Corinthians 11:10 NKJV). We'll get to the angels in a minute. But for now, let's focus on that word *symbol*, or *sign*.

Symbols are culturally specific. An item might symbolize one thing in one culture, and something totally different in another. When I was growing up in the sixties, the symbol of a woman's anger at and rebellion against men was the burning of her undergarments. In Paul's day, a Christian woman symbolized her submission to her husband by wearing a head covering. Rebellious women, including prostitutes, did not burn their undergarments as a symbol of their rebellion; they shaved their heads.

key point

Paul warned his female readers that by entering the church worship service with their heads uncovered they sent the same signal as if they had shaved *their* heads (1 Corinthians 11:6). He is simply asking the Christian women in Corinth to wear the culturally relevant symbol of their submission—a veil or head covering. If Paul was writing to Christian women today, he would not exhort them to wear head coverings since that symbol is no longer culturally relevant.

Paul's reference to the angels is quite interesting. Angels evidently take a keen interest in how we Christians worship. For example, Paul made a charge to Timothy "before . . . the elect angels" (1 Timothy 5:21 NKJV). Peter pointed out that the Old Testament prophets revealed truth meant for us, "things which angels desire to look into" (1 Peter 1:12 NKJV).

go to

**evil**
2 Peter 2:4

Angels are intrigued by our human behavior since they are obviously not human. They are curious about our salvation since God instituted no plan to save or redeem <u>evil</u> angels. Angels take an active interest in the goings-on in our churches, since angels do not have church services of their own.

It is sobering for us to realize that God's holy angels take an active interest in our lives as they curiously watch our behavior as Christians. Such a realization ought to motivate us to honor God in everything we do, even when it appears that no one is watching. Because the angels always are.

something to ponder

**what others say**

**J. Vernon McGee**

Another purpose of the mystery is revealed here. God's created intelligences are learning something of the wisdom of God through the church. They not only see the love of God displayed and lavished upon us, but the wisdom of God is revealed to His angels.[7]

## Conduct at the Communion Table

1 CORINTHIANS 11:17–22 *Now in giving these instructions I do not praise you, since you come together not for the better but for the worse. For first of all, when you come together as a church, I hear that there are divisions among you, and in part I believe it. For there must also be factions among you, that those who are approved may be recognized among you. Therefore when you come together in one place, it is not to eat the Lord's Supper. For in eating, each one takes his own supper ahead of others; and one is hungry and another is drunk. What! Do you not have houses to eat and drink in? Or do you despise the church of God and shame those who have nothing? What shall I say to you? Shall I praise you in this? I do not praise you.* (NKJV)

We will now shift gears completely and talk about a seemingly unrelated issue, the Corinthian Christians' abuses of the Lord's Supper. The custom of the early church in Jerusalem properly placed a high value on their observance of Communion. We read that "[they continued] daily with one accord in the temple, and breaking bread from house to house, they ate their food with gladness and simplicity of heart, praising God and having favor with all the people. And the Lord added to the church daily those who were being saved" (Acts 2:46–47 NKJV).

Apparently, fellowship meals in connection with Communion were commonplace among the early Christians, a tradition that no doubt expanded to other churches as they were established throughout the Roman Empire, including Corinth. Like most everything else in that troubled church, the Communion table in Corinth became tainted when touched by the carnal Christians there. If you feel yet another of Paul's sharp rebukes coming, you are right.

Among other things, Communion celebrates our unity in Christ. When we gather together around the Lord's Table, we come as one family united in Christ's love. We leave our petty differences behind. When we hold in our hands the powerful symbols of Christ's broken body and shed blood (something we'll say more about in the next section), we ought to feel compelled to examine ourselves (1 Corinthians 11:28), confess all of our known sins, and reflect upon Christ's sacrifice on our behalf. In Corinth, instead of one body of believers uniting around the table, each of the different factions was represented. Some of the believers there sincerely sought to worship Christ and obey Him as Lord. Those were the ones to whom Paul referred as *approved*. As translated in the Contemporary English Version, "It is easy to see which of you have God's approval" (1 Corinthians 11:19).

key point

But clearly, the vast majority of so-called Christians in the church did not meet with God's approval, nor with Paul's. They turned the sacred celebration of the Lord's Supper and its corresponding fellowship meal into a gluttonous, drunken affair. And to add insult to that injury, as certain wealthier people brought their sumptuous cuisine to the potluck they refused to share their food with others who were less fortunate and hungry (v. 21).

Understandably exasperated, Paul said, "What! Do you not have houses to eat and drink in? Or do you despise the church of God and shame those who have nothing? What shall I say to you? Shall I praise you in this? I do not praise you" (1 Corinthians 11:22 NKJV).

go to

supper
John 13:2

irreverent
treating God with
blatant disrespect

> **what others say**
>
> **Lloyd Ogilvie**
>
> The author is placing before his readers and hearers the guidelines of Christian conduct and deportment in the church and the world. The foundation has been laid in a magnificent exposition of the theme, Christ-in-His-church; now the structure must be erected, with its complementary theme, the church-in-Christ, or more properly, Christ's church in its relations with society.[8]

What could Paul say to compel the **irreverent** Corinthians to bring some measure of reverence to the Lord's table? He did the only thing he could do. He reminded them of the meaning of Communion.

## A Most Meaningful Picture

1 CORINTHIANS 11:23–26 *For I received from the Lord that which I also delivered to you: that the Lord Jesus on the same night in which He was betrayed took bread; and when He had given thanks, He broke it and said, "Take, eat; this is My body which is broken for you; do this in remembrance of Me." In the same manner He also took the cup after supper, saying, "This cup is the new covenant in My blood. This do, as often as you drink it, in remembrance of Me." For as often as you eat this bread and drink this cup, you proclaim the Lord's death till He comes. (NKJV)*

Some call it Communion, the Lord's Supper, or the Eucharist. Call it what you will, it commemorates Jesus's last supper on earth with His disciples before His arrest, trials, and execution. Jesus broke bread with His men. As He distributed the pieces He attached a sobering significance to them when He said, "Take, eat; this is My body which is broken for you; do this in remembrance of Me." As He passed around the cup of wine, He said, "This cup is the new covenant in My blood. This do, as often as you drink it, in remembrance of Me."

He then made clear His intention that the church should commemorate His death on the cross with these same two elements, thereby calling to memory His sacrifice for us. From its inception in Acts 2 to the present day, local church congregations around the world have regularly participated in this beautiful observance called Communion. Churches will continue to do so until Christ's return (v. 26). Thus we can understand how horrifying it must have been to Paul to receive a report that such a singularly spiritual exercise had, along with everything else in the church at Corinth, been so corrupted by the Christians there.

## A Serious Misstep

*1 CORINTHIANS 11:27–34 Therefore whoever eats this bread or drinks this cup of the Lord in an unworthy manner will be guilty of the body and blood of the Lord. But let a man examine himself, and so let him eat of the bread and drink of the cup. For he who eats and drinks in an unworthy manner eats and drinks judgment to himself, not discerning the Lord's body. For this reason many are weak and sick among you, and many sleep. For if we would judge ourselves, we would not be judged. But when we are judged, we are chastened by the Lord, that we may not be condemned with the world. Therefore, my brethren, when you come together to eat, wait for one another. But if anyone is hungry, let him eat at home, lest you come together for judgment. And the rest I will set in order when I come. (NKJV)*

Woe to the one who participates in the Lord's Supper in "an unworthy manner." That was Paul's warning to the church in Corinth.

What did Paul mean by the words "unworthy manner"? Any action or attitude that detracted from the significance of the Lord's Supper failed to attribute to its observance the worth, value, or respect that Communion not only deserves but demands. The behavior of many of the Christians at the Communion table—the factions that were present in the church, the drunkenness, the gluttony—turned the Lord's Supper into a hypocritical farce that heaped scorn on the crucifixion of their Lord and His sacrifice for their sins.

Jesus intended for Communion to be a time of quiet reflection on what Jesus did for us, an examination as we pray, "Search me, O God, and know my heart; try me, and know my anxieties; and see if there is any wicked way in me, and lead me in the way everlasting" (Psalm 139:23–24 NKJV). The so-called Christians at Corinth utterly destroyed the sanctity of the Communion service to the point where "many of you are sick and weak and . . . a lot of others have died"

key point

(1 Corinthians 11:30 CEV). God actually visited judgment on many of those who desecrated their Lord's Supper.

Let this be a warning to us that we'd better not treat something as sacred as the Lord's Supper with a blatant disregard for the sanctity of its significance.

Paul concluded his discussion by assuring them that when he returned to Corinth for an apostolic visit, he would have much more to say about their disturbing desecration of the Communion table.

## Chapter Wrap-Up

- The first half of 1 Corinthians 11 can seem controversial, but Paul is really tackling concepts and questions about the behavior of men and women that relate directly to the Corinthian culture of that era.

- One of those concepts involves submission (or subordination) of women. In that time and place, women's submission to men was an unfortunate fact of life, yet Paul seemed to be endorsing it for all times and places.

- However, many people do not read the *rest* of Paul's admonitions in this regard, in which he instructed men to love, honor, and respect their wives. He also made it plain that "the head of man is Christ," even as the head of the family should, in most situations, be the man. These two truths are every bit as important as anything else Paul ever said.

- The members of the Corinthian church had debased the whole concept of Holy Communion. Paul did not tell them to discontinue taking Communion per se, but to stop turning what should have been a holy, elevating experience into something entirely different.

## Study Questions

1. Before you read this chapter what was your conception of Paul's recommendations for how women should behave, and how they should be treated by men? Has that conception changed? If so, how?

2. What part of Paul's admonitions about how women should behave is often left out of the equation? Why is it so important?

3. What were some of the abuses the Corinthians were committing with respect to Holy Communion?

4. Why were these abuses so horribly wrong?

# 1 Corinthians 12–14
# What About Spiritual Gifts?

## Let's Get Started

One of the most encouraging topics of discussion in the New Testament is that of spiritual gifts. It's both edifying and humbling to realize that the moment someone becomes a true follower of Jesus Christ, he receives a spiritual gift—a God-given, supernatural, Spirit-empowered ability to serve Christ and others in an effective way.

go to

receives
John 1:12

Think of it this way: Prior to becoming a Christian, a person is "dead in trespasses and sins" (Ephesians 2:1 NKJV). The moment that person <u>receives</u> Christ, or invites Christ into his or her life, immediately that person is spiritually "made alive," or in Jesus's words, "born again" (John 3:3 NKJV). He or she experiences a spiritual birthday. And as a spiritual birthday present, he receives a spiritual gift. In that sense, every follower of Jesus is enormously gifted. How exciting is that?

But as exciting as the reality, the subject of spiritual gifts is fraught with confusion and controversy. That was true in Corinth; it is equally true today.

Spiritual gifts is one of those subjects about which the Bible leaves a lot of latitude as far as our understanding is concerned. Indeed, even today, two thousand years removed from Corinth, churches have been torn asunder over differing views on spiritual gifts. Likewise, as we'll soon see, the divisions within the Corinthian church were exacerbated by the same kind of conflicting actions and opinions.

something to ponder

Questions still abound, both from the Christians in Corinth and from us today. How many gifts does a person receive? Are all of the gifts listed in 1 Corinthians 12–14 operational today? What about the gift of healing? What about the gift of tongues? What is the baptism of the Spirit? Does the baptism of the Spirit happen at the point of salvation or can someone be baptized by the Spirit later on?

Some of these questions can be answered definitively. The answers to other questions are open to a couple of plausible interpretations, because the verses that address these questions are, quite honestly, a bit unclear or indefinite as to Paul's intended meaning.

So I make you this promise. Throughout our study of these three great chapters—1 Corinthians 12, 13, and 14—I'll do my best to celebrate the reality of the fact that as Christ's followers, you and I are supremely gifted. At the same time, I'll carefully and scripturally navigate us through these sometimes confusing waters, arriving at what I believe to be the best and most accurate understanding of Paul's teaching concerning this exciting subject.

key point

Given what I told you in the introduction to this chapter, it's not surprising that Paul began this discussion with the ominous words, "Now concerning spiritual gifts, brethren, I do not want you to be ignorant" (1 Corinthians 12:1 NKJV). He doesn't want *us* to be ignorant, either.

## First Things First

1 CORINTHIANS 12:1–3 *Now concerning spiritual gifts, brethren, I do not want you to be ignorant: You know that you were Gentiles, carried away to these dumb idols, however you were led. Therefore I make known to you that no one speaking by the Spirit of God calls Jesus accursed, and no one can say that Jesus is Lord except by the Holy Spirit. (NKJV)*

The use and abuse of spiritual gifts in the Corinthian congregation was a big deal to Paul, so much so that he devoted three entire chapters, nearly 20 percent of this letter, to correcting their faulty understanding of this most important topic. The problems created by their misunderstanding can be divided into two main categories:

First, while it is humbling for us to realize that God has graciously given us spiritual gifts, in Corinth these gifts became points of pride. As we will see when we get to 1 Corinthians 13 and 14, people were actually competing with one another for positions of power and influence based upon their mistaken belief that they had the better gifts. Therefore they thought they were entitled to be up front in full view of the congregation.

Second, as indicated in the passage quoted above, many of the Christians brought into the church some of the pagan religious practices that they had participated in prior to committing their lives to Christ. Paul was so disturbed by this that he addressed this concern right at the top of this discussion.

These pagan worship rituals often included ecstatic utterances from participants who worked themselves up into a religious frenzy. We have already noted that temple prostitution was often included in the mix, as well as drunkenness (Ephesians 5:18). This is exactly what Paul meant when he spoke of them being "carried away" in the worship of their idols.

Apparently, during these alcohol-induced frenzies, some of the Corinthian Christians committed the grievous sin of blasphemy—they actually cursed the Jesus they now claimed to love and worship. So Paul drew this line in the sand right from the get-go: "No one speaking by the Spirit of God calls Jesus accursed, and no one can say that Jesus is Lord except by the Holy Spirit" (1 Corinthians 12:3 NKJV).

**what others say**

**Robert L. Thomas**

"No one can say, 'Jesus is Lord,' except by the Holy Spirit" (12:3). This step involves full confession of the Lordship of Jesus along with full allegiance to Him. Any time anyone makes this acknowledgment with conviction, it is a cry of adoration and an act of homage on his part.[1]

Understand that Paul was talking here of a verbal confession of an inward reality. He was not referring to a "talk is cheap" type of flippant or causal expression. A person who lives under the influence of the Holy Spirit will affirm Jesus's lordship in his life and will back up that affirmation by his lifestyle. I stress this because, on the surface, 1 Corinthians 12:3 appears to be in direct contradiction of Jesus's words in Matthew 7:21, "Not everyone who says to Me, 'Lord, Lord,' shall enter the kingdom of heaven" (NKJV). The words "Jesus is Lord" in and of themselves mean nothing unless the person who speaks them "walks the talk" as evidenced by a surrendered, obedient life. As Jesus continued His thought, He stated quite succinctly that His true followers seek to do "the will of My Father in heaven." The talk without the walk is meaningless.

something to ponder

So here the Corinthian Christians worked themselves up into an ecstatic frenzy, all in the name of the Holy Spirit, all the while cursing the very Jesus they thought they were praising. What a stinging rebuke when Paul suggested that they were worse than the idols they used to worship. At least their false gods sat mute; these so-called Christian believers were verbally blaspheming the Son of the one true God.

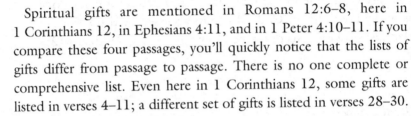

the big picture

**1 Corinthians 12:4–11**

Paul pointed out that while there are many different gifts manifested in any church, the same Holy Spirit is the one who dispenses the gifts according to His will. The gifts are given for the mutual benefit of everyone in the body.

## For the Profit of All

Spiritual gifts are mentioned in Romans 12:6–8, here in 1 Corinthians 12, in Ephesians 4:11, and in 1 Peter 4:10–11. If you compare these four passages, you'll quickly notice that the lists of gifts differ from passage to passage. There is no one complete or comprehensive list. Even here in 1 Corinthians 12, some gifts are listed in verses 4–11; a different set of gifts is listed in verses 28–30. What are we to make of this?

It seems to me that the only plausible interpretation is that God never intended for us to get too hung up on identifying our own particular gifts. Nowhere in 1 Corinthians 12–14 did Paul encourage his readers to identify their gifts. Instead, he emphasized that as the people walked in the fullness of the Spirit they would automatically, by virtue of the Holy Spirit's work in and through them, exercise their gifts to the benefit of others.

Perhaps it is enough to know that we each have a spiritual gift; that it was given to us by the Holy Spirit through no merit of our own; that our gifts are expressions of God's grace to us; and that as we live in the power of the Holy Spirit we will use our gifts to benefit others whether we can identify our own particular gifts or not.

According to 1 Corinthians 12:8–10, these are the gifts that were in operation in Corinth: word of wisdom, word of knowledge, faith, healing, miracles, prophecy, discerning of spirits, tongues, interpretation of tongues (NKJV). Put them side by side and they might look like this:

# The Gifts of the Spirit in the Church in Corinth

| Gift | Definition | Scriptural Examples |
|---|---|---|
| Word of Wisdom | The God-given ability to apply biblical truth to everyday life situations. | Acts 6:10; James 3:13, 17; 2 Peter 3:15 |
| Word of Knowledge | The God-given ability to understand and teach the truths of Scripture to others. | Romans 16:25; Ephesians 3:3; Colossians 2:2 |
| Faith | The God-given ability to trust God regardless of one's circumstances, and to impart that trust to others. | Romans 1:12; 2 Corinthians 8:7 |
| Healing | The God-given ability to restore someone to physical health. | Acts 3:1–10; 9:36–43 |
| Miracles | The God-given ability to counteract the laws of nature. | Hebrews 2:4 |
| Prophecy | The God-given ability to proclaim biblical truth in a way that brings people to a place of repentance. | Acts 7:54; 21:9 |
| Discerning of Spirits | The God-given ability to identify deceptive or erroneous doctrines taught under the influence of a demonic spirit. | Acts 8:14–23; 1 Timothy 4:1–3 |
| Tongues | The God-given ability to speak and to pray in a language that the speaker has not previously learned. | Acts 2:5–12; 10:46; 19:6 |
| Interpretation of Tongues | The God-given ability to translate a foreign language that the translator doesn't know. | 1 Corinthians 14:26–33 |

For example, the writer to the Hebrews said, "How shall we escape if we neglect so great a salvation, which at the first began to be spoken by the Lord, and was confirmed to us by those who heard Him, God also bearing witness both with signs and wonders, with various miracles, and gifts of the Holy Spirit, according to His own will?" (Hebrews 2:3–4 NKJV). While the writer does not tell us a complete list of which gifts were foundational to establishing the church and authenticating the ministries of the apostles, he does tell us that "signs, wonders and various miracles" were given for that purpose.

what others say

**Sam Storms**

I believe in the absolute centrality of the cross of Christ and its power to save lost souls (Romans 1:16). Quite obviously, so did Paul, a man who described his gospel ministry as one characterized by the "power of signs and wonders, in the power of the (Holy) Spirit" (Romans 15:19).[2]

**sick**
Philippians 2:27

**heals**
James 5:14–15

**carnality**
1 Corinthians 3:1

Yet, in spite of the fact that "signs and wonders" authenticated Paul's ministry, it is intriguing to me that when Epaphroditus got <u>sick</u>, Paul could not heal him; God healed him. God often <u>heals</u> today, but not necessarily through a gift of healing that God gives to some but not to others.

As far as tongues and the interpretation of tongues are concerned, Paul clearly stated the first purpose of these two gifts when he wrote, "Tongues are for a sign, not to those who believe but to unbelievers; but prophesying is not for unbelievers but for those who believe" (1 Corinthians 14:22 NKJV). The second purpose, which most advocates authenticate via the fourteenth chapter of 1 Corinthians but also on the basis of Romans 8:26, Ephesians 6:18, and Jude 20, is praying to God in an unknown tongue, as the "the Spirit Himself makes intercession for us" (Romans 8:26 NKJV).

Paul further detailed the evidence of the filling of the Spirit as "speaking to one another in psalms and hymns and spiritual songs, singing and making melody in your heart to the Lord, giving thanks always for all things to God the Father in the name of our Lord Jesus Christ" (Ephesians 5:19–20 NKJV).

## Baptized into the Body

> 1 CORINTHIANS 12:12–13 *For as the body is one and has many members, but all the members of that one body, being many, are one body, so also is Christ. For by one Spirit we were all baptized into one body—whether Jews or Greeks, whether slaves or free—and have all been made to drink into one Spirit. (NKJV)*

The word translated *baptized* is a transliteration of the Greek word *baptidzo*, which means "to dip or immerse," often used of a piece of cloth being dipped or immersed into a dye. The word *all* is most instructive. In spite of their <u>carnality</u>, every believer in Christ in Corinth was "by one Spirit . . . baptized into one body" (1 Corinthians 12:13 NKJV). There is simply no such thing today as a Christian who has not been baptized by the Holy Spirit. As Paul told the Christians in Rome, "If anyone does not have the Spirit of Christ, he is not His" (Romans 8:9 NKJV).

Baptism thus becomes the formal welcoming of every follower of Christ into the body of Christ, a beautiful designation of the church—the family of God that includes every follower of Christ from the inception of the church on the Day of Pentecost in Acts 2 to the <u>rapture</u> of the church at the end of the age. The baptism of the Spirit emphasizes our <u>unity</u> since we are organically joined together as one.

## <u>Diversity in the Midst of Unity</u>

go to

**rapture**
1 Thessalonians
4:16–18

**unity**
Ephesians 4:3–6

**head**
Ephesians 5:23

**the big picture**

**1 Corinthians 12:14–31**

There is no place in the body of Christ for feelings of spiritual superiority, because spiritual gifts are not earned—just received. Nor is there a place for feelings of spiritual inferiority since we are all equally important to Jesus and vital to His ministry through the church regardless of what our gifts might be.

Using the human body as a metaphor for the church, Paul reminded his readers that the smallest or humblest parts of the body are as essential to the health of the whole as the seemingly more important parts. There is a touch of the ironic to Paul's examples when he asks, "If the whole body were an eye, where would be the hearing? If the whole were hearing, where would be the smelling?" (1 Corinthians 12:17 NKJV). We each have a differing role within the body, and different spiritual gifts to enable us to fulfill our roles effectively. Both our roles and our gifts are determined by Christ through no merit of our own. Therefore, the Corinthians needed to stop all their fussing about who had the most important gifts or the most powerful roles within their church. Such prideful considerations were offensive to Christ Himself, the <u>head</u> of His church.

God never intended that everyone should be an apostle, prophet, teacher, miracle worker, or healer. He did not give everyone the ability to preach the gospel in the foreign languages of others, or to translate that preaching. God gave the Corinthian Christians the gifts He wanted them to have to promote their unity and spiritual growth. They had compromised His purposes for giving them gifts by flaunting their gifts before one another, thus making others feel inferior if they did not possess the more visible gifts such as preaching or teaching.

something to ponder

what others say

**Bryan Carraway**

All Christians (not just pastors and famous evangelists) have
been given specific gifts by the Holy Spirit to enable them to
do their part in "the work of the ministry." If you have been
called to be saved, then you have been called to serve.[3]

key point

Our churches are equally susceptible to Corinthian carnality in the
area of spiritual gifts. We have been given gifts to use in serving one
another, not in pridefully competing with one another for the platform or positions of power. Whenever someone feels that they
deserve or are entitled to their place in the sun, they have compromised their calling to humbly "through love serve one another"
(Galatians 5:13 NKJV). As we are about to learn in 1 Corinthians 13,
they were not serving others in love; they were serving themselves in
a self-satisfying, self-absorbed quest for attention and power.

The Corinthian Christians were not displaying love toward one
another. Quite the contrary. They were busily trying to outdo each
other by elevating some spiritual gifts above others, some positions
of power above others, by seeking places on the platform to the
exclusion of others. No wonder Paul chided them a bit when he suggested that when an unbeliever visited their church, "will they not
say that you are out of your mind?" (1 Corinthians 14:23 NKJV).

Paul pointed a finger in their faces and essentially told them that
without love it didn't matter what gifts the Holy Spirit distributed in
their church. The manifestation of their gifts meant nothing without
love.

## A World Without Love

1 CORINTHIANS 13:1–3 *Though I speak with the tongues of
men and of angels, but have not love, I have become sounding
brass or a clanging cymbal. And though I have the gift of
prophecy, and understand all mysteries and all knowledge, and
though I have all faith, so that I could remove mountains, but
have not love, I am nothing. And though I bestow all my goods
to feed the poor, and though I give my body to be burned, but
have not love, it profits me nothing.* (NKJV)

When I read this passage, I am reminded of Paul's words to Timothy: "The purpose of the commandment is love from a pure heart, from a good conscience, and from sincere faith" (1 Timothy 1:5 NKJV). It's always been interesting to me that Paul did not say that the goal of his instruction was doctrinal purity, though doctrinal purity is of vital importance. Sure, we can dot every theological "i" correctly, and cross every theological "t" accurately. But if we don't love each other, what's the point? In fact, in the first twelve chapters of this great letter Paul has yet to correct any doctrinal error in the church. His corrections have related to their deep divisions and faulty practices. Doctrinally, they apparently had it all together. But it didn't matter one twit because they did not love each other. This was especially apparent in the exercise of their spiritual gifts.

Paul used hyperbole to emphasize his point. He made several extreme statements to underscore the absolute priority of loving others. For example, if he could speak every language in heaven or on earth fluently, but didn't love others, his linguistic abilities meant nothing. Contrary to the belief of some, Paul was not suggesting that there exists a language unique to the angels that you and I are meant to master.

Some make a connection between "tongues of angels" and the gift of tongues, thereby suggesting that there is some heavenly language that God wants every Spirit-filled Christian to speak. Those who hold this view suggest that when they speak in some unknown tongue they are, in reality, speaking this heavenly language. Many who hold this view, like the Corinthians before them, evidently prize this gift above all others; they attach a level of importance to the gift of tongues that is clearly contradicted by Scripture. Some even go so far as to suggest that a person has not been baptized by the Spirit until he manifests this form of ecstatic speech.

We can dismiss this interpretation out of hand, given Paul's use of hyperbole. To be consistent, one who holds the view that we ought to speak in the language of angels must then also believe that there is some merit to a Christian giving his or her "body to be burned." That statement is obviously hyperbolic, as if to say that we can speak all languages fluently, understand all knowledge flawlessly, and give of ourselves sacrificially. But if those actions are not motivated by love, they mean nothing.

# Love from the Inside Out

1 CORINTHIANS 13:4–8a *Love suffers long and is kind; love does not envy; love does not parade itself, is not puffed up; does not behave rudely, does not seek its own, is not provoked, thinks no evil; does not rejoice in iniquity, but rejoices in the truth; bears all things, believes all things, hopes all things, endures all things. Love never fails. (NKJV)*

Paul did not pen these verses in a vacuum. He did not intend for them to form the basis of some sort of Valentine's Day devotional. He very much meant to confront the Corinthian Christians about their egregious abuse of their spiritual gifts by using them to serve themselves and their self-interests rather than to humbly serve one another in love.

**key point**

Each of the following attributes of love can be turned inside out and used to describe what life was like in the loveless church in Corinth. Paul was addressing exactly what was going on (which shouldn't have been), and what was not going on (which should have been) in the Corinthian church. Keep that in mind as we move through this list of attributes. Also understand that the words Paul used are quite colorful, with a whole array of rich meanings. By comparing different translations of this passage, we begin to see the beauty of the tapestry that Paul presents to us here.

Paul declared love to be patient; we can therefore conclude that those in the Corinthian congregation were acting impatiently toward one another. Love is kind; evidently those in Corinth were treating each other unkindly. Love is never jealous, yet in Corinth people were jealous of one another's gifts. Love does not boastfully parade itself in front of others, and is not proud or self-centered.

Love is always others-centered, putting the needs of others ahead of oneself. Loving people do not treat people rudely, but politely. Loving people are not selfish or self-focused or out for themselves. They are not quick tempered or easily provoked to anger. Love does not keep a record of the wrongs of others, or hold grudges, but is quick to forgive. Love does not function as a cheerleader for sinful people, nor does it encourage others to continue to sin. Love rejoices when truth is taught and obeyed. Love assumes the best about others; never the worst. Loving people are always supportive of one another and loyal to one another, even during times of tension. Love holds out hope for the best and trusts and endures to the end. "Love never fails."

Love, not the exercise of one of the spiritual gifts, is the mark of a Spirit-filled individual. Indeed, love is the <u>fruit</u> of a Spirit-controlled life

**fruit**
Galatians 5:22–23

## Abiding Love

1 CORINTHIANS 13:8b–13 *But whether there are prophecies, they will fail; whether there are tongues, they will cease; whether there is knowledge, it will vanish away. For we know in part and we prophesy in part. But when that which is perfect has come, then that which is in part will be done away. When I was a child, I spoke as a child, I understood as a child, I thought as a child; but when I became a man, I put away childish things. For now we see in a mirror, dimly, but then face to face. Now I know in part, but then I shall know just as I also am known. And now abide faith, hope, love, these three; but the greatest of these is love.* (NKJV)

Paul readily admits that in the here and now, where "we see in a mirror, dimly," the exercise of our spiritual gifts is both temporary and imperfect. We don't know everything there is to know. We do indeed "prophesy [or preach] in part" precisely because our knowledge and understanding are limited. The day will indeed come when preaching will cease (it won't be needed), the gift of tongues will be silenced (some would even argue that it already has been), and our imperfect, incomplete knowledge will disappear like a mist in the full face of the sun because one day we will know what we do not now know.

Paul likens himself and the Corinthian Christians to children whose knowledge is limited. There is an intended jab in those words. Paul had to wonder why some of the Christians were boasting that they had special insight that others were lacking when, in reality, we're all just like children.

Why did Paul bring all this up? To underscore the fundamental fact that while preaching, tongues, and knowledge—spiritual gifts all—will one day cease, faith (our belief and trust in God), hope (our unshakable confidence that God will one day fulfill all His promises for our bright and beautiful future), and love (our selfless commitment to seek the very best for the one so loved) will last forever. Those were the

**go to**

**greatest**
Matthew 22:36–37

attributes that the Corinthians should have been seeking; not some temporary spiritual gift that puffed them up and made them feel superior toward others. And of the three—faith, hope, and love—the greatest is and ever shall be love, because our "God is love" (1 John 4:16 NKJV), the fruit of the Spirit is love, and the greatest commandment is that we love God and love one another.

## The Truth About Tongues

For some strange reason, the Corinthian Christians elevated the gift of tongues to a higher status than any of the other gifts. The resulting confusion and competition in the church prompted the apostle Paul to set the record straight about the purpose of tongues, the proper operation of tongues within the church, and the priority of prophecy as a gift to be sought in the church more than tongues.

> **the big picture**
>
> **1 Corinthians 14:1–19**
>
> Paul expressed his concern that no one benefited from the exercise of the gift of tongues in the church in Corinth because they were not using the gift properly. Paul exhorted them to place a higher priority on the gift of prophecy, because the preaching of God's Word edified others.

As we break the seal on 1 Corinthians 14, we must understand that the tone of the entire chapter is one of rebuke. Paul was confronting the misuse of the gift of tongues, and correcting the abuse of this gift.

Portions of this chapter drip with sarcasm. For example, Paul declared, "He who speaks in a tongue does not speak to men but to God, for no one understands him; however, in the spirit he speaks mysteries" (1 Corinthians 14:2 NKJV). When Paul said this he was literally throwing his hands up in disgust and shouting: *No one understands what you are saying, except God! Don't do that unless there's someone there to interpret for you.*

Likewise, when Paul said, "He who speaks in a tongue edifies himself, but he who prophesies edifies the church" (1 Corinthians 14:4 NKJV), he was offering a rebuke, as if to say, *Don't you understand that all you are doing is building yourself up when you ought to be concerned about building others up?* So Paul delivered a much-needed one-two punch: Pursue love, he told them, and work a little harder

**key point**

at seeking the spiritual gift of prophecy, which can then be better manifested in your church.

To prophesy simply means "to speak forth." We often associate prophesying with foretelling the future because a good deal of the content of the Old Testament prophetic revelations was still in the future. But a careful examination of the seventeen prophetic books—Isaiah through Malachi—reveals that much of the preaching of the prophets of old applied specifically to situations that the prophets were encountering at the time that they preached. Note, for example, Malachi's preaching in Malachi 2:1–9. He began, "And now, O priests, this commandment is for you" (2:1 NKJV). There was nothing in the future tense about that.

Prophesying is not so much foretelling as it is forth-telling. The word we might commonly use today to describe the gift of prophecy is preaching. From Paul's point of view, a spiritually rich church is a church rich in biblical preaching. Apart from the Spirit-empowered declaration of biblical truth, a church simply will not spiritually grow. So Paul made his case: "I wish you all spoke with tongues, but even more that you prophesied; for he who prophesies is greater than he who speaks with tongues, unless indeed he interprets, that the church may receive edification" (1 Corinthians 14:5 NKJV).

With respect to tongues, the word translated "tongues" is the same word used in Acts 2:1–12; 10:46; and 19:6. The Acts 2 passage clearly defines for us the spiritual gift of tongues: "They were all filled with the Holy Spirit and began to speak with other tongues, as the Spirit gave them utterance. And there were dwelling in Jerusalem Jews, devout men, from every nation under heaven. And when this sound occurred, the multitude came together, and were confused, because everyone heard them speak in his own language" (Acts 2:4–6 NKJV). Note especially the last phrase, "everyone heard them speak in his own language."

The spiritual gift of speaking in tongues, in public, is the God-given ability for someone to declare "the wonderful works of God" (Acts 2:11 NKJV) in a foreign language that the speaker does not know.

Luke (the author of Acts) specifically wrote Acts 2:8 and 11 virtually side by side to stress this very fact. He wrote: "How is it that we hear, *each in our own language* in which we were born? Parthians and Medes and Elamites, those dwelling in Mesopotamia, Judea and

**Law**
Joshua 1:8

Cappadocia, Pontus and Asia, Phrygia and Pamphylia, Egypt and the parts of Libya adjoining Cyrene, visitors from Rome, both Jews and proselytes, Cretans and Arabs—*we hear them speaking in our own tongues* the wonderful works of God" (Acts 2:8–11 NKJV, emphasis added).

To properly understand this chapter, whenever we read the word *tongue* or *tongues*, we should substitute the word *language* or *languages*. When we do, Paul's intended meaning becomes crystal clear.

To further punctuate his point, Paul compared speaking in tongues with the playing of a musical instrument. A flute, harp, or trumpet will only make a meaningless noise unless there is "a distinction in the sounds" (1 Corinthians 14:7 NKJV). So it is with tongues.

## The Purpose for Tongues

**the big picture**

**1 Corinthians 14:20–25**

Paul told the Corinthian Christians God's intended purpose for the gift of tongues.

Paul stated as a fact, "Tongues are for a sign, not to those who believe but to unbelievers" (1 Corinthians 14:22 NKJV). Think of it this way: When God gave the <u>Law</u>, He gave it to one people (the Jews) and He gave it in one language (Hebrew). Yet the first time the gospel, "the message of the cross" (1 Corinthians 1:18 NKJV), was preached, it was preached to everyone, in every language. The miraculous sign that validated this new message (the gospel) and these new messengers (the apostles) was that each of these foreign-speaking individuals heard this new message delivered by these new messengers in his own language, even though the apostles did not speak these languages.

This happened in Acts 2, the first time the gospel was preached to the Jews. It happened in Acts 10, the first time the gospel was preached to the Gentiles. And it happened in Acts 19, the first time the gospel was preached to followers of John the Baptizer.

Precisely because the Christians in Corinth perverted God's intended purpose for the gift of tongues, reducing it to a confusing free-for-all as multiple people all spoke at once, Paul was forced to lament, "If the whole church comes together in one place, and all speak with tongues, and there come in those who are uninformed or unbelievers, will they not say that you are out of your mind?" (1 Corinthians 14:23 NKJV).

I do not know if Paul was bald. But assuming he had a full head of hair, I can see him pulling it out by the handfuls when he got wind of what was really going on in Corinth's worship services. Clearly, things had gotten completely out of hand as far as any semblance of decorum in the Corinthian church worship services was concerned. Paul's readers desperately needed some direction, a steady hand at the wheel. So among other things, Paul responded by setting down some basic rules.

## The Proper Use of the Gift of Tongues

**the big picture**

**1 Corinthians 14:26–40**

Paul established some guidelines that the Corinthians could use to restore order in a church whose worship services had gotten completely out of control.

God is a God of order. So, Paul made the appeal that in their worship services, the Corinthian Christians had to "let all things be done decently and in order" (1 Corinthians 14:40 NKJV). He did so by laying out some basic guidelines that apply equally to us in our churches today. Different commentators have different "takes" on what some of those guidelines should be—and how rigidly Paul meant for them to be applied—but most will agree on the following:

- *Guideline #1:* Unbelievers should be present in the worship services where the gift of tongues is being used. Otherwise there is usually little need for the exercising of that gift (1 Corinthians 14:22).

- *Guideline #2:* There should be no more than "two or at the most three" people speaking in tongues in any given worship service, and they should speak "each in turn" or one at a time (1 Corinthians 14:27 NKJV).

- *Guideline #3:* An interpreter should be present (1 Corinthians 14:27), who should be enabled by the Holy Spirit to translate the message being spoken in a foreign language so that the rest of the congregation will know what is being said.

Finally, Paul adds this closing charge to anyone who might disagree with his teaching about this gift. If anyone tried to place himself above Paul's teaching by suggesting that he was more spiritual than Paul, or that Paul missed the mark, Paul said, "If anyone thinks himself to be a prophet or spiritual, let him acknowledge that the things which I write to you are the commandments of the Lord" (1 Corinthians 14:37 NKJV).

In other words, Paul wasn't just giving his opinions. Paul wrote with apostolic authority under the inspiration of the Holy Spirit. His words were the Word of God. Any self-proclaimed teacher or leader who disagreed with Paul's teachings exposed himself as *ignorant* of God's written revelation.

key point

If a person's experience contradicts Scripture, biblical truth must trump experience. The Bible does not submit to people's experience; people must submit their experiences to the truth of the Word of God.

# Chapter Wrap-Up

- Every sincere believer receives spiritual gifts from God—but they might not be what we expect or desire! And they are seldom given to us to use as dramatically and indiscriminately as we sometimes seem to suppose.

- We must never feel prideful about our spiritual gifts, whatever they might be. They are gifts from God, not rewards for our own goodness! And they are to be used *only* in His service.

- Paul specifically mentioned nine different gifts that were given to the congregation in Corinth.

- Whether all these gifts are in operation today is an open question. Some believe they all are; some believe that some were limited to use in the early church and are no longer part of our "spiritual arsenal" today.

- Paul gave the Corinthians an extensive lesson about true "love" in this chapter—but his definition does not fit the popular, modern mode!

# Study Questions

1. What were the nine spiritual gifts that Paul said were "in use" within the Corinthian congregation?

2. What guidelines did Paul give us that define how we are to use the gift of tongues?

3. Do you believe that Christians are given the gift of tongues even today?

4. How might we summarize all that Paul said about spiritual gifts, balanced against his extensive definition of love?

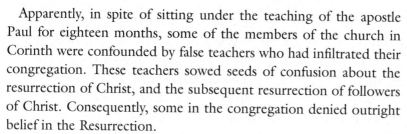

# 1 Corinthians 15
# The Resurrection: Hoax or History?

## Let's Get Started

Well, it was only a matter of time before Paul moved from issues of behavior—divisions, singleness and marriage, meat offered to idols, and the like—to a matter of belief. Specifically, in 1 Corinthians 15 Paul wrote for his readers the single most extensive explanation of the Resurrection in the New Testament.

Apparently, in spite of sitting under the teaching of the apostle Paul for eighteen months, some of the members of the church in Corinth were confounded by false teachers who had infiltrated their congregation. These teachers sowed seeds of confusion about the resurrection of Christ, and the subsequent resurrection of followers of Christ. Consequently, some in the congregation denied outright belief in the Resurrection.

Others were confused about the nature of the resurrection, both Christ's and theirs. In response, Paul devoted a full fifty-eight verses to straightening out their misunderstanding of the bodily resurrection of all of Christ's followers, ending with the victory chant borrowed from Isaiah 25:8 and Hosea 13:14, "Death is swallowed up in victory. O Death, where is your sting? O Hades, where is your victory?" (1 Corinthians 15:54–55 NKJV).

The resurrection of Christ is absolutely central to the gospel—the good news that God can save sinners. As Paul later wrote in this chapter, "If Christ is not risen, your faith is futile; you are still in your sins!" (1 Corinthians 15:17 NKJV). It's no wonder, then, that much of the attack of our <u>adversary</u>—the devil—is aimed directly at the Resurrection. Corrupt the message of the Resurrection, and you corrupt the message of the gospel itself. Remove the foundation of the resurrection of Christ, and all of Christianity will collapse under its own weight. Everything we hold near and dear rises or falls on the reality of the Resurrection.

**go to**

adversary
1 Peter 5:8

**key point**

go to

dead
James 2:26

# Essential Elements of the Gospel

*1 CORINTHIANS 15:1–8a Moreover, brethren, I declare to you the gospel which I preached to you, which also you received and in which you stand, by which also you are saved, if you hold fast that word which I preached to you—unless you believed in vain. For I delivered to you first of all that which I also received: that Christ died for our sins according to the Scriptures, and that He was buried, and that He rose again the third day according to the Scriptures, and that He was seen by Cephas, then by the twelve. After that He was seen by over five hundred brethren at once, of whom the greater part remain to the present, but some have fallen asleep. After that He was seen by James, then by all the apostles. Then last of all He was seen by me also, (NKJV)*

The gospel was the cornerstone of Paul's ministry to the Corinthians. He *preached* it; they *received* it; they were *saved* by it; and now they were *holding fast* to it. At least some of them were. Apparently there were some whose faith in Christ was on shaky ground, forcing Paul to say, "unless you believed in vain." In other words, some in that church had an empty faith, what James called a <u>dead</u> faith. Indeed, at the close of 2 Corinthians, Paul exhorted his readers to "examine yourselves as to whether you are in the faith. Test yourselves. Do you not know yourselves, that Jesus Christ is in you?—unless indeed you are disqualified" (2 Corinthians 13:5 NKJV).

And yet, even in the middle of this chapter Paul made the disturbing observation that some members of the church in Corinth did not have a personal relationship with God (1 Corinthians 15:34). Those individuals aside, the majority of those in the church in Corinth responded with genuine saving faith to the gospel message that Paul preached.

something to ponder

If you'd like to perform an interesting experiment, the next time you are with a group of your Christian friends, ask them the question, "What are the elements that *must* be included in a proper presentation of the gospel?" and see what they say. Before you read any further, why not make up your own list? Ask yourself, "What are the absolute essentials required for a complete presentation of the gospel?"

My experience has been that it's rare to get two people to agree on what should make the list. For example, some will say that people need to believe in the virgin birth to be saved. Others will insist that belief in a literal six-day creation is essential. Another might add that someone must be **Pre-Trib** in his **eschatology**. Others would scratch their heads and say, "Huh? Pre-Trib? What's that mean?" Does someone need to believe in the infallibility of Scripture to become a Christian? How about belief in the Trinity? Is that an essential aspect of the gospel message?

When you boil it down to its irreducible minimum, there are only three truths that must be included in any gospel presentation. The sheer simplicity of the gospel that Paul preached is breathtaking to behold.

Read 1 Corinthians 15:3–4 and you'll see that the three essential elements are these: (1) We are sinners. (2) Christ died to save us from our sins. (3) Jesus arose from the dead and is alive today.

So simple that a young <u>child</u> can understand it. And yet so profound that for more than two thousand years the best theological minds the world has ever produced have yet to plumb the depths of these three truths.

Let's consider them individually.

1. *We are sinners.* A person cannot be saved unless he understands what he is being saved from. The Bible declares, "All have sinned and fall short of the glory of God" (Romans 3:23 NKJV).

God is <u>holy</u>. Holiness, the absolute standard of moral excellence, is the central attribute or characteristic of His being. Think of God's holiness as the hub of a wheel around which every other attribute revolves. For example, God is love. But love apart from holiness leads to compromise. God is just. But justice apart from holiness leads to harshness. Holiness guarantees that God exercises every one of His attributes in a morally proper way.

Every single one of us has fallen far short of God's holiness. We do not consistently exhibit moral excellence. The Old Testament prophet Isaiah put it this way: "All we like sheep have gone astray; we have turned, every one, to his own way" (Isaiah 53:6 NKJV). Consequently, the penalty of our <u>sins</u> is spiritual death, our eternal separation from God. That is precisely the reason "Christ died for our sins."

**child**
Mark 10:13

**holy**
1 Peter 1:16

**sins**
Romans 6:23

**Pre-Trib**
the belief that Jesus will return before the beginning of the seven-year Tribulation, during which there will be much suffering on the earth

**eschatology**
the biblical doctrine of the end times

**go to**

**hand**
Acts 7:55

**rise**
Matthew 12:40;
John 2:19

**iniquity**
sins

**2.** *Christ died to save us from our sins.* And this He did "according to the Scriptures" (1 Corinthians 15:3 NKJV). Back to the Isaiah passage: "The LORD has laid on Him the **iniquity** of us all" (53:6 NKJV). Paul put it this way, "God made Christ, who never sinned, to be the offering for our sin, so that we could be made right with God through Christ" (2 Corinthians 5:21 NLT). The holiness of God demands that we live a morally perfect life. The justice of God demands that when we don't we must pay a penalty for our sins. The love of God provided the payment—His "only begotten Son" (John 3:16 NKJV). As Jesus hung on the cross, all of our sins—past, present, and future—were placed on Jesus Christ. Thus He paid the penalty in our place. Because of His sacrificial death on the cross, God's justice has been satisfied and we can now "be made right with God."

**3.** *Jesus arose from the dead and is alive today.* A dead Savior is no use to anyone. But Jesus is not a dead Savior. He is our living Savior, standing at the right <u>hand</u> of God. Jesus validated His claim to be God by insisting that He would <u>rise</u> from the dead. This Jesus did "according to the Scriptures," for the Old Testament Scriptures declare, "I am your chosen one. You won't leave me in the grave or let my body decay" (Psalm 16:10 CEV).

> **what others say**
>
> **Eugene Peterson**
>
> In the letters Paul wrote, there are fifty-three references to the resurrection of Jesus. The resurrection of Jesus is the event which sets and keeps in motion the entire gospel enterprise. Most of these resurrection texts assert either the centrality of Jesus's resurrection or the certainty of our final resurrection, or both.[1]

Jesus "rose again the third day according to the Scriptures, and . . . He was seen" (1 Corinthians 15:4–5 NKJV). The resurrection of Jesus Christ stands today as a historically proven fact, established on the basis of multiple eyewitness accounts spanning several days and hundreds of people. He was seen alive by *Cephas* (Peter), all of the apostles, and even by as many as *five hundred people at one time*, "of whom the greater part remain" (15:6 NKJV), meaning they were still alive at the time of Paul's writing.

I love that. That was Paul's way of saying, "Hey, don't take my word for it. Jesus appeared to more than five hundred people, most of whom are still alive. If you don't believe me, ask them!" And of course, the very-much-alive Jesus appeared to Paul on the road to Damascus. And when He did, Paul fell to the ground and submitted his life to Christ as his "Lord" (Acts 9:6 NKJV).

That's the moment—on the road to Damascus—that all the pieces of the salvation puzzle came together for Paul in vivid, three-dimensional relief. The gospel that Paul understood was as basic as ABC. Paul **A**dmitted that he was a sinner, **B**elieved that Jesus died to save him from his sins, and **C**onfessed that Jesus was his risen Lord. Such is the utter simplicity of the gospel message. That's when Paul became a follower of Jesus. Which begs the question, When did you?

## Better Late Than Never

1 CORINTHIANS 15:8b–11 *as by one born out of due time. For I am the least of the apostles, who am not worthy to be called an apostle, because I persecuted the church of God. But by the grace of God I am what I am, and His grace toward me was not in vain; but I labored more abundantly than they all, yet not I, but the grace of God which was with me. Therefore, whether it was I or they, so we preach and so you believed. (NKJV)*

**born again**
John 3:3

**chief**
1 Timothy 1:15

**persecuted**
Acts 9:5

**chief**
worst

Paul came to faith in Christ too late to become one of the original twelve disciples. In that sense, he was "born out of due time." But he was spiritually <u>born again</u> in time to enjoy a fruitful ministry that included the planting of multiple churches and writing much of the New Testament. He didn't become a follower of Jesus before His resurrection, but he sure made up for lost time after he met the resurrected Christ!

Once again, we are reminded that Paul never lost sight of what he was in his BC or "before Christ" days—a persecutor of the church, a tormentor of Christians. He never lost the wonder of it all—that by God's grace he, the **chief** of sinners, could now serve the One against whom he had so grievously sinned, the One whom he had so viciously <u>persecuted</u>.

If God can save and use Paul, the chief of sinners, just imagine how God can save and use us.

key point

# Denying the Undeniable

**rise**
1 Thessalonians 4:16

Skeptics have been around since time immemorial. In recent times—from (1) the celebrated *Passover Plot*, which alleges "Jesus was a mortal man, a young genius who believed himself to be the Messiah and brilliantly and deliberately planned his entire ministry according to the Old Testament prophecies even to the extent of plotting his own arrest, crucifixion and resurrection,"[2] to (2) *The Da Vinci Code*, which perpetrated the blasphemous notion that Jesus and Mary Magdalene had a son, to (3) James Cameron of *Titanic* fame, who claimed to have found the burial bone boxes of Jesus, Mary Magdalene, and their supposed son, Judah—we who believe in the Resurrection have been treated to a constant river of ridicule as one author or "scholar" or filmmaker after another markets his or her latest theory on why the resurrection of Christ is the most heinous deception ever perpetrated on the human race.

This is nothing new. As we are about to learn, essentially the same thing happened in Corinth.

# A Futile Faith

> the big picture
>
> ## 1 Corinthians 15:12–19
>
> There were some in the Corinthian congregation who were teaching "that there is no resurrection of the dead" (v. 12 NKJV). Paul addressed this serious doctrinal and historical heresy in his customary confrontational style, pointing out in no uncertain terms that the implications of this heresy were wide ranging.

"If Christ is not risen your faith is futile" Paul declared to his readers. "You are still in your sins!" (1 Corinthians 15:17 NKJV).

Such is the seriousness of the false teaching that echoed through the church in Corinth. Paul's argument was a study in logic, a classic example of correctly connecting the dots so as to arrive at the proper conclusion.

Paul's line of reasoning basically went like this. We apostles are eyewitnesses to the undeniable fact that Jesus rose from the dead. We too will <u>rise</u> from the dead. But if the resurrection from the dead is a false doctrine, if this life is all there is, if we are mere mortals with

key point

no eternal souls, if there is no life after death, then not only will we not be raised; Jesus was not raised. If Jesus was not raised, not only are we false witnesses, but the whole purpose of Jesus's crucifixion and resurrection is made null and void. If Jesus was not raised, if He too was a mere mortal no different from us, then we are still in our sins.

Therefore our faith, the cornerstone of which is Christ's resurrection, is meaningless. Every Christian who has died is gone, lost forever. If our faith in Christ is meaningless and there truly is no life after death, then we are to be pitied—for believing a lie; for trying to live a disciplined Christian life in obedience to a Jesus who's dead, buried, and gone; for limiting our personal freedom in the name of biblical morality; for denying ourselves limitless pleasure; for following a Christ who in the final analysis is no different from any of us.

This is sobering stuff. The implications of denying a bodily resurrection are staggering in the extreme. Just imagine the impact on your faith if it could be proven that "the dead do not rise" (1 Corinthians 15:15 NKJV). The ripple effect of that theological thunderclap would touch every dimension of our lives. Suddenly, any sense of purpose would be gone. All would be futile. Our existence on planet Earth would have no meaning, no significance. We would be robbed of every semblance of dignity and worth. All laws that define our morality would be purely arbitrary. Murdering a fellow human being would be no more serious than swatting a gnat. Suicide might be elevated to a virtue as the ultimate solution to the pains of daily life. The adage "One man's terrorist is another man's freedom fighter" would take on a new significance. The survival of the fittest would become the new ethic. Kierkegaard, Camus, et al. would be right; life would become absurd.

**what others say**

**William Lane Craig**

Modern man thought that when he had gotten rid of God, he had freed himself from all that repressed and stifled him. Instead, he discovered that in killing God, he had also killed himself. For if there is no God then man's life becomes absurd.[3]

# Christt the Firstfruits

**the big picture**

**I Corinthians 15:20–28**

Paul assured his readers that Christ did indeed rise from the dead, and that because He lives, we shall live also. He introduced the concept of "firstfruits" (v. 23 NKJV) in order to encourage the Christians in Corinth that they will live again.

"Firstfruits." Now that's an interesting word, certainly an uncommon one by our standards. Yet, the concept of "firstfruits" was an integral part of Paul's reasoning concerning our resurrection from the dead.

The idea of firstfruits goes all the way back to Exodus 23:16, which says, "Celebrate the Feast of Harvest with the firstfruits of the crops you sow in your field" (NIV). God instructed His people to celebrate His goodness in providing a bountiful harvest by eating from the first crops of that harvest. In Exodus 23:19 we read of an offering of firstfruits when God instructs His people, "The first of the firstfruits of your land you shall bring into the house of the LORD your God" (NKJV).

Picture the Israelites gathering the first portion of their harvest and bringing it into the Tabernacle as a thanksgiving offering to God. In both examples, "firstfruits" referred to the first part of a much larger harvest.

The New Testament reveals that at the end of the age there will be a mass resurrection, a vast harvest of souls raised from the dead. As Paul wrote to the church in Thessalonica, "The Lord Himself will descend from heaven with a shout, with the voice of an archangel, and with the trumpet of God. And *the dead in Christ will rise first.* Then we who are alive and remain shall be caught up together with them in the clouds to meet the Lord in the air. And thus we shall always be with the Lord" (1 Thessalonians 4:16–17 NKJV, emphasis added).

We referenced this passage earlier when we talked about the rapture of the church. Note the order of things: First, when Christ returns, all of His followers who have died will rise from the dead. Then all of Christ's followers who are alive when He returns will be caught up (or raptured) in a glorious, heavenly reunion with their dearly departed loved ones. We're talking about multiplied millions of people who have come to faith in Christ over the past two millennia—a vast harvest indeed. None of which would be possible, however, unless Christ was Himself first raised from the dead as the "firstfruits" of the harvest.

With that understanding in mind, as unfamiliar as the word *firstfruits* might sound to us, the concept is really quite simple. The NLT version of 1 Corinthians 15:23 perhaps says it best: "There is an order to this resurrection: Christ was raised as the first of the harvest; then all who belong to Christ will be raised when he comes back." A wonderful concept indeed! But it gets even better.

After Christ returns, "then comes the end" (1 Corinthians 15:24 NKJV). Every ruler, every authority, every power—both spiritual and political—that opposes God's sovereign rule on the earth will be destroyed. We will see a grand and glorious fulfillment of Psalm 2 where God asks of the nations of the world, "Why do the nations rage, and the people plot a vain thing? The kings of the earth set themselves, and the rulers take counsel together, against the LORD and against His Anointed, saying, 'Let us break Their bonds in pieces and cast away Their cords from us'" (vv. 1–3 NKJV).

Is God threatened or intimidated by the saber rattling of these rogue rulers? Not a chance. Indeed, "In heaven the LORD laughs as he sits on his throne, making fun of the nations. The LORD becomes furious and threatens them. His anger terrifies them as he says, 'I've put my king on Zion, my sacred hill'" (Psalm 2:4–6 CEV). God has installed His King, His Son, the "KING OF KINGS AND LORD OF LORDS" (Revelation 19:16 NKJV), on His holy mountain, and nothing will destabilize His rule on the earth.

key point

With Jesus, there won't ever be any sort of regime change, even though the armies of hell itself march against Him. And that's a promise, a God-given promise, a promise made by God to His Son, a promise that Jesus claimed when He said, "I will declare the decree: The LORD has said to Me, 'You are My Son, today I have begotten You. Ask of Me, and I will give You the nations for Your inheritance, and the ends of the earth for Your possession. You shall break them with a rod of iron; you shall dash them to pieces like a potter's vessel'" (Psalm 2:7–9 NKJV).

feet
1 Corinthians 15:27,
Psalm 8:6

In light of what's coming, God gave these rulers this ominous warning: "Be wise, O kings; be instructed, you judges of the earth. Serve the LORD with fear, and rejoice with trembling. Kiss the Son, lest He be angry, and you perish in the way, when His wrath is kindled but a little. Blessed are all those who put their trust in Him" (Psalm 2:10–12 NKJV).

God will fulfill this psalm in magnificent detail. Once all of Christ's enemies have been put under Christ's <u>feet</u>, a picture of a vanquished king assuming a place of submission before a conquering king, Jesus will then hand it all back to God the Father, so that God "will be utterly supreme over everything everywhere" (1 Corinthians 15:28 NLT) forever and ever.

Such is the significance of the biblical doctrine of our resurrection from the dead. We can now understand why Paul was so offended by those in Corinth who denied the reality of the Resurrection, and by so doing, rendered the faith of their followers as *futile*, empty, and worthless.

key point

Paul had much to say about our coming resurrection from the dead. He painted a glorious picture of what will happen to us when we close our eyes down here and open our eyes up there. The resurrection from the dead is arguably the single most hope-filled doctrine in the Bible. And yet, false teachers who had infiltrated the Corinthian congregation sought to rob the people there of this glorious truth.

## Making His Case

*1 CORINTHIANS 15:29–34 Otherwise, what will they do who are baptized for the dead, if the dead do not rise at all? Why then are they baptized for the dead? And why do we stand in jeopardy every hour? I affirm, by the boasting in you which I have in Christ Jesus our Lord, I die daily. If, in the manner of men, I have fought with beasts at Ephesus, what advantage is it to me? If the dead do not rise, "Let us eat and drink, for tomorrow we die!" Do not be deceived: "Evil company corrupts good habits." Awake to righteousness, and do not sin; for some do not have the knowledge of God. I speak this to your shame. (NKJV)*

In this passage, some suggest that *baptized* is to be taken metaphorically, such as referring to those who are being baptized into the ranks of the dead through martyrdom. Others proffer the idea that the word *dead* might itself be metaphorical, referring to those who were being baptized with a view toward their own eventual deaths, or their coming reunion with loved ones who had previously died.[4]

Some take it to mean that this refers to those who came to faith in Christ because of the witness or influence of Christians who had since died. Others interpret the verse as a reference to those who are being baptized "over the sepulchers of the dead." Still others suggest that Paul referred to those who are filling the vacancies left by the dead. And still others believe that the baptism is the baptism of suffering.[5]

I believe that we should take the verse at face value. Let's remember Paul's argument: He is confronting those who have rejected a belief in the resurrection of the dead. He is arguing that to reject that foundational belief of orthodox Christianity is to deny the bodily resurrection of Christ. His purpose here is to return his readers to an understanding and acceptance of the glorious truth, that when we die we shall be raised to an eternal life.

Paul next asked them why, if there is no resurrection from the dead, he and the other apostles place their lives in jeopardy every hour of every day? As one example, Paul referenced a situation with which his original readers were familiar. It happened in Ephesus and it wasn't pretty. A guy by the name of Demetrius incited a crowd and stirred them into a rage against Paul.

Paul's reference to "beasts at Ephesus" (1 Corinthians 15:32 NKJV) might have been a reference to the unruly mob that threatened his life. Or it might refer quite literally to Paul facing wild animals—an incident not mentioned in Acts. Point is, why would Paul be willing to face death every day if there were no life after death? Say what they wanted about the apostle, they knew that Paul was no fool. But if this life is all there is, then Paul was surely acting like a fool. They had too much respect for him to ignore the sacrifices he was making and the dangers he was enduring to preach the resurrection of Christ, and the resurrection of His followers.

**evil one**
John 17:15

Paul then ended this section by reiterating what he had already stated: If there is no resurrection, then life becomes absurd. "Let us eat and drink, for tomorrow we die!" (15:32 NKJV), for that's where we end up. If this life is all there is, if there is no life after death, then the only sensible approach to life is to get all of the pleasure, possessions, and power that you can.

But Christ did rise from the dead. There is life after death. The dead in Christ will be raised. So Paul figuratively grabbed his readers by the lapels and tried to shake some sense into them by shouting, "Do not be deceived: 'Evil company corrupts good habits'" (15:33 NKJV). In other words, stop tolerating the false teachers among you. Stop hanging out with those people. Reject them. They are corrupting you. Don't you see that? "For some do not have the knowledge of God" (15:34 NKJV). In other words, some of them aren't even Christians. "I speak this to your shame" (15:34 NKJV).

apply it

Paul's point is well taken. "Evil company corrupts good habits." In the words of the New Living Translation, "Bad company corrupts good character." Our Christian character (how we live) and convictions (what we believe) must be guarded relentlessly against spiritual attack. One of the ploys of the <u>evil one</u> is to get us to hang around people who bring us down spiritually. We dare not tolerate those who teach error either through their words or their actions. We simply have too much to lose.

## Time for a Trade-In

*the big picture*

### 1 Corinthians 15:35–49

Paul revealed to the Christians in Corinth that just as our earthly bodies are suitable for life on this planet, so our resurrection bodies will be perfectly suited to life in heaven.

Questions abounded. "How are the dead raised up?" (1 Corinthians 15:35 NKJV) asked one person. "With what body do they come?" (15:35 NKJV) asked another. Calling upon a lesson from nature, Paul reminded his readers that when a grain of wheat falls to the earth and dies, God provides the perfect body for the stock of grain that springs from the dead seed. Likewise, God provides each of the animals, fish, and birds with bodies that are perfectly suited to their environments.

God will do the same for us. He provided us with "terrestrial bodies" that enable us to live and thrive on this planet. But a day is coming when, like a grain of wheat, our bodies will die. But out of that death, God will bring life. And when He does, He will provide for us "celestial bodies," better translated "heavenly bodies,"⁶ perfectly suited for our eternal, heavenly abode.

Our earthly bodies degenerate with age, and will begin a process of decomposition at the time of our deaths—what Paul referred to as the *corruption* of our bodies. But we will be raised with bodies *incorruptible*! Our bodies of flesh are easily enticed, given over to our sinful impulses—what Paul called *dishonor*. But our resurrected bodies will be glorious! Our earthly bodies are weak, but our new bodies will be strong, raised to life by the same power that raised Jesus from the dead. Yes, our *natural* bodies will die one day. But our new bodies will be tailor-made for the spiritual realm in which we will be living forever and ever.

key point

This contrast between our earthly and resurrected bodies is perhaps most clearly seen by placing Adam (*the first man*) and Jesus (*the second Man*) side by side. Adam, "the first man was of the earth, made of dust; the second Man is the Lord from heaven" (1 Corinthians 15:47 NKJV). Adam was created with a natural, earthly body. When he died, his body returned to the dust; as the Scripture says, "For dust you are, and to dust you shall return" (Genesis 3:19 NKJV). Jesus too was created with a natural body. But He was raised with a heavenly body. So too will we be.

For just as Adam's earthly body was a prototype of our earthly bodies, so Jesus's resurrection body was a prototype of our heavenly bodies. Or as Paul told the church in Philippi, "Our citizenship is in heaven, from which we also eagerly wait for the Savior, the Lord Jesus Christ, who will transform our lowly body that it may be conformed to His glorious body, according to the working by which He is able even to subdue all things to Himself" (Philippians 3:20–21 NKJV).

If you want a glimpse of what our new, resurrection bodies will be like, take a look at Jesus. He was raised with the same kind of body that we will be given when we are raised to live forever.

If there is no resurrection from the dead, life becomes futile. But because the dead will indeed be raised, life has meaning—a glorious meaning that's worth embracing, a life lived with an eternal perspective.

## That Mysterious "Rapture"

*1 CORINTHIANS 15:50–54 Now this I say, brethren, that flesh and blood cannot inherit the kingdom of God; nor does corruption inherit incorruption. Behold, I tell you a mystery: We shall not all sleep, but we shall all be changed—in a moment, in the twinkling of an eye, at the last trumpet. For the trumpet will sound, and the dead will be raised incorruptible, and we shall be changed. For this corruptible must put on incorruption, and this mortal must put on immortality. So when this corruptible has put on incorruption, and this mortal has put on immortality, then shall be brought to pass the saying that is written: "Death is swallowed up in victory." (NKJV)*

Place 1 Corinthians 15:50–54 side by side with 1 Thessalonians 4:15–18 and you get quite an exciting picture of the future that awaits us. In both of these passages Paul is painting a portrait of what is arguably the single most amazing doctrine in all of Scripture: the rapture of the church.

Paul refers to this doctrine as a "mystery," but not in the sense that it makes no sense or that we trying to solve some puzzle and he's giving us the clues. The word is a precise term that refers to a New Testament truth not previously revealed in the Old Testament. Indeed, the first hint at this notion that Christ will return and rapture—or take all living Christians immediately into His presence—came from Jesus Himself when He promised His disciples, "Let not your heart be troubled; you believe in God, believe also in Me. In My Father's house are many mansions; if it were not so, I would have told you. I go to prepare a place for you. And if I go and prepare a place for you, I will come again and receive you to Myself; that where I am, there you may be also" (John 14:1–3 NKJV).

He made that promise on the night before He died on the cross. I am sure that in the dark days that followed the Crucifixion the disciples mentally and emotionally retreated into the comfort of those reassuring words.

Paul fleshed out that promise in some detail as he wrote to the churches of Thessalonica and Corinth. He began by reiterating the fact that "flesh and blood cannot inherit the kingdom of God"

(1 Corinthians 15:50 NKJV). As we have already noted, our earthly bodies are perfectly suited to life down here; they are not designed for life in heaven. Rest assured, Paul informed his readers, new bodies are on the way!

Paul then revealed that Christians who are alive when Jesus returns to the earth will never die. Paul used the metaphor of *sleep* to refer to death, because for the Christian, death is a doorway and not a wall. When we die, it's as if we will fall asleep here and wake up there. But whether we die or live to see Christ's return, we will all be changed "in a moment, in the twinkling of an eye" (15:52 NKJV).

A trumpet will sound, the same trumpet referred to in 1 Thessalonians 4:16. This trumpet will herald the coming of the King, much as the arrival of a sovereign was trumpeted during biblical times. And it's precisely at that moment that "the dead [in Christ] will be raised" (15:52 NKJV) with bodies that are *incorruptible*—brand-new bodies just like that of the risen Jesus, eternal bodies designed for our eternal home in heaven.

And, because they are incorruptible they will never die, or fall prey to disease, or suffer aches and pains, or have any human limitation whatsoever. This is physical healing in the ultimate sense. The blind will see, the deaf will hear, the lame will walk, the sick will be cured. We will shed our bodies much like a caterpillar sheds its cocoon and emerges as a bright and beautiful butterfly. "Mortal must put on immortality" (15:53 NKJV). In the words of Isaiah 25:8, "Death [will be] swallowed up in victory" (15:54 NKJV). And we will sing. Boy, will we sing!

**what others say**

**Billy Graham**

In contrast to the anguish and anxiety of the person with no eternal hope, Christians can look to Christ for hope and encouragement. Because of our faith in Christ we do not "grieve like the rest of men who have no hope" (1 Thessalonians 4:13b).[7]

## Our Victory Song

1 CORINTHIANS 15:55–58 *"O Death, where is your sting? O Hades, where is your victory?" The sting of death is sin, and the strength of sin is the law. But thanks be to God, who gives us the victory through our Lord Jesus Christ. Therefore, my beloved*

*brethren, be steadfast, immovable, always abounding in the work of the Lord, knowing that your labor is not in vain in the Lord. (NKJV)*

The prophet Hosea looked death squarely in the face and taunted it. We will sing his words, quoted from Hosea 13:14, "O Death, where is your sting? O Hades, where is your victory?" Or if I might paraphrase, "Listen, O Death, who's afraid of you now? Can you hear me, O Grave, Jesus declared war against you and now proclaims His victory!"

key point

After we die and are resurrected, our glorious bodies will never again be tempted to rebel against God. Never again will we be enticed to break His laws. There will be no sins committed in heaven, not by us or by anyone. We will dwell in absolute safety and security with one another, never to suffer or fear the heinous actions of those who would sin against us or our loved ones. We have a glorious day coming. There is a life after death—more glorious than we can possibly imagine—despite the denials the false teachers in Corinth dared to spread throughout that struggling church. Paul restored to them the God-given joy that these men had taken away.

All of which prompted Paul to give to his beloved brothers and sisters in Corinth, and to us, this closing benediction: "My beloved brethren, be steadfast, immovable, always abounding in the work of the Lord, knowing that your labor is not in vain in the Lord" (1 Corinthians 15:58 NKJV).

## Chapter Wrap-Up

- The resurrection of Christ is central to the gospel, and Paul made this very clear in the fifteenth chapter of 1 Corinthians.
- Paul preached the gospel; his hearers received it, were saved by it, and were holding fast to it.
- Paul cleared away a world of confusion when he clearly identified the three essential elements of the gospel—the *only* three that really matter!
- Paul went to great lengths to prove, via the historical evidence, that Christ *did in fact* rise from the dead and is alive today. And, that we will one day do the same when we exchange our earthly bodies for eternal ones.

## Study Questions

1. What were the three central elements of the gospel that Paul preached?

2. Name just one proof (of many!) that Christ arose from the dead.

3. What is the word Paul used in place of "dead," in referring to our own physical deaths? Why did he do so?

4. What is the word commonly used to refer to the moment when faithful believers will be resurrected from their graves and "snatched up" into the air to be with Christ forever—after which the faithful who are still alive on earth will be "taken up" as well?

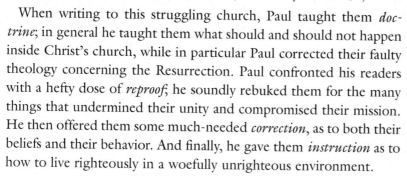

# 1 Corinthians 16
# The Joy of Giving

*Chapter Highlights:*
- A Famine in the Land
- A Gift of Love
- An Open Door
- Two Trusted Friends
- Closing Commands
- Final Farewell

## Let's Get Started

All good things must end. And that's certainly true of Paul's paternal letter to a congregation he loved, the church he founded in Corinth. Paul's first letter to this church in crisis certainly illustrates Paul's reminder to Timothy, that "all Scripture is given by inspiration of God, and is profitable for doctrine, for reproof, for correction, for instruction in righteousness" (2 Timothy 3:16 NKJV).

When writing to this struggling church, Paul taught them *doctrine*; in general he taught them what should and should not happen inside Christ's church, while in particular Paul corrected their faulty theology concerning the Resurrection. Paul confronted his readers with a hefty dose of *reproof*; he soundly rebuked them for the many things that undermined their unity and compromised their mission. He then offered them some much-needed *correction*, as to both their beliefs and their behavior. And finally, he gave them *instruction* as to how to live righteously in a woefully unrighteous environment.

As we turn the page to this final chapter, Paul concluded his letter with one last bit of teaching, this time concerning the financial responsibilities of those in the church. He then ended his letter with his customary personal touch, mentioning several individuals by name, bestowing God's grace on his readers, and assuring them of his enduring love—a sobering conclusion to this confrontational first letter.

**stoned**
Acts 7:58

## A Famine in the Land

> 1 CORINTHIANS 16:1 *Now concerning the collection for the saints, as I have given orders to the churches of Galatia, so you must do also:* (NKJV)

Tough times had hit the people of God who were living in Jerusalem and in all of Judea. In addition to the hostility that these early believers were facing—remember that Stephen had been recently <u>stoned</u> just outside the city wall of Jerusalem—a severe famine had hit the land.

**John**
Galatians 2:9

**Pentecost**
Acts 2:1

Luke, author of the book of Acts, made reference to this famine when he wrote: "In these days prophets came from Jerusalem to Antioch. Then one of them, named Agabus, stood up and showed by the Spirit that there was going to be a great famine throughout all the world, which also happened in the days of Claudius Caesar. Then the disciples, each according to his ability, determined to send relief to the brethren dwelling in Judea. This they also did, and sent it to the elders by the hands of Barnabas and Saul" (Acts 11:27–30 NKJV).

The pressing needs of these Christians, especially those in the overcrowded city of Jerusalem, were very much on Paul's mind and heart as he brought this first letter to the Corinthians to a conclusion. Paul shared this pressing need with the churches throughout *Galatia*. Indeed, when James, Peter, and <u>John</u> commissioned Paul and Barnabas to take the gospel to the Gentiles, "they desired only that we should remember the poor, the very thing which I also was eager to do" (Galatians 2:10 NKJV).

The *poor*, of course, referred primarily to the Christians in Jerusalem who were struggling financially in the wake of both the famine and the enormous numbers of people who were receiving Christ in that city. Indeed, for years after the initial Day of <u>Pentecost</u>, in which three thousand were baptized as Christian believers, the members of the Jerusalem church were pressed financially.[1]

We often forget the hardships that the early Christians—and indeed Christians throughout all periods of church history—have had to endure. Perhaps we have been lulled into a false sense of security and prosperity because no one has driven us from our homes or threatened us with imprisonment or bodily harm because of our Christian faith. A unique "prosperity" theology has developed in our time that suggests financial blessing is the sign of God's favor, and that every obedient, Spirit-filled Christian is entitled to monetary prosperity. But the Christians living throughout Judea in the first century would vehemently disagree, as would Christians living today in oppressive cultures and countries hostile to Christianity.

The situation in Judea, and particularly in Jerusalem, was so dire that "those from Macedonia and Achaia [made] a certain contribution for the poor among the saints who [were] in Jerusalem" (Romans 15:26 NKJV). The church in Corinth wanted to contribute toward this need as well. So, in their list of questions, they asked Paul what they could do to help. The words "Now concerning" in 1 Corinthians 16:1 (NKJV) tip us off to this; the same two words introduced Paul's discussion of singleness and marriage (7:1), the unmarried (7:25), meat offered to idols (8:1), and spiritual gifts (12:1).

**seventh**
Genesis 2:1–3

## A Gift of Love

> 1 CORINTHIANS 16:2–4 *On the first day of the week let each one of you lay something aside, storing up as he may prosper, that there be no collections when I come. And when I come, whomever you approve by your letters I will send to bear your gift to Jerusalem. But if it is fitting that I go also, they will go with me.* (NKJV)

Paul's instructions were simple and straightforward—they were to take a special offering during their worship services for the suffering Christians of Judea. But there are some interesting observations that can be made from Paul's answer to the Corinthians' question concerning the collection.

First, note the phrase "On the first day of the week." By anyone's reckoning, this was a reference to Sunday, not Saturday. The early church began the tradition of meeting not on the Jewish Sabbath (Saturday, the <u>seventh</u> day of the week), but on Sunday, the first day of the week.

This isn't the first indication that the early church met on Sunday. The church in Troas met "on the first day of the week, when the disciples came together to break bread" (Acts 20:7 NKJV). Likewise John, when he received the revelations that became the book of Revelation, "was in the Spirit on the Lord's Day" (Revelation 1:10 NKJV). In many early Christian writings the phrase "the Lord's Day" refers to Sunday, the day of our Lord's resurrection. Indeed, *The Message* translates Revelation 1:10 as follows: "It was Sunday and I was in the Spirit, praying." So we have clear and compelling evidence that the early church established the tradition that unlike their Jewish contemporaries who met for worship on Saturday, they would meet for worship on the Lord's Day, Sunday, Resurrection Day.

This is not to suggest that we are biblically mandated to meet for worship on Sunday. There is no command of Scripture to do so. So even though this tradition has endured the centuries and continues

**tithe**
Numbers 18:21–32

to our day, if some churches choose to add a Saturday night service or a Friday night service, they are perfectly at liberty to do so.

Second, the phrase "storing up as he may prosper" (1 Corinthians 16:2 NKJV) is quite significant. Many Christians believe that tithing—putting 10 percent of their income into the offering plate—is a biblical command. Now it is true that "the law of Moses required that the priests, who are descendants of Levi, must collect a <u>tithe</u> from the rest of the people of Israel, who are also descendants of Abraham" (Hebrews 7:5 NLT). The tabernacle and, later, the temple priests derived their incomes from these tithes. But there is no similar command in Scripture that mandates we give a tithe of our income to the church.

Having said that, tithing is a good principle to follow as a basic guideline for giving. But God did not place upon Christians the legal requirement of the tithe. Instead, He wants us to give out of the generosity of our hearts, not because we have to but because we want to. He wants us to give not based on a rigid 10 percent law, but according to this principle of sowing and reaping: "He who sows sparingly will also reap sparingly, and he who sows bountifully will also reap bountifully. So let each one give as he purposes in his heart, not grudgingly or of necessity; for God loves a cheerful giver. And God is able to make all grace abound toward you, that you, always having all sufficiency in all things, may have an abundance for every good work" (2 Corinthians 9:6–8 NKJV).

**what others say**

**Mark Allan Powell**

"Where you put your treasure—that's where your heart will end up." The point isn't that how we spend our money *reveals* what sort of people we are, but how we spend our money *determines* what sort of people we *become*.[2]

**Kennon Callahan**

Living is giving. This is the first principle for giving. We live life best as we give our strengths, gifts, and competencies in the service of God's mission. We are called to serve, not survive. Our giving makes a difference in our families, our work, our community, our world, and our church.[3]

Paul wanted the Corinthians to take up their collection every Lord's Day in the weeks leading up to Paul's arrival in Corinth. He asked them to choose those who would hand-carry these financial gifts to Jerusalem. Paul even offered to personally accompany their messengers if they would feel a greater level of comfort having him do so.

In customary fashion, Paul ended his letter by addressing some personal matters regarding his present and future plans.

## An Open Door

*1 CORINTHIANS 16:5–9 Now I will come to you when I pass through Macedonia (for I am passing through Macedonia). And it may be that I will remain, or even spend the winter with you, that you may send me on my journey, wherever I go. For I do not wish to see you now on the way; but I hope to stay a while with you, if the Lord permits. But I will tarry in Ephesus until Pentecost. For a great and effective door has opened to me, and there are many adversaries. (NKJV)*

Paul wrote 1 Corinthians toward the end of his three-year stay in Ephesus. At the time, Paul was enjoying a fruitful ministry among the Ephesians, so fruitful in fact that he said of his time there that "a great and effective door has opened to me." However, as is always the case when spiritual progress is being made, "there are many adversaries."

Indeed, the situation got far worse before it got better. We get a glimpse into the suffering that Paul endured shortly after writing 1 Corinthians. In 2 Corinthians 1:8–10, Paul wrote, "We do not want you to be ignorant, brethren, of our trouble which came to us in Asia: that we were burdened beyond measure, above strength, so that we despaired even of life. Yes, we had the sentence of death in ourselves, that we should not trust in ourselves but in God who raises the dead, who delivered us from so great a death, and does deliver us; in whom we trust that He will still deliver us" (NKJV).

We can take comfort in the fact that someone as illustrious as Paul was constantly embroiled in an ongoing spiritual battle. When Paul wrote to the church in Thessalonica he acknowledged, "We wanted to come to you—even I, Paul, time and again—but Satan hindered us" (1 Thessalonians 2:18 NKJV). So now, in Ephesus, Paul was making headway as he labored night and day for three years to establish a church in that influential city. But he was challenged by "many adversaries." We should expect the same.

key point

If you ever feel overwhelmed by the *adversaries* that stalk you on your spiritual journey, you are not alone. So did Paul. "Yes, and all who desire to live godly in Christ Jesus will suffer persecution" (2 Timothy 3:12 NKJV).

Paul planned to visit Corinth when he passed through Macedonia. Depending on the timing of his arrival, he even considered spending the winter with them. But for now, he planned to remain in Ephesus, wrapping up his ministry there by Pentecost (some time in late spring). So it is quite likely that Paul planned to arrive in Corinth just before winter.

## Two Trusted Friends in the Faith

> 1 CORINTHIANS 16:10–12 *And if Timothy comes, see that he may be with you without fear; for he does the work of the Lord, as I also do. Therefore let no one despise him. But send him on his journey in peace, that he may come to me; for I am waiting for him with the brethren. Now concerning our brother Apollos, I strongly urged him to come to you with the brethren, but he was quite unwilling to come at this time; however, he will come when he has a convenient time. (NKJV)*

Two trusted friends in the faith made their appearance here at the end of Paul's letter, both of whom have already been mentioned in this letter. The first is Timothy, of whom we read, "I have sent Timothy to you, who is my beloved and faithful son in the Lord, who will remind you of my ways in Christ, as I teach everywhere in every church" (1 Corinthians 4:17 NKJV).

As we just mentioned, "Paul purposed in the Spirit, when he had passed through Macedonia and Achaia" that he would visit Corinth, possibly to spend the winter. From Corinth Paul intended "to go to Jerusalem" to deliver the Corinthians' financial gift. In preparation for that trip, "he sent into Macedonia two of those who ministered to him, Timothy and Erastus" (Acts 19:21–22 NKJV). Timothy was then to go to Corinth.

Paul wanted Apollos to accompany Timothy and Erastus (Remember Apollos from 1 Corinthians 1:12?) But Apollos felt strongly that he should remain in Ephesus. So strong were his convictions that Paul respected and supported his decision, assuring his readers that Apollos would indeed visit the church in Corinth "when he has a convenient time" (1 Corinthians 16:12 NKJV).

**The Smart Guide to the Bible**

# Closing Commands

1 CORINTHIANS 16:13–14 *Watch, stand fast in the faith, be brave, be strong. Let all that you do be done with love.* (NKJV)

Through nearly sixteen chapters, we have read Paul's words of correction and confrontation. We can easily forget that Paul possessed a tender heart. He truly cared about people. He summarized the longing of his rather sizable heart when he wrote, "[Christ] we preach, warning every man and teaching every man in all wisdom, that we may present every man perfect in Christ Jesus. To this end I also labor, striving according to His working which works in me mightily" (Colossians 1:28–29 NKJV). Paul did what he did and wrote what he wrote, all to that end. As we come to the conclusion of this great letter, we will see Paul's tender heart shine as he pours out his love for his dear readers.

In his closing commands, Paul left his Corinthian readers with five final imperatives that he had determined were especially needful given the level of compromise in the Corinthian assembly. Even though they were written specifically to the believers in Corinth, these five commands serve as a helpful checklist for each of us to consider as a barometer of our own spiritual health.

## Paul's Five Parting Imperatives to Ensure Spiritual Health

| Command | Significance | Scriptural Support |
|---|---|---|
| Watch | Be alert to spiritual danger; be aware of your weaknesses as potential areas of spiritual attack. | 1 Peter 5:8: "Stay alert! Watch out for your great enemy, the devil. He prowls around like a roaring lion, looking for someone to devour" (NLT). |
| Stand Fast in the Faith | Firmly establish your biblical convictions; purpose in your heart that you will not compromise your convictions regardless of the cost. | Daniel 1:8: "But Daniel purposed in his heart that he would not defile himself" (NKJV). |
| Be Brave | Face your challenges with the absolute confidence that you do not fight this spiritual battle on your own; God is ever on your side! | 1 Samuel 17:47: "All those gathered here will know that it is not by sword or spear that the LORD saves; for the battle is the LORD's, and he will give all of you into our hands" (NIV). |

**go to**

**tentmakers**
Acts 18:1–3

**Paul's Five Parting Imperatives to Ensure Spiritual Health (cont'd)**

| Command | Significance | Scriptural Support |
|---|---|---|
| Be Strong | Know that you fight not in your own power, but in the power of the Spirit of God. | Ephesians 6:10: "Be strong in the Lord and in the power of His might" (NKJV). |
| Let All That You Do Be Done with Love | As you serve God and serve others, make certain that your motivation is always centered upon love—seeking the very best for the other person. | 1 Corinthians 13:3: "If I give everything I own to the poor and even go to the stake to be burned as a martyr, but I don't love, I've gotten nowhere. So, no matter what I say, what I believe, and what I do, I'm bankrupt without love" (MSG). |

# Paul's Final Farewell

**the big picture**

### 1 Corinthians 16:15–24

Paul ended his letter with his heartfelt greetings to several in Corinth who had been a blessing to Paul personally, as well as to the church.

We see something of the heart of the apostle in his closing comments to the Corinthians. Paul routinely ended his letters with personal greetings and even some musings about individuals or situations relative to his original audience. He did the same here.

Paul referred to the household of Stephanas as "the firstfruits of Achaia" (1 Corinthians 16:15 NKJV). The word *firstfruits* should by now be a familiar term to us. Used in this context, Paul identified Stephanas and his family as being among the first converts (*firstfruits*) to the Christian faith in Corinth, which was located in Achaia, the southern province of Greece.

You might remember that in 1 Corinthians 1:16 Paul wrote, "Yes, I also baptized the household of Stephanas" (NKJV). We know nothing specific about Stephanas's family. We do know that at the time Paul wrote 1 Corinthians, Stephanas, Fortunatus, and Achaicus were visiting with Paul (v. 17). It is quite possible that they were the ones who delivered the letter from Corinth to Paul in which they asked him the questions that Paul answered in chapters 7–16.

Aquila and Priscilla were quite the couple. We know that they were <u>tentmakers</u> with whom he worked and even lived when he got to

Corinth. They followed Paul to Ephesus, ministered with him there, and even opened their home to the church that Paul established in Ephesus. Paul felt such a closeness to this couple that when he wrote his second letter to Timothy, literally from his deathbed, he asked Timothy to "greet Prisca and Aquila" (2 Timothy 4:19 NKJV).

**Galatia**
Galatians 1:8

The reference in verse 19 to the "holy kiss" has definite cultural overtones. It was customary in biblical times, and even today in some Middle Eastern countries, for men to greet men with a kiss on the check, and for women to do the same to women. It was purely an expression of sincere Christian affection between two people, with no sexual significance whatsoever.

Paul wrote the final salutation himself, an indication that the bulk of the letter was dictated to a scribe. This was a common practice of Paul, possibly because he suffered from poor eyesight. Indeed, he wrote to the churches in Galatia, "I bear you witness that, if possible, you would have plucked out your own eyes and given them to me" (Galatians 4:15 NKJV). At the end of the same letter he added, "See with what large letters I have written to you with my own hand!" (Galatians 6:11 NKJV). If Romans 16:22 is any indication, Paul routinely used the services of a scribe; in the case of Romans, the scribe's name was Tertius, Paul's personal secretary to whom Paul dictated the letter.

Finally, Paul expressed his desire for those in the Corinthian congregation who did not truly love Jesus, and who were therefore causing so many of the problems that Paul addressed in the letter, to be set apart for divine judgment. Paul used the word *anathema*, translated here as *accursed*, the same word he used in reference to those in Galatia who were wreaking havoc in the churches there. Strong language by anyone's standard, but appropriate language given the eternal consequences of leading someone away from Christ and causing dissension in the church.

key point

Paul then prayed that Jesus would soon return, and reminded his readers to walk in Christ's love until that glorious day.

And so ends this amazing book we call 1 Corinthians. As we'll soon see, this wouldn't be the last word of Paul to this troubled church, nor does this mark the end of our study. One to two years later, having left Ephesus for Macedonia, Paul wrote 2 Corinthians, an equally amazing letter that it will now be our privilege to study.

## Chapter Wrap-Up

- By the time Paul brought 1 Corinthians to a close he had successfully done at least four things within the letter, as he defined "Scripture," later on, in 2 Timothy 3:16.
- Paul was not afraid to talk about money, nor to ask for it when it was truly deserved, for others but also even for himself!
- Paul indicated that he was, indeed, human in all respects, by talking briefly about some of the sufferings he'd had to endure.
- Paul introduced two good friends who were also faithful servants of God, and were also of tremendous help to Paul in his own work.

## Study Questions

1. What four things mentioned in 1 Corinthians did Paul do for the church in Corinth?

2. What "natural disaster" had hit the people in Jerusalem and, indeed, in all of Judea?

3. What five imperatives did Paul leave the Corinthians with in the closing portion of 1 Corinthians?

4. How did Aquila and Priscilla make a living? Who else do we know who did the same kind of work?

# 2 Corinthians

# Part Three
# Seven Essential Concepts

# 2 Corinthians 1:1–7
# The Purpose of Pain

**Chapter Highlights:**
- Setting the Scene
- Beneath the Surface
- God of All Comfort
- Times of Tribulation
- Inward or Outward
- Proper Perspective

## Let's Get Started

In my Bible, barely one page separates 1 and 2 Corinthians. But the reality on the ground in the troubled seaside city of Corinth reveals that a vast separation of circumstances divided one letter from the other.

Times were tough for the apostle Paul. It's safe to say that he wrote 2 Corinthians with a heavy heart. He was in the throes of intense spiritual warfare on several fronts. While in his beleaguered state, problems at his beloved church in Corinth hung over him like a dark cloud that would not go away.

go to

**standing**
2 Corinthians 4:7

**weaknesses**
2 Corinthians 3:5;
12:5

**accusations**
2 Corinthians
11:16–17

## Setting the Scene

Paul's opening greeting sounds eerily similar to that of 1 Corinthians. One almost gets the feeling of "déjà vu all over again." But as we will soon see, the tenor and tone of 2 Corinthians are radically different from 1 Corinthians.

Second Corinthians is perhaps the most introspective and self-revealing of all Paul's letters. The apostle made himself remarkably vulnerable as he spoke of his lowly <u>standing</u>, human <u>weaknesses</u>, and his reluctance to defend himself in the face of an onslaught of false <u>accusations</u>. Through the next several chapters, we will again and again get a glimpse into the soul of one of God's choicest servants.

key point

what others say

**David K. Lowery**

Few portions of the New Testament pose as many problems for translators and interpreters as does 2 Corinthians. Few, therefore, are the preachers who undertake a systematic exposition of its contents. For those undaunted by its demands, however, an intimate picture of a pastor's heart may be found as the apostle Paul shepherded the wayward Corinthians and revealed a love which comes only from God.[1]

go to

**justifying**
1 Corinthians 6:11

**Lord**
1 Corinthians 1:2

**Syria**
Acts 18:18

**report**
1 Corinthians 1:11

**questions**
1 Corinthians 7:1

# Beneath the Surface

*2 Corinthians 1:1–2 Paul, an apostle of Jesus Christ by the will of God, and Timothy our brother, to the church of God which is at Corinth, with all the saints who are in all Achaia: Grace to you and peace from God our Father and the Lord Jesus Christ. (NKJV)*

We learned at the beginning of our study of 1 Corinthians that Paul planted himself in Corinth for an eighteen-month stay. During this year and a half, Paul led his first converts to Christ, established the church, and systematically laid a solid theological framework for these new believers—so much so that Paul wrote, "You were enriched in every thing by Him [Christ] in all . . . knowledge" (1 Corinthians 1:5 NKJV).

His was a turbulent time in Corinth. Suffice it to say that the townspeople were not especially appreciative or receptive of Paul's ministry. So hostile was this city against Paul and his gospel message, in fact, that God had to appear to Paul in a vision to assure his fearful apostle, "Do not be afraid, but speak, and do not keep silent; for I am with you, and no one will attack you to hurt you; for I have many people in this city" (Acts 18:9–10 NKJV).

*For I have many people in this city.* God was going to do a great work in Corinth—washing, sanctifying, and <u>justifying</u> the many who would receive Christ and submit to Him as <u>Lord</u>.

key point

At the conclusion of his year-and-a-half-long ministry, Paul left Corinth for <u>Syria</u>. You might remember that some time after leaving Corinth, Paul received a disturbing <u>report</u> about the many problems that had arisen in the church in Corinth. At about the same time, the Corinthian Christians wrote Paul a letter in which they asked him a series of <u>questions</u> about a number of pressing issues. In response to the disturbing report and the Corinthians' questions, Paul wrote, signed, sealed, and sent them 1 Corinthians.

However, if Paul hoped that his letter would heal the rifts, solve the problems, and answer the questions of these immature believers, he was soon sadly disappointed. A new and potentially deadly problem now plagued the church. False teachers who claimed apostolic authority arrived in Corinth, infiltrated the church, cast doubts on Paul's character and teaching, and led the church into doctrinal error.

Much to his chagrin, Paul wrote, "I am jealous for you with godly jealousy. For I have betrothed you to one husband, that I may present you as a chaste virgin to Christ. But I fear, lest somehow, as the serpent deceived Eve by his craftiness, so your minds may be corrupted from the simplicity that is in Christ. For if he who comes preaches another Jesus whom we have not preached, or if you receive a different spirit which you have not received, or a different gospel which you have not accepted—you may well put up with it!" (2 Corinthians 11:2–4 NKJV).

You may well put up with it! What an indictment! Paul proceeded to describe these teachers as "false apostles, deceitful workers, transforming themselves into apostles of Christ" (2 Corinthians 11:13 NKJV).

As soon as Paul received word of this new threat, he immediately left Ephesus and made a beeline straight to Corinth, a visit he would characterize as painful or _sorrowful_. Apparently someone in the church, possibly one of the false teachers, <u>wrongly</u> went on the attack and caused Paul much grief. Upon his return to Ephesus, Paul in his anguish wrote another letter to the church in Corinth—a letter not preserved as a part of the New Testament canon—that he sent with Titus. This is the letter to which Paul referred when he wrote, "Out of much affliction and anguish of heart I wrote to you, with many tears, not that you should be grieved, but that you might know the love which I have so abundantly for you" (2 Corinthians 2:4 NKJV).

Paul eventually left Ephesus and traveled to Troas, where he hoped to meet up with Titus to receive a report about the continuing problems in Corinth. We get some sense of the angst Paul felt over the Corinthian situation when he wrote, "When I came to Troas to preach Christ's gospel, and a door was opened to me by the Lord, I had no rest in my spirit, because I did not find Titus my brother; but taking my leave of them, I departed for Macedonia" (2 Corinthians 2:12–13 NKJV). While in Macedonia, Paul finally met up with Titus. "His presence was a joy, but so was the news he brought of the encouragement he received from you. When he told us how much you long to see me, and how sorry you are for what happened, and how loyal you are to me, I was filled with joy!" (2 Corinthians 7:7 NLT).

**go to**

**sorrowful**
2 Corinthians 2:1

**wrongly**
2 Corinthians 7:12

**third**
2 Corinthians 13:1

Yet the church was hardly out of the woods. A segment of the congregation was still strongly influenced by the continuing presence and teaching ministry of the self-proclaimed apostles. Paul planned a <u>third</u> visit to Corinth, hoping once and for all to right the ship. As a part of his preparation for that trip, Paul wrote 2 Corinthians from Macedonia, a letter in which he vigorously defended his apostolic authority, reminded them of the continuing financial need of the Christians in Judea and Jerusalem, and leveled his strongest rebuke yet of the church's tolerance of the false teachers in their midst.

But before he got into any of that, Paul gave us a remarkable insight into his personal sufferings, much of which came at the hands of the Corinthian Christians. What follows is one of the most complete and compelling answers to the age-old question of why God allows bad things to happen to good people.

## The God of All Comfort

We each go through them—periods of intense, unexpected, unwelcomed suffering. No one lived a more dedicated, disciplined, God-pleasing life than the apostle Paul. Yet, Paul's life, like that of Job, of whom it was said, "[Job] was blameless and upright, and one who feared God and shunned evil" (Job 1:1 NKJV), reads like a case study in suffering. You'll remember that Paul was the man who wrote from a prison cell, "I have suffered the loss of all things" and one who longed "to know [Christ] and the power of His resurrection, and the *fellowship of His sufferings*" (Philippians 3:8, 10 NKJV, emphasis added). Those statements refer to Paul's sufferings in the abstract. Let's get specific and discover exactly what was going on in Paul's life and ministry at the time he wrote 2 Corinthians.

## Trying Times of Tribulation

> 2 CORINTHIANS 1:3–4a *Blessed be the God and Father of our Lord Jesus Christ, the Father of mercies and God of all comfort, who comforts us in all our tribulation,* (NKJV)

When referencing his sufferings, Paul used a very specific word that is translated in the NKJV as *tribulation*. When you read that word both here and in other passages in Scripture, think of the most intensive type of suffering imaginable. The word conveys the image of someone having his life crushed out of him as if a weight of immense proportions has fallen on the individual. *Tribulation* does *not* refer to the little annoyances or inconveniences that we encounter every day. It does call to mind suffering in the extreme, the kind that is potentially paralyzing or bone-crushing to those who are under its load.

key point

Indeed, in verse 5, Paul wrote that his sufferings "abound in us" (NKJV). In other words, Paul was getting hit from all sides, fighting spiritual battles on multiple fronts. Everywhere he looked he stared straight into the face of suffering.

In the introduction to this chapter, we mentioned in some detail the heaviness of Paul's burden as it related to the situation in Corinth. Let's expand on that just a bit. As we'll discuss when we get to 2 Corinthians 11, Paul contrasted his sufferings with those of the self-appointed false apostles who had infiltrated the Corinthian church.

"Are they ministers of Christ?—I speak as a fool—I am more: in labors more abundant, in stripes above measure, in prisons more frequently, in deaths often. From the Jews five times I received forty stripes minus one. Three times I was beaten with rods; once I was stoned; three times I was shipwrecked; a night and a day I have been in the deep; in journeys often, in perils of waters, in perils of robbers, in perils of my own countrymen, in perils of the Gentiles, in perils in the city, in perils in the wilderness, in perils in the sea, in perils among false brethren; in weariness and toil, in sleeplessness often, in hunger and thirst, in fastings often, in cold and nakedness—besides the other things, what comes upon me daily: my deep concern for all the churches" (2 Corinthians 11:23–28 NKJV).

Paul lived in a biblical world in which "others were tortured, not accepting deliverance, that they might obtain a better resurrection. Still others had trial of mockings and scourgings, yes, and of chains and imprisonment. They were stoned, they were sawn in two, were tempted, were slain with the sword. They wandered about in sheepskins and goatskins, being destitute, afflicted, tormented—of whom the world was not worthy. They wandered in deserts and mountains, in dens and caves of the earth" (Hebrews 11:35–38 NKJV).

Likewise, no one delighted God more than His Son, Jesus, in whom God the Father was "well pleased" (Matthew 3:17 NKJV). Yet,

He suffered the most torturous beatings and death—indeed, the full fury of the wrath of men in concert with the unbridled wrath of God—that anyone has ever endured. If the lives of Jesus and Paul tell us anything, it's that humans suffer. But we never suffer without purpose! Keep reading.

what others say

**Charlyn Singleton**

Taking a stand for God in this crazy world of ours sometimes carries with it unexpected consequences. Like Joseph, you might get fired for doing the right thing, you might lose a friend, or you might suffer economic consequences. Whatever the cost, it's always right and proper to take a stand for the Lord—on your job, in your home, in your community, and in the world at large.[2]

## An Inward or an Outward View?

**2 CORINTHIANS 1:4b–5** *that we may be able to comfort those who are in any trouble, with the comfort with which we ourselves are comforted by God. For as the sufferings of Christ abound in us, so our consolation also abounds through Christ. (NKJV)*

Paul knew suffering up close and personal. He also knew God's comfort in ways that only one who suffers in the extreme can possibly experience.

It's fascinating to note that Paul never attempted to answer the "Why?" question. The Bible simply acknowledges that every person will suffer. As a matter of fact, the Bible promises that we will. Jesus assured His disciples, "In the world you *will have* tribulation; but be of good cheer, I have overcome the world" (John 16:33 NKJV, emphasis added). Likewise, Paul promised young Pastor Timothy that "all who desire to live godly in Christ Jesus *will suffer* persecution" (2 Timothy 3:12 NKJV, emphasis added). Job's friend Eliphaz observed that "man is born to trouble, as the sparks fly upward" (Job 5:7 NKJV).

The question for the Christian is not *why* we suffer but *how* we respond to our suffering and *what* to do with it when it comes. Paul decided not to wallow in his suffering, not to succumb to his personal pain, not to feel sorry for himself. He chose to channel his suffering in a positive direction by using his pain as a platform from which he could help other sufferers.

what others say

**Denise George**

Over time, however, Job became weary, worn down by pain. He believed God had not heard his prayers. He looked into heaven and cried out in frustration, "If only I knew where to find him" (Job 23:3). "If I go to the east, he is not there; if I go to the west, I do not find him" (23:8). Finally, Job admitted he couldn't find God. He thought God was gone or not listening. He opened his fists and let his hands fall limply to his sides. "I cry out to you, O God, but you do not answer," Job whispered (30:20).

But Job hung on to his faith. He decided to keep praying, not to give up. He made a great statement of faith: "But He knows the way that I take; when He has tested me, I shall come forth as gold" (23:10 NKJV).

In the end, Job experienced God in a dramatic way (see Job 38–42). God "blessed the latter days of Job more than his beginning" (42:12 NKJV).

Job protested his suffering. He didn't suffer quietly. God allowed Job to question him, to challenge him, to directly confront him. And, as a result, God taught Job some powerful lessons.[3]

Keeping Paul's overall purpose for writing 2 Corinthians in mind, the apostle was establishing the predicate for the remainder of this book. Unlike the false, self-appointed apostles who were actively discrediting Paul's apostolic authority, Paul paid a hefty personal price for following Christ as one of His true apostles. He let his readers know right from the start that his apostolic credentials were written in his blood. But rather than grouse about how unfairly he had been treated, or complain about the injustices he was forced to endure, Paul gloried in the fact that as God had faithfully comforted him in his trials, so Paul could be a comfort to others in theirs.

What's true for Paul is equally true for us. We can choose to wallow in our sufferings. Or we can turn that negative emotional energy in a positive direction and offer to others the same comfort that God offers to us. Once we adjust our theology to conform to the biblical truth that in this fallen world we will suffer, we can train ourselves to focus on all of the positives that God gives us, rather than on the negatives of our painful circumstances. That adjustment puts us into a mental, emotional, and spiritual frame of mind to recognize and receive God's comfort. And when we do, we can then be a comfort to those around us who are also in pain.

apply it

**martyrdom**
2 Timothy 4:6

**devour**
1 Peter 5:8

Paul was perfectly positioned to offer his encouragement to those in the Corinthian church who were suffering. It's a credit to Paul that he continued to love and to support this church that had caused him so much personal pain. He reached out to them in love and established a common bond by assuring them that he was aware of the many in the church who were suffering, and that he wanted to come alongside them in order to offer them his comfort.

## Putting Our Problems into Their Proper Perspective

**2 CORINTHIANS 1:6–7** *Now if we are afflicted, it is for your consolation and salvation, which is effective for enduring the same sufferings which we also suffer. Or if we are comforted, it is for your consolation and salvation. And our hope for you is steadfast, because we know that as you are partakers of the sufferings, so also you will partake of the consolation. (NKJV)*

Paul understood that our salvation is paid for in blood. The blood of Christ to be sure, as Ephesians 2:13 makes abundantly clear: "Now in Christ Jesus you who once were far off have been brought near by the blood of Christ" (NKJV). But as Tertullian so aptly said in the third century, "The blood of martyrs is the seed of the Church." Paul viewed his present suffering and likely <u>martyrdom</u> as a price that must be paid to bring the good news of the gospel to others.

Pain is a part of the price we pay to live obedient lives in a way that influences others to receive Christ. We have already noted that "all who desire to live godly in Christ Jesus will suffer persecution" (2 Timothy 3:12 NKJV)—the persecution of losing a job promotion because we refuse to compromise our standards, the persecution of receiving a poor grade on a school assignment because fulfilling the requirement violates our convictions, the persecution of losing a friend because we won't engage in certain activities when pressured to do so.

But in addition to that, there is the relentless attack of an enemy determined to defeat or destroy or <u>devour</u> us. Satan will happily inflict upon us undeserved pain if he believes that suffering will derail our commitment to Christ. Just ask Job.

Paul faced all of that and so much more. He was able to endure it all only by God's grace to the point where he could triumphantly declare, "I take pleasure in infirmities, in reproaches, in needs, in persecutions, in distresses, for Christ's sake. For when I am weak, then I am strong" (2 Corinthians 12:10 NKJV).

Wouldn't it be great if our responses to unwanted, undeserved, and unwelcomed suffering could mirror that of the apostle Paul?

> ### what others say
>
> **Philip Yancey**
>
> God wants us to choose to love him freely, even when that choice involves pain, because we are committed to him, not to our own good feelings and rewards. He wants us to cleave to him, as Job did, even when we have every reason to deny him hotly. That, I believe, is the central message of Job. Satan had taunted God with the accusation that humans are not truly free. Was Job being faithful simply because God had allowed him a prosperous life? Job's fiery trials proved the answer beyond doubt. Job clung to God's justice when he was the best example in history of God's apparent injustice. He did not seek the Giver because of his gifts; when all gifts were removed he still sought the Giver.[4]

We now know enough about the culture of compromise that was Corinth, and about the inner workings of the church in Corinth, to begin to understand something of the incredible pressure that was placed on the godly people within the congregation. Just try to imagine what it must have been like to maintain a consistent Christian walk with all that was going on around them. It wasn't enough to be battered, bloodied, and bruised every day as these amazing men, women, and young people tried to stand firm against the sinful forces that came at them from every direction in their world. But when they went to church on Sunday in the hope of receiving much-needed instruction and inspiration to make it through one more week, they were hit in the face with false teaching and a culture of compromise in the church that rivaled everything going on outside of the church. To this godly remnant within the congregation, Paul offered these words of encouragement from one suffering saint to another: "Our hope for you is steadfast, because we know that as you are partakers of the sufferings, so also you will partake of the consolation" (2 Corinthians 1:7 NKJV).

So there you have it. Second Corinthians—a letter written in anguish by one beleaguered believer to another. In this letter we get a glimpse into the heart of one of God's choice servants in a way that no other New Testament book will allow. This was a man on the ropes, attacked both from within and without the church. This was a guy who, in a sense, was fighting for his very survival. This was someone against whom the forces of darkness had declared an all-out war.

For Paul, Corinth became a field of battle. The souls of the precious people in the sin-sick city of Corinth were the spoils of that war. A church's destiny hung in the balance. Let's now look and listen as we watch the apostle become fully engaged in spiritual warfare of the most intensive type imaginable.

## Chapter Wrap-Up

- Paul's second letter to the Corinthians is probably the most introspective and self-revealing of all. His first letter to them had not entirely solved all the problems they were bringing upon themselves, and he was also fighting other spiritual battles.
- Paul called his sufferings "tribulation," meaning "suffering in the extreme."
- Even so, Paul knew that God truly could comfort him, and reminded the Corinthians of the same eternal truth.
- Paul went on to put his own problems—and those of the Corinthians as well—into an understandable perspective. Thus he revealed his own wisdom—which, however, was given to him by God!

# Study Questions

1. Why was Paul feeling so vulnerable when he wrote 2 Corinthians?

2. Paul used the term *tribulation* to refer to his own troubles. In what other, much larger context is this term commonly applied to end-times events?

3. What well-known Old Testament character might Paul's sufferings be compared to?

4. What was the "spiritual dynamic" that Paul put into play in the opening portion of 2 Corinthians, with respect to his own suffering?

# 2 Corinthians 1:8–2:13
# A Rationale for Restoration

**Chapter Highlights:**
- Death Sentence
- God Who Delivers Us
- A Time to Boast
- A Change of Plans
- Seal of Approval
- Heartfelt Concern

## Let's Get Started

Paul was on the ropes. At the time of his writing 2 Corinthians, Paul was up to his hips in spiritual warfare. The tone of this entire letter—particularly the first and second chapters—sounds understandably dire.

The celebrated apostle found himself fighting on multiple fronts. The work in Ephesus, from where Paul wrote 2 Corinthians, was going well. But any progress there came at quite a price.

The situation in Corinth showed some signs of improvement. But as we have previously discussed, cracks formed in the foundation of the church—its doctrinal and organizational unity was coming apart. Schisms developed around various factions within the church that threatened to undermine the only witness for Christ in that sinful seaside city. Additionally, as we will learn throughout our study of 2 Corinthians, false teachers infiltrated this infant church, causing significant doubt in the minds of many of the members concerning Paul's apostolic authority.

As if that wasn't enough, Paul did hand-to-hand combat with the devil himself. Paul referenced in 2 Corinthians 12:7 that "a messenger of Satan [came] to buffet me" (NKJV).

Paul was indeed on the ropes. How did the apostle respond to the darkness that descended upon him like a fog? Keep reading. There is much strength and inspiration to be found throughout 2 Corinthians. In terms of your own spiritual battles, I truly believe that you'll be encouraged to stay in the fight even when everything around you seems to be going south in a hurry.

key point

## Death Sentence

Add to all of the above that something happened that caused Paul to despair "even of life" (2 Corinthians 1:8 NKJV). In a masterstroke of understatement, allow me to make the observation that these were not good days for Paul. The pressure was on, and Paul found himself trapped in the pressure cooker.

There are times when, try as we might to make right choices and do the right things, everything hits the wall. We sometimes find ourselves battling the problems and pressures of life on multiple fronts—our families, our jobs, our friendships, our finances, our health. If you have ever had a bad day, or a whole bunch of bad days, you'll find much comfort in the next few pages.

## Our God Who Delivers Us

> 2 CORINTHIANS 1:8–11 *For we do not want you to be ignorant, brethren, of our trouble which came to us in Asia: that we were burdened beyond measure, above strength, so that we despaired even of life. Yes, we had the sentence of death in ourselves, that we should not trust in ourselves but in God who raises the dead, who delivered us from so great a death, and does deliver us; in whom we trust that He will still deliver us, you also helping together in prayer for us, that thanks may be given by many persons on our behalf for the gift granted to us through many.* (NKJV)

As we observed in our study of 1 Corinthians 13:1–3, there are times when the apostle Paul is given to using hyperbole as a characteristic of his writing style. Having said that, let me assure you that you'll not find one syllable of hyperbole in 2 Corinthians 1:8–11. In 2 Corinthians 1:8–11, Paul wrote literally and compellingly about the hardships he endured just prior to composing this great letter.

Something happened in or around Ephesus that convinced Paul that he was going to die. He did not tell his Corinthian readers the specifics of his life-threatening circumstances—he assumed that they already knew. Consequently, we will never know for sure to what event or events Paul referred. But we do know that whatever it was, it was bad—really, really bad.

Paul knew exactly what he was doing when he decided to paint this portrait of suffering as the backdrop for this letter. Once we get into the meat and potatoes of this epistle, we will read the words of a man under singular attack from both within and without the church at Corinth. In the face of those who tried to discredit him, as one of his strongest arguments in defense of his credibility and authority as an apostle, Paul referred to the price he paid to conduct the ministry to which God had called him. Unlike the self-proclaimed, pseudo-apostles who tried to undermine him in Corinth, his ministry exacted an enormous toll from Paul personally. We get quite a picture of some of that suffering as we read the passage before us.

Listen to the words and phrases that Paul used to express the level of pain that he was in as he wrote this letter—*trouble; burdened beyond measure, above strength; despaired even of life; sentence of death.* Clearly, whatever difficulties Paul faced were way beyond his human ability to handle or endure. He was overwhelmed with despair.

apply it

I hope that Paul's words resonate with you. There are times when life becomes overwhelming. Problems and pressures come at us from every direction and are just too much for us to handle. And when this happens, our problems are often compounded by the enormous load of guilt that we carry when we almost crumble under the pressure.

There is a Christian cliché that we often quote, but one that is simply not biblical. It goes like this: "God will never give us more than we can handle." Do you really believe that? Does the Bible truly teach that? When I have asked people to give me scriptural support for such a statement, they invariably turn to a verse we have already studied, 1 Corinthians 10:13: "No temptation has overtaken you except such as is common to man; but God is faithful, who will not allow you to be tempted beyond what you are able, but with the temptation will also make the way of escape, that you may be able to bear it" (NKJV).

Some are quick to point out that *temptation* can also be translated *trial* or *testing.* I won't dispute that point, but I will make this one: Whether you translate the word as "temptation" or "trial" or "testing," this verse does not convey the notion that God will never give us more than *we* can handle. What it does say is that God will never give us more than *He* can handle. I don't know about you, but I would far rather compare my sufferings to God's limitless strength rather than my own limited strength.

key point

God is the One who "will also make the way of escape." He is the One who gives us His strength so that we "may be able to bear it." He is the One in whom we can *trust* (2 Corinthians 1:9) when we exhaust our own physical, mental, or emotional resources. He is the

**intercessory prayers**
praying for others

One who delivers us "from so great a death" (2 Corinthians 1:10 NKJV).

You and I can claim the same promise today that Paul claimed so long ago: "[God] does deliver us . . . He will still deliver us" (2 Corinthians 1:10 NKJV).

> **what others say**
>
> **Major Ian Thomas**
>
> The Christians of the early church have been described as being "incorrigibly happy, completely unafraid, and nearly always in trouble." That is gloriously true, and Paul gives us an illustration of this attitude in the second epistle to the Corinthians when he was in a situation that was beyond human endurance. "We were burdened beyond measure," he says, ". . . so that we despaired even of life." Then he goes on, "Yes, we had the sentence of death in ourselves that *we should not trust in ourselves but in God* who raises the dead" (2 Corinthians 1:8–9). He was adopting this attitude: Our present difficulty is not our problem; it is *His* problem. It is in the hands of our God, who raises the dead.[1]

One of the great mysteries of spiritual warfare is the role of our **intercessory prayers** in the midst of the battle. You might remember the Ephesians 6 "armor of God" passage in which Paul encouraged the Christians in Ephesus to "put on the whole armor of God, that you may be able to stand against the wiles of the devil" (Ephesians 6:11 NKJV). After listing the primary pieces of armor, Paul then made a most thought-provoking request. He flat-out asked the Ephesian believers to continue "praying *always* with *all* prayer and supplication in the Spirit, being watchful to this end with *all* perseverance and supplication for *all* the saints—and for me" (Ephesians 6:18–19 NKJV, emphasis added).

Let's break that down: *When do we pray?* "Always." *How do we pray?* "In the Spirit," or as the Holy Spirit prompts our hearts to pray. *What should characterize our prayers?* "Perseverance"; we never stop praying. *For whom do we pray?* "All the saints."

Somehow, our prayers help those who are in the midst of spiritual warfare. When he found himself embroiled in the battle, Paul asked the Christians in Ephesus to pray for him. It's clear from 2 Corinthians 1:11 that the Christians in Corinth did pray for him. The moment they hit their knees they were literally "helping together in prayer for us" (NKJV). Paul thanked them for their prayers because in response to their prayers God granted to Paul "the gift" of his deliverance.

Part of Paul's deliverance came about in response to the prayers of God's people.

key point

## A Time to Boast

*2 CORINTHIANS 1:12–14 For our boasting is this: the testimony of our conscience that we conducted ourselves in the world in simplicity and godly sincerity, not with fleshly wisdom but by the grace of God, and more abundantly toward you. For we are not writing any other things to you than what you read or understand. Now I trust you will understand, even to the end (as also you have understood us in part), that we are your boast as you also are ours, in the day of the Lord Jesus. (NKJV)*

Paul's critics came at him with all guns blazing. They attacked his integrity with false accusations of Paul's alleged dishonesty and insincerity. They attacked his veracity by falsely accusing him of being a manipulator, schemer, and deceiver. They attacked his authority by alleging that Paul's motives were self-serving, his words were self-inflating, and his actions were self-gratifying.

Paul was defenseless in the face of these false accusation. He had only one court of appeal—his clear conscience before God. He knew that in God's eyes he had conducted himself in *simplicity*, the opposite of duplicity, and *sincerity*, a word that means "to hold up to the sunlight and to see no cracks." Not that Paul was perfect. We have already discussed some of Paul's many weaknesses and failings. But he was a man who truly sought to please his Lord in everything he did. Like King David, Paul was a man after God's own <u>heart</u>. He was truly submitted to the lordship of Christ. In that sense, Paul's conscience was clear.

**Kay Arthur**

### what others say

The Greek word for sincerity is *eilikrineia* which means clearness. The two parts of this word were derived from *heile*, the sun's rays, and from *krino*, which means "to distinguish." Thus this word has the connotation of being judged by sunlight

go to

**heart**
Acts 13:22

and tested as genuine. Understanding this word gives us quite a picture, doesn't it, of the purity of Paul's teaching? This is good to know, because what you're about to see is pure truth—reality. And in it, Beloved, you'll discover why you are adequate, where the adequacy comes from, and how it happens.[2]

In fact, let me see if I can paraphrase what Paul said about all this:

key point

> With the confidence that can only come from maintaining a clear conscience before God, everything I have said and everything I have done has been with absolute sincerity. Before you and before a watching world we have conducted ourselves with no duplicity whatsoever. This letter, as with all of my letters, is written to you with no hidden agenda. I am going to be straight with you, just as I have always been. It is my hope that one day your confidence in me will be restored, even though others have shaken that confidence. If so, then on the day when the Lord Jesus returns, you will gladly stand side by side with me in the same way that I am standing with you.

Paul's accusers seized upon every opportunity to discredit him. Even something as innocent and unavoidable as a change in his schedule generated a wave of criticism in the church. Despite his good and noble intentions, Paul found himself on the defensive, having not only to defend himself against these unwarranted accusations but defending his love for the Corinthians as well.

## An Innocent Change of Plans

2 CORINTHIANS 1:15–20 *And in this confidence I intended to come to you before, that you might have a second benefit—to pass by way of you to Macedonia, to come again from Macedonia to you, and be helped by you on my way to Judea. Therefore, when I was planning this, did I do it lightly? Or the things I plan, do I plan according to the flesh, that with me there should be Yes, Yes, and No, No? But as God is faithful, our word to you was not Yes and No. For the Son of God, Jesus Christ, who was preached among you by us—by me, Silvanus, and Timothy—was not Yes and No, but in Him was Yes. For all the promises of God in Him are Yes, and in Him Amen, to the glory of God through us. (NKJV)*

This is a confusing passage, to say the least. If you found yourself scratching your head as you tried to make some sense out of the above yeses and noes, I can assure you that you are not alone. Ironically, the gist of what Paul was saying is very easy to understand.

**wolves**
Matthew 7:15

Here's how it went down: In the aftermath of Paul's last "painful" visit, and the subsequent "severe" letter (see below) that he wrote in response, Paul desperately wanted to visit Corinth twice, once on his way to Macedonia and then again on his way from Macedonia to Judea. He felt that he needed to extend to the Corinthians this "second benefit," or more clearly translated, "the benefit of two visits instead of just one," because the problems in the church were so monumental that they required Paul's personal involvement, and because his commitment to the church in Corinth had been called into question.

It's important to keep in mind that travel in biblical times was much more treacherous and inconvenient than travel is today. It wasn't just a matter of Paul hopping on a plane and getting to his destination within a matter of hours or even days. If you think weather delays in airports are a colossal irritation for us, just try to imagine what it must have been like to contend with storms on the Mediterranean and unexpected delays on overland trade routes. Even with the best of planning, trips of the magnitude that Paul was suggesting could take weeks to get from point to point. That being said, think of how often we change our travel plans even though we can get from Point A to Point B in relative ease. We can cut Paul a lot of slack when it comes to his change of plans, something his critics were utterly unwilling to do.

Those false teachers, the self-appointed apostles we have talked so much about, used Paul's change of plans as clear and compelling evidence that Paul did not truly love the Christians at Corinth, did not view the church as a priority of his ministry, at best could not be trusted to keep his word, and at worst was an outright liar and deceiver. Remember how we mentioned that Paul was on the ropes? Now you know why.

This opening chapter of 2 Corinthians certainly demonstrates that the situation in Corinth had reached critical mass. We have evidence that Satan singled out this church for severe spiritual attack. He sent his emissaries, <u>wolves</u> in sheep's clothing, to this church in order to ingratiate themselves with the church people, gain a platform among them, and spew disruptive and divisive venom throughout the congregation. Those self-appointed pseudo-apostles would stop at nothing to discredit Paul and cast doubt upon his character and ministry.

**key point**

In the parlance of Jesus's parables, these men were <u>tares</u> whom the enemy sowed among the wheat—unbelievers who masqueraded as believers—to do the devil's bidding. What could Paul say in response to these verbal assaults on his character and credibility? He appealed to a higher power. Just as God is faithful, just as God does not waver between yes and no, just as God said what He meant and meant what He said, so Paul was a faithful, honest, and trustworthy messenger of his God, whose word could be trusted.

Paul's statement in 2 Corinthians 1:19 is especially strong and compelling. He wrote, "Jesus Christ, the Son of God, does not waver between 'Yes' and 'No.' He is the one whom Silas, Timothy, and I preached to you, and as God's ultimate 'Yes,' he always does what he says" (NLT). By invoking the name of Christ, and His title as the "Son of God," Paul clued us in that Jesus was under attack in the church, as well as His true messengers—Silas (another form of the name *Silvanus*), Timothy, and Paul.

## Seal of Approval

> 2 CORINTHIANS 1:21–22 *Now He who establishes us with you in Christ and has anointed us is God, who also has sealed us and given us the Spirit in our hearts as a guarantee.* (NKJV)

These last two verses of this section of 2 Corinthians ought to bring great joy and encouragement to the hearts of every true servant of God. Without a lot of fanfare, Paul declared the truth of his situation.

**go to**

**tares**
Matthew 13:24–30

**ambassador**
2 Corinthians 5:20

**tares**
weeds that look like wheat

**1.** First, God *established* Paul in Christ. Jesus was the foundation of Paul's life. No verbal assault on his character could shake his standing before his Lord.

**2.** Second, God *anointed* him, or set him apart as a special person for a special purpose—namely, to be God's <u>ambassador</u> in the world, reconciling people just like the sinful Corinthians to their holy God.

**3.** Third, God sent the Holy *Spirit* to live in Paul's heart as both a *seal* and a *guarantee*. When you think of a seal, think of a king who seals a decree by placing his ring into a bowl of warm wax, thereby forever marking the decree as the official declaration by the king. God declared Paul as His own, and sealed that declaration with the Holy Spirit, thereby guaranteeing that Paul is God's own.

**write**
2 Corinthians 2:4

As you might suspect, everything God did for Paul He has done for us. We are established in Christ. We are set apart by God as special people for a special purpose—to represent Him in the world. We are sealed with the Holy Spirit as God's guarantee that we are His own. With that endorsement in hand, what more do we need?

## One Further Explanation

> 2 Corinthians 1:23–2:2 *Moreover I call God as witness against my soul, that to spare you I came no more to Corinth. Not that we have dominion over your faith, but are fellow workers for your joy; for by faith you stand.*
> *But I determined this within myself, that I would not come again to you in sorrow. For if I make you sorrowful, then who is he who makes me glad but the one who is made sorrowful by me?* (NKJV)

There was more to Paul's change in plans than at first meets the eye. Paul vividly remembered his last visit, the painful "in sorrow" visit that Paul mentioned in 2 Corinthians 2:1. Remember, Paul returned to Ephesus after his "painful" visit, and in his anguish proceeded to <u>write</u> another letter, the "severe" letter to the church in Corinth that *was not preserved* as a part of the New Testament canon. As a result, though Paul originally intended to visit Corinth on his way to Macedonia, he thought better of it until he learned how the Corinthian Christians would respond to that letter. Both for his sake and for theirs, Paul did not want to have to endure yet another confrontational visit to the church.

Paul didn't want to further assume the posture of a father rebuking his disobedient children. That's what he meant by the phrase "Not that we have dominion over your faith." Rather, he wanted to come to them as a servant, a "fellow worker" who would bring them joy.

Thus Paul decided *not* to pay the Corinthian Christians a visit that he knew would be excruciatingly painful, both for himself and for them. Instead, he wrote them what some have called the "severe" letter,[3] written between 1 and 2 Corinthians, which was not preserved.

You get the sense that, at this point in his ministry, after all Paul had gone through during his last visit to Corinth and then just recently in or around Ephesus, Paul was battle weary. He readily admitted that he needed someone to make *him* glad (NKJV), to cheer *him* up (CEV), to refresh *him* (MSG). Safe to say that Paul was exhausted.

If our sense of Paul is that of a man who was tireless in his ministry, able to rise above every circumstance and face every trial with superhuman strength, always on top of it, never one to get down or discouraged, then we have read him all wrong. Paul was human just like us, subject to every human weakness that we face every minute of every day. Like us, he needed to establish boundaries. There were times when he needed to say no. He said no to a visit to the church in Corinth, one that he knew would tax him beyond his ability to endure.

And of course, in fine Corinthian fashion, they attacked him for it. So be it. He needed a break and he took a break. And he told them why.

## Hoping for the Best

### the big picture

### 2 Corinthians 2:3–11

Paul had high hopes for the "severe" letter that he wrote the Corinthian Christians after his "painful" or "sorrowful" visit. Apparently, in response to that letter, some of the sinning members genuinely repented of their sins. Paul instructed the church as to how to respond to those who had caused him and the church much grief.

Call him the eternal optimist, but Paul held high hopes for his "severe" letter. Its tone must have been highly confrontational—much more so even than 1 Corinthians. He feared that they would react negatively to the letter, causing him the grief of their rejection rather than the joy of their obedience. But he was hopeful that they would receive it in the spirit with which he wrote it, as he expressed at the end of 2 Corinthians 2:4, "I didn't want to grieve you, but I wanted to let you know how much love I have for you" (NLT).

His optimism seems to have been rewarded. One *man*, at least, seems to have responded in genuine, behavior-changing repentance. Now we come to an interpretive challenge. Just who exactly *is* the man Paul referred to in verse 6? Here are the two options:

The least likely option is that Paul is referring to the immoral man mentioned in 1 Corinthians 5:1, the man who "has his father's wife" (NKJV). While this is a commonly held view, I say "least likely" because in the context of 2 Corinthians 1 and 2 it would seem completely out of place for Paul to suddenly and unexpectedly reach all the way over the "severe" letter, all the way back to 1 Corinthians, and bring up such old news.

key point

I believe that most who hold to this view do so because they fail to take into account the chronology surrounding 2 Corinthians. One would have to ignore Paul's "sorrowful" visit and assume that the "severe" letter to which Paul referred in 2 Corinthians 2:3–4 is in reality 1 Corinthians—even though over half of 1 Corinthians consists of written answers to the Corinthians' questions and isn't confrontational at all. Only then does this interpretation make sense. But given the fact that between the writing of 1 and 2 Corinthians Paul did indeed make his "sorrowful" visit to Corinth and then wrote a "severe" letter, it seems highly unlikely that Paul would suddenly revisit his discussion of the immoral man.

The more likely view is that Paul is referring either specifically to one man who was particularly troublesome both to Paul and to the church, or generally to men of that ilk who had fueled the fires of division and conflict within the church. I favor the view that, in response to Paul's "severe" letter, one of the ringleaders of the rebellion within the church genuinely repented of his sins, both against Paul and against the church. If this is indeed the case, Paul wanted to instruct the church as to how they should respond to this individual now that he had repented.

Keep in mind that biblical repentance is always indicated by words accompanied by deeds, what John the Baptizer called "fruits worthy of repentance" (Matthew 3:8 NKJV). Since one of the troublemakers did indeed repent, we can assume that he did so in front of the entire

**forgiveness**
Matthew 18:21

**head**
Ephesians 5:23

congregation—confessing his sins, asking the church for forgiveness, and changing his behavior. Paul was quite specific in pointing out that this man hurt Paul, but more significantly, hurt "all of you" (2 Corinthians 2:5 NKJV). Apparently, a number of the church members "opposed him" in his sin (2:6 NLT), further prompting his repentant response.

This sounds exactly like Matthew 18:15–20, the biblical blueprint for church discipline. Here in 2 Corinthians 2 we have a man who was confronted about his sins against Paul and the church, both by members of the Corinthian congregation and by Paul's letter. The man repented. Just as Jesus followed up His teaching on church discipline with a lesson on <u>forgiveness</u>, so too Paul instructed the church that they needed to forgive the man.

It's easy to understand why some in the church would be tempted to hold a grudge against one of the ringleaders of the rebellion. Paul certainly had ample reason to become bitter toward this individual. But Paul reminded his readers that "you ought rather to forgive and comfort him, lest perhaps such a one be swallowed up with too much sorrow. Therefore I urge you to reaffirm your love to him" (2 Corinthians 2:7–8 NKJV). It was time for the healing to begin, at least as far as *this* man was concerned.

**key point**

Why would the repentant man be "overcome by discouragement"? Because once he repented he would surely be ostracized by the "bad guys," the group of troublemakers he had chosen to leave. Yet, if the "good guys" held a grudge and failed to warmly receive him, he would feel ostracized by them as well. He would truly be "a man without a country." In spite of the damage that he did to the church, the church people needed to be ready and willing to embrace him and welcome him back into the fold.

Paul may have had Matthew 18 in mind when he wrote 2 Corinthians 2:10: "Whom you forgive anything, I also forgive. For if indeed I have forgiven anything, I have forgiven that one for your sakes in the presence of Christ" (NKJV). Paul knew that when he encouraged the church to forgive the man, he was doing so under the authority of Jesus Christ, the <u>head</u> of the church. How could he be so sure? Because his teaching amplified and applied Christ's teachings concerning church discipline and forgiveness.

If the church had failed to <u>restore</u> the repentant man, they would have sunk to the level of those who caused the problems in the first place. They would have been perpetuating a spirit of contention and division in the church, playing right into the hands of the enemy. So Paul punctuated his point about forgiveness by reminding his readers that if they refused to restore their repentant brother, "Satan should take advantage of us; for we are not ignorant of his devices" (2 Corinthians 2:11 NKJV)—namely his divide-and-conquer devices.

**restore**
Galatians 6:1

## Heartfelt Concern

2 CORINTHIANS 2:12–13 *Furthermore, when I came to Troas to preach Christ's gospel, and a door was opened to me by the Lord, I had no rest in my spirit, because I did not find Titus my brother; but taking my leave of them, I departed for Macedonia.* (NKJV)

Even though God opened a door of ministry for Paul in Troas, he "had no rest in [his] spirit." His mind and heart were ever centered on Corinth. He knew that the tone of the first half of 1 Corinthians was confrontational. He remembered the "painful" visit that he had made to Corinth after hearing of their continuing problems. He feared that his "severe" letter was too severe, and that the church would rebel rather than repent. You might remember that Paul asked Titus to deliver that "severe" letter to them. He waited anxiously to hear firsthand from Titus about their response. But he couldn't find Titus, so he traveled to Macedonia to look for him there.

That's where Paul leaves us at this point in 2 Corinthians 2. We have to fast-forward to 2 Corinthians 7 to find out what happened next. There we read that, glory be to God, Paul found Titus! And when he did, the report that Titus gave him came as music to his ears.

We'll talk about this in more detail when we get to 2 Corinthians 7. But for now, just listen to Paul's upbeat recollection of that joyful reunion with his trustworthy friend:

"When we came to Macedonia, our bodies had no rest, but we were troubled on every side. Outside were conflicts, inside were fears. Nevertheless God, who comforts the downcast, comforted us by the coming of Titus, and not only by his coming, but also by the consolation with which he was comforted in you, when he told us of your earnest desire, your mourning, your zeal for me, so that I rejoiced even more" (2 Corinthians 7:5–7 NKJV).

Paul's "severe" letter was well received. Very well received! So much so that Paul continued: "Even if I made you sorry with my letter, I do not regret it; though I did regret it. For I perceive that the same epistle made you sorry, though only for a while. Now I rejoice, not that you were made sorry, but that your sorrow led to repentance. For you were made sorry in a godly manner, that you might suffer loss from us in nothing" (2 Corinthians 7:8–9 NKJV).

key point

what others say

**Sandy Wilson**

Paul did not regret having brought sorrow to the people of Corinth when he confronted them about their sin, because he knew that God uses sorrow to bring about repentance and healing.[4]

In response to Paul's letter, a large segment of the congregation in Corinth repented of their sins. One of the ring leaders of the rebellion repented as well. Those who had been influenced to doubt Paul's sincerity and authority as an apostle realized that they had been duped. Their confidence in Paul was restored. And for the first time in a long time, the future of the church in Corinth looked bright and hopeful.

# Chapter Wrap-Up

- Paul admitted that he had been "burdened beyond measure" in recent days, so these were not "good times" for him. And despite his frequent use of hyperbole, there was no hyperbole on the horizon at all in this section of the Corinthian letters.

- Paul responded to some of the attacks against his character by something he called "boasting," which was actually more like a simple, honest listing of some of his actions and attributes.

- Apparently, many of the members of the church at Corinth were highly displeased with Paul for changing his travel schedule, even though he did so for extremely good reasons.

- Paul still hoped for a positive response to the "severe" letter he felt he'd been forced to send the Corinthians, in between the two Corinthian letters that we are familiar with.

# Study Questions

1. What was Paul's basic reaction to the most severe troubles that beset him?

2. What did Paul do "on paper" to offset the troubles he was having?

3. What were the three irrefutable claims that Paul made with respect to his commission to serve God?

4. Did Paul ever identity the "one man" who had apparently caused a majority of the trouble within the church at Corinth? Do we know what that person did?

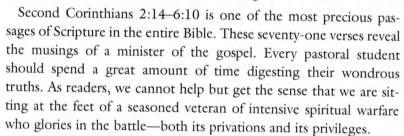

# 2 Corinthians 2:14–6:10 Blessings from the Battlefield

**Chapter Highlights:**
• Sincerity and Authority
• A Sweet Fragrance
• A Notable Contrast
• A Glory Transformed
• Light from Darkness

## Let's Get Started

Buckle your seat belt, hold on to your hat, and get ready for a radical right turn. Paul makes such a dramatic content shift in 2 Corinthians 2:14 that it's almost as if we're pulling some serious "G's" as we move from Paul's lament of the situation in Corinth to his praise to God for the privileges of being His servant.

Second Corinthians 2:14–6:10 is one of the most precious passages of Scripture in the entire Bible. These seventy-one verses reveal the musings of a minister of the gospel. Every pastoral student should spend a great amount of time digesting their wondrous truths. As readers, we cannot help but get the sense that we are sitting at the feet of a seasoned veteran of intensive spiritual warfare who glories in the battle—both its privations and its privileges.

Fact is, every single one of us is embroiled in the same warfare into which Paul was drafted. Like him, we have experienced the hardships and rewards of the battle. We will find much in Paul's ruminations to encourage us as we face our own unique challenges, and to endear us to Paul as a fellow soldier reflecting on his blessings from the battlefield.

warfare
Ephesians 6:11–13

## With Sincerity and Authority

When we last left Paul he was ecstatic over the good report that he had received from his faithful companion in the ministry, Titus. Paul's heart was buoyed by the news that his "severe" letter had been well received, that some in the church had repented of their sins, that many of the people who had come under the influence of those who tried to discredit Paul were once again respecting his apostolic authority, and that the overall situation in Corinth was much improved. As Paul reflected upon these good things, he (as he so often did) burst into spontaneous, heartfelt praise to God.

**Davidic**
those written by
David

While up until now the tone of 2 Corinthians has been somewhat somber, it will now become quite jubilant. It's almost as if Paul placed a bold-faced parenthesis in his manuscript—one that included 2 Corinthians 2:14 and 6:10—and reflected on the blessings that he received from the hand of his God, blessings that came his way even while he was embroiled in his bloody spiritual battles. As we break the seal on this marvelous section, Paul praised God for the many spiritual victories that had been won despite the significant setbacks.

## A Sweet-Smelling Fragrance

2 CORINTHIANS 2:14–16 *Now thanks be to God who always leads us in triumph in Christ, and through us diffuses the fragrance of His knowledge in every place. For we are to God the fragrance of Christ among those who are being saved and among those who are perishing. To the one we are the aroma of death leading to death, and to the other the aroma of life leading to life. And who is sufficient for these things? (NKJV)*

**key point**

Paul here followed a pattern strikingly familiar to that found in most of the **Davidic** psalms. In many of his psalms, David begins on a negative note; Psalm 28:1 comes to mind: "To You I will cry, O LORD my Rock: Do not be silent to me, lest, if You are silent to me, I become like those who go down to the pit" (NKJV). These are not exactly the words of someone caught in the euphoria of celebration. David then characteristically moves from despair to a discussion of some aspect of God's goodness and faithfulness—"The LORD is my strength and my shield" (Psalm 28:7 NKJV)—and then invariably concludes by praising God—"With my song I will praise Him" (28:7 NKJV).

Do you see the similarities between Paul's opening chapters of 2 Corinthians and the typical structure of a Davidic psalm? Paul began this letter by rehearsing for his readers the trials and tribulations he had recently encountered in and around Ephesus. He bared his soul as he recounted the pain of his last visit and the tone of his last letter. But now, in chapter 2, Paul completely shifts his focus by reflecting upon the greatness of his God and the privilege of serving Him—"Now thanks be to God who always leads us in triumph in Christ" (v. 14 NKJV). Paul is clearly taking a page out of the Hebrew Psalter as he begins this section.

The subject and tone of 2 Corinthians 2:14 is so dramatically different from the preceding verses that one has to wonder why the editors did not make a chapter break immediately after 2:13. Fact is, you could rip 2 Corinthians 2:14–6:10 right out of the letter, and the flow of 2 Corinthians wouldn't skip a beat. Indeed, set 2:13 side by side with 6:11–12 and here's what you get: "I still had no peace of mind, because I did not find my brother Titus there. So I said good-by to them and went on to Macedonia. . . . We have spoken freely to you, Corinthians, and opened wide our hearts to you. We are not withholding our affection from you, but you are withholding yours from us" (NIV).

Do you get the flow of the narrative? Paul was so consumed in his heart with his concern for the church in Corinth that he dropped everything to find Titus. How he longed to see the Corinthians reciprocating by opening their hearts to him! Thus we can regard 2 Corinthians 2:14–6:10 as a lengthy rabbit trail on which Paul reflects on his many blessings, even while embroiled in a battle for the soul of this precious church.

But Paul also touched on a theme that doesn't play well in our current climate of political correctness. That theme is this: Biblical Christianity is an exclusive religion. In fact, Paul's worldview was centered upon the notion that the human race can be divided into one of two categories—"those who are being saved" and "those who are perishing" (2 Corinthians 2:15 NKJV). This dualistic worldview should sound familiar; we discussed the exact same phraseology in 1 Corinthians 1:18. The line of demarcation that separates the two groups is their response to the "message of the cross" and to the messengers of that message.

The one group—*those who are perishing*—find in Paul and those of his ilk "the aroma of death leading to death." To the other group—*those who are being saved*—the messengers of the message of the Cross are "the aroma of life leading to life." If Christ's servants operate under the assumption that the world will love and adore us because we are such wonderful people, we are setting ourselves up for a big disappointment. As Jesus warned His disciples, "If the world hates you, you know that it hated Me before it hated you" (John 15:18 NKJV). One cannot live a life of absolute, uncompromising devotion to the God of the Bible and expect to be popular in the eyes of the masses. No wonder Paul asked, "To the one we are

**go to**

**written**
Galatians 6:11

the aroma of death leading to death, and to the other the aroma of life leading to life. And who is sufficient for these things?" (2 Corinthians 2:16 NKJV).

## A Notable Contrast

2 CORINTHIANS 2:17 *For we are not, as so many, peddling the word of God; but as of sincerity, but as from God, we speak in the sight of God in Christ. (NKJV)*

Paul bluntly stated that an elder or pastor of a church must never be someone who is "greedy for money" (1 Timothy 3:3 NKJV). Peter warned elders against performing their duties with the motivation of "dishonest gain" (1 Peter 5:2 NKJV).

**key point**

We can well understand these warnings. Even so, Paul went out of his way to ensure that he never did anything that even hinted at manipulation. He could write the church in Corinth with a clear conscience and unblemished record regarding his attitude toward money when he said, "We are not, as so many, peddling the word of God; but as of sincerity, but as from God, we speak in the sight of God in Christ" (2 Corinthians 2:17 NKJV). Paul did what he did under the ever-watchful eye of almighty God, and in absolute dependence upon His power.

Paul, prolific writer that he was, knew all about <u>written</u> letters. Indeed, thirteen of his written letters (fourteen if you believe that Paul wrote Hebrews) are preserved in the New Testament. But when we come to 2 Corinthians 3, Paul had a different kind of letter in mind. Here he wrote about "living letters," the kind of letter written in the lives of people—the Christians in Corinth in whom Paul had invested so much of his time and energy. It was now time for Paul in particular and Corinth in general to receive a return on that sizable investment.

## Letters of Recommendation

2 CORINTHIANS 3:1–3 *Do we begin again to commend ourselves? Or do we need, as some others, epistles of commendation to you or letters of commendation from you? You are our epistle written in our hearts, known and read by all men; clearly you are an epistle of Christ, ministered by us, written not with ink*

*but by the Spirit of the living God, not on tablets of stone but on tablets of flesh, that is, of the heart. (NKJV)*

Paul was not a man who cherished championing his own cause. He never felt comfortable blowing his own horn or boasting of his achievements. Self-promotion was never his strong suit. Ever mindful of the critics' attacks against him, Paul chose a different tactic than reminding the Corinthians of his impressive résumé, or bringing to them letters of recommendation establishing his credentials as an apostle.

"You are our letters of recommendation," Paul said. "You are the evidence that our ministry is genuine. Just look at your changed lives. When we came to you the first time, you received our message—the message of the cross of Christ—and by the Spirit of the living God, it did its work in you. People have seen your changed lives. They have read in the letter of your lives the genuineness, authenticity, and sincerity of our ministry. You are all we need to establish the validity of our credentials." That was Paul's argument. A compelling argument indeed. Compelling because if anyone had a reason to doubt Paul's genuineness, all they had to do was look into a mirror.

## Ministers of the New Covenant

**2 CORINTHIANS 3:4–6** *And we have such trust through Christ toward God. Not that we are sufficient of ourselves to think of anything as being from ourselves, but our sufficiency is from God, who also made us sufficient as ministers of the new covenant, not of the letter but of the Spirit; for the letter kills, but the Spirit gives life. (NKJV)*

In the grand scheme of things, Paul obviously knew his place. In and of himself, he did not possess the resources necessary to maintain an effective ministry for Christ. His dependence was exactly where it should have been, exactly where ours should be—"our sufficiency is from God."

That being said, Paul then threw out a three-word phrase that ought to give us some pause. Up until this point in 1 and 2 Corinthians, Paul only used this phrase once before—very, very briefly—in 1 Corinthians 11:25. There he was talking about the Communion cup when he wrote, "In the same manner He also took

**Mount Sinai**
Exodus 19:20

**divided**
1 Kings 12:20–24

the cup after supper, saying, 'This cup is the new covenant in My blood. This do, as often as you drink it, in remembrance of Me'" (NKJV). Here, in 2 Corinthians 3:6, Paul described himself as a minister of "the new covenant" (NKJV). Which causes us to ask, What exactly is the new covenant?

The definitive declaration of the new covenant is found in Jeremiah. There we read: "Behold, the days are coming, says the LORD, when I will make a new covenant with the house of Israel and with the house of Judah—not according to the covenant that I made with their fathers in the day that I took them by the hand to lead them out of the land of Egypt, My covenant which they broke, though I was a husband to them, says the LORD. But this is the covenant that I will make with the house of Israel after those days, says the LORD: I will put My law in their minds, and write it on their hearts; and I will be their God, and they shall be My people. No more shall every man teach his neighbor, and every man his brother, saying, 'Know the LORD,' for they all shall know Me, from the least of them to the greatest of them, says the LORD. For I will forgive their iniquity, and their sin I will remember no more" (Jeremiah 31:31–34 NKJV).

There's obviously a lot there for us to consider. So let's take a moment to unpackage it. First of all, the old covenant, referred to here as "the covenant I made with their forefathers when I took them by the hand to lead them out of Egypt," harkens back to God's giving of the Law to Moses high atop Mount Sinai.

A lot of history took place between the establishment of the old covenant in Exodus and the promise of a new covenant in Jeremiah 31—far too much history for us to consider here. Suffice it to say that by the time of Jeremiah's writing, the once-unified nation of Israel had divided into two kingdoms—the Northern Kingdom (Israel) and the Southern Kingdom (Judah). The people of the Northern Kingdom had violently rejected God and had given themselves over to the worship of idols. They flagrantly disobeyed the Ten Commandments given by God on Mount Sinai. Even after a series of prophets called those of the Northern Kingdom back to the one true God, the people persisted in their rebellion.

God's own words, as recorded by Jeremiah, tell the sad tale: "They broke My covenant." Consequently, God permitted the Assyrians to descend upon the Northern Kingdom and to obliterate it. The official fall of the Northern Kingdom occurred in 722 BC. It wasn't a pretty sight.

It also wasn't long before the Southern Kingdom followed suit. The southerners rejected the words of God's prophets too, and determined to defy Him at every turn. This time, God used the Babylonians to decimate Judah. However, their tactics were a bit different from those of the Assyrians. The Assyrians captured those they did not kill and scattered them throughout the Assyrian Empire.

After 722 BC, Israel was no more. The Babylonians also differed in their treatment of those they vanquished. They took the people of Judah captive and led them in chains to Babylon, where they languished throughout what turned out to be a seventy-year captivity.

All hope was not lost on the Jewish people, however. There was a silver lining behind this dark cloud. God promised a new day with a new covenant. God's laws would be written in their hearts, in contrast to the stone tablets of the Ten Commandments. He would be their God and they would be His people. The Jewish people as a whole would come to faith in their God and would enjoy His blessings.

Obviously, this covenant has not been entirely fulfilled. But the day is coming when "all Israel will be saved" (Romans 11:26 NKJV). The non-Jewish, Gentile Christians in Corinth, as well as every non-Jewish follower of Jesus today, "were grafted in among them, and with them became a partaker of the root and fatness of the olive tree," the olive tree being a symbol of God's people, the Jews (Romans 11:17 NKJV).

This new covenant was secured on the cross and sealed with Christ's blood. Hence Jesus's words at the Last Supper: "He took the cup, and gave thanks, and gave it to them, saying, 'Drink from it, all of you. For this is My blood of the new covenant, which is shed for many for the remission of sins'" (Matthew 26:27–28 NKJV).

## A Glory Transformed

**2 Corinthians 3:7–18**

the big picture

Paul contrasts the darkness and death of the old covenant with the glory and life of the new.

**key point**

The old covenant, with its system of laws, could not save anyone. It was never intended to save anyone. The purpose of Old Testament, or old covenant Law, was to drive people to a place of desperation and dependence upon God to save them. The verdict of the Law is always the same for every human being: "All have sinned and fall short of the glory of God" (Romans 3:23 NKJV). The condemnation of God's Law is final—"The wages of sin is death" (Romans 6:23 NKJV).

The intended purpose of the Law was that every Jew and Gentile would come before God broken and desperate for God's saving grace, much like the tax collector in the book of Luke, who, "standing afar off, would not so much as raise his eyes to heaven, but beat his breast, saying, 'God, be merciful to me a sinner!' I tell you, this man went down to his house justified rather than the other; for everyone who exalts himself will be humbled, and he who humbles himself will be exalted" (Luke 18:13–14 NKJV).

Don't misunderstand. The giving of the Law (the ministry of death, as Paul called it) was a glorious thing. God's glory shone on Mount Sinai, and Moses' face reflected that glory when he came down the mountain. The giving of the Law was glorious, because we learned so much about God's holy nature. Lines were drawn by which we could measure our lives. Knowing where those lines were, we then knew how God wanted us to live. God's Law emphasized how perfectly holy God is, and constantly reminds us of how sinful we are. Responded to properly, God's Law drives us to our God of all grace.

**what others say**

**Philip Yancey**

The many uses of the word in English convince me that *grace* is indeed amazing—truly our last best word. It contains the essence of the Gospel as a drop of water can contain the image of the sun. The world thirsts for grace in ways it does not even recognize; little wonder the hymn "Amazing Grace" edged its way onto the Top Ten charts two hundred years after composition. For a society that seems adrift, without moorings, I know of no better place to drop an anchor of faith.[1]

Using Moses' <u>shining</u> face as a metaphor, Paul reminded his readers that when Moses came down the mountain with the Law engraved on stone tablets, his face did indeed reflect God's glory. In order for the Israelites to look upon him, Moses had to cover his face with a <u>veil</u>. That glory gradually faded, as did the glory of the old covenant. Now the new covenant of forgiveness through the shed blood of Jesus has a glory all its own, a glory that will never fade. In that sense, the glory of the new covenant is "much more glorious" than the glory of the old covenant.

In a metaphorical sense, the glory of the old covenant, equated in verse 14 with the Old Testament, is veiled with a veil that is Christ. In other words, when someone lifts the veil and reads the Old Testament with an open mind and an open heart, Christ shines through every page. Without Christ, the Old Testament leaves the reader feeling aimless and hopeless, forever condemned by a Law that he can never hope to fulfill.

Superimpose Jesus Christ on the Old Testament, and the reader is struck by the fact that every word on every page points the reader to a Redeemer, a promised Savior, a coming Messiah who, in the words of the Old Testament prophet Isaiah, "was wounded for our transgressions, He was bruised for our iniquities; the chastisement for our peace was upon Him, and by His stripes we are healed. All we like sheep have gone astray; we have turned, every one, to his own way; and the LORD has laid on Him the iniquity of us all" (Isaiah 53:5–6 NKJV).

How much clearer could that be? Someone would have to have his or her spiritual eyes, or heart, veiled not to see that. Only the Holy Spirit can remove that veil from our faces. And when He does, "We all, with unveiled face, beholding as in a mirror the glory of the Lord, are being transformed into the same image from glory to glory, just as by the Spirit of the Lord" (2 Corinthians 3:18 NKJV).

Paul was never one to lose heart. His heart shines in this next section of Scripture. As we study it together, we'll discover from what resources Paul was able to draw in order to maintain his heart for the ministry, especially when he was in the heat of the battle.

go to

**shining**
Exodus 34:29

**veil**
Exodus 34:33

Something to ponder

# Light Out of Darkness

**the big picture**

## 2 Corinthians 4:1-6

Paul gets right to the core of spiritual warfare, revealing for his readers that the one we battle is in reality the "god of this age" (v. 4 NKJV), who has blinded the minds of those who oppose Christ's ministry.

**key point**

"We do not lose heart" (2 Corinthians 4:1 NKJV). Though there is a period following that sentence in the New King James Version, we could properly place an exclamation point at the end of Paul's triumphant declaration. In making that victorious statement, Paul used a military metaphor that literally refers to someone who cowers in a corner after his surrender to his enemy. Paul was utterly unwilling to surrender. There was no such thing as surrender in Paul's worldview. He refused to retreat. Called by God to be a minister of the "message of the cross" (1 Corinthians 1:18 NKJV), or what he refers to in this letter as the new covenant, and strengthened by God's mercy in the midst of merciless attacks, Paul would not lay down his arms and cower in the face of Christ's enemy.

Unlike those who served the enemy of God rather than the Son of God, Paul was not "walking in craftiness nor handling the word of God deceitfully" (2 Corinthians 4:2 NKJV). He *renounced*, or refused to stoop to such shameful tactics. As we have already established, unlike the pseudo-apostles who tried so desperately to undermine Paul's genuine apostolic authority, Paul never resorted to gimmickry or manipulation techniques for his own personal profit. He preached biblical truth in a way that everyone with a clear or undefiled conscience would recognize, and in a way that met with God's approval since he was ministering "in the sight of God."

Paul's perspective was commendable and instructive. Every one of God's servants will experience opposition. In fact, tares had been planted in the church in Corinth. False teachers had infiltrated the congregation and were sowing their seeds of deception and division. Now we know the source of these tares—the "god of this age [who] has blinded [those] who do not believe" (2 Corinthians 4:4 NKJV). They are perishing, a word that has now become all-too-familiar to the readers of 1 and 2 Corinthians. Their minds are darkened to the truth, they do not believe the truth, and they have put a lid on "the light of the gospel of the glory of Christ" (4:4 NKJV).

So take heart, especially if you are on the ropes spiritually. Spiritual warfare is the name of the game when it comes to serving Christ. Paul told Timothy the ministry is "the good fight" (1 Timothy 1:18 NIV). We fight. But we do not fight alone. "The God who commanded light to shine out of darkness" (2 Corinthians 4:6 NKJV) has called you to shine the light of truth in the darkness of error and spiritual opposition. He will sustain you in the battle, just as He sustained Paul by His grace.

## We Do Not Despair

the big picture

### 2 Corinthians 4:7–15

Paul was encouraged to remain in the fight because his was an eternal perspective. This is one of Paul's most transparent passages, one in which he gives us a glimpse into the humble soul of this great apostle.

The gospel is a treasure. This treasure has been entrusted to us, men and women who are nothing more than "earthen vessels" (2 Corinthians 4:7 NKJV). God did this purposefully because, given our human weaknesses, the impact of the gospel is an evidence not of the power of people but of the power of God.

Expanding upon his earthen vessels theme, Paul penned one of his most transparent statements. If we had any doubt about the severity of the struggles that had engulfed this battle-weary apostle, doubt no more. I dare say that Paul suffered through indignities that few of us will ever see or even imagine. Paul and those who ministered with him truly were lights shining out of a dark place.

Paul knew that, apart from God's presence and power in his life, he was nothing special—just an unadorned jar of clay. Likewise with his fellow sufferers, who were also battered by troubles. But their spirits were not crushed. At times their heads were spinning with confusion, yet they did not despair. They were persecuted relentlessly, yet never felt abandoned by God. They may have been knocked down, but they could not be knocked out.

**martyred**
2 Timothy 4:6

The suffering that they were experiencing was merely a continuation of the suffering endured by Jesus. What had been done to Jesus—the false accusations, the beatings, the mockery, His murder—was exactly what was being done to them. In that context they felt privileged to suffer on Christ's behalf. As Paul wrote to the church in Colossae, "I now rejoice in my sufferings for you, and fill up in my flesh what is lacking in the afflictions of Christ, for the sake of His body, which is the church" (Colossians 1:24 NKJV).

The ironic twist was this: Paul's suffering and eventual death at the hands of the enemies of Christ (Paul was eventually <u>martyred</u> for his faith) actually resulted in scores of people (including the Christians in Corinth) receiving eternal life.

Citing Psalm 116:10, a hymn of praise for God's deliverance of the psalmist's soul from death, Paul asserted his unshakable confidence that even if they killed him, "He who raised up the Lord Jesus will also raise us up with Jesus" (2 Corinthians 4:14 NKJV). Because Paul believed that with absolute confidence, he was able to speak on Christ's behalf with equal confidence. It's as if he was saying to the Corinthians, "Hey, what's the worst thing they can do to me? Kill me? Ha! Even if they do that, God will raise me from the dead and let me live with Him forever. So what do I have to lose?" His truly was an eternal perspective.

> ### the big picture
>
> **Billy Graham**
> The desire to gain a better understanding of death has been called the "new obsession." I certainly don't want to be unbalanced in thinking about this subject, but I am convinced that when we know where death leads, we will know the "hope of the glory" spoken of by Paul in Colossians 1:27.[2]

## Renewed Day by Day

**2 CORINTHIANS 4:16–18** *Therefore we do not lose heart. Even though our outward man is perishing, yet the inward man is being renewed day by day. For our light affliction, which is but for a moment, is working for us a far more exceeding and eternal weight of glory, while we do not look at the things which are seen, but at the things which are not seen. For the things which are seen are temporary, but the things which are not seen are eternal. (NKJV)*

Paul got it right. All things considered, relatively speaking, his afflictions were *light* when compared to the blessings he was receiving day by day. One of those daily blessings was God's renewing of Paul's soul. Yes, they could beat Paul's body. But they could not touch that inner part of him, his essence, his soul.

This sounds reminiscent of Jesus's words to His disciples: "Do not fear those who kill the body but cannot kill the soul. But rather fear Him who is able to destroy both soul and body in hell" (Matthew 10:28 NKJV). Paul knew that his body was expendable and that his soul was safely in God's hands. So despite the problems and pressures that he faced every day, he was able to throw himself into his God-given ministry, knowing all the while that "our light affliction, which is but for a moment, is working for us a far more exceeding and eternal weight of glory" (2 Corinthians 4:17 NKJV).

Paul described himself as an ambassador for Christ, and his ministry as one of reconciliation. Everywhere he went, in everything he wrote or said, and in everything he did he had that identity in mind. He saw himself as a citizen of heaven, temporarily assigned to earth to reconcile people with their God.

**go to**

**tentmaker**
Acts 18:3

## At Home with the Lord

**the big picture**

### 2 Corinthians 5:1–8

Many people wonder what happens when we die. In this passage of Scripture, Paul gives us the definitive answer to that most important question.

Paul's narrative runs seamlessly from the end of 2 Corinthians 4 to the beginning of chapter 5. The man who "despaired even of life" (2 Corinthians 1:8 NKJV) was thinking about heaven.

You've got to love how he described death. To Paul, death was no different than someone on a camping trip folding up his tent and going home. An apt metaphor, given that Paul was a <u>tentmaker</u> by trade. He knew that his body—his tent, as it were—was a temporary dwelling place; Paul's true home was "a house not made with hands, eternal in the heavens" (2 Corinthians 5:1 NKJV). That's where his focus was, so much so that he inwardly *groaned* under the load of

something to ponder

suffering he was called upon to endure here, and also *groaned* in anticipation of moving to his heavenly home.

Paul faced death with the absolute confidence of a man who was granted a rare glimpse behind the veil into the eternal realm. We will talk more about Paul's heavenly vision when we get to chapter 12. He knew exactly where he was going because he had already seen it.

So it was with a remarkable certainty and well-earned credibility that Paul gave us a basic chronology of what happens the moment we die. Here's how it works: (1) While we are at home in our earthly bodies—our temporary tents—we are "absent from the Lord" (2 Corinthians 5:6 NKJV). Sure, we can talk to Him in prayer, but we cannot see Him, we cannot visit Him, we cannot cry on His shoulder or sit at His feet and learn from Him. But (2) the moment we fold our tents, when the moment of death comes, when we lay our bodies down and are *absent* from our bodies, we will immediately be transported into the presence of Jesus. One of the most blessed promises in all of the Scriptures is found in 2 Corinthians 5:8: "We are confident, yes, well pleased rather to be absent from the body and to be present with the Lord" (NKJV).

## The Power of Persuasion

> **2 CORINTHIANS 5:9–11** *Therefore we make it our aim, whether present or absent, to be well pleasing to Him. For we must all appear before the judgment seat of Christ, that each one may receive the things done in the body, according to what he has done, whether good or bad. Knowing, therefore, the terror of the Lord, we persuade men; but we are well known to God, and I also trust are well known in your consciences.* (NKJV)

Do you remember our discussion of the bema seat of Christ way back in 1 Corinthians 3? Paul revisited that sobering scene here in 2 Corinthians 5. Now, understand that when we "all appear before the judgment seat of Christ" we do so for the purpose of reward, not punishment. It's a scene familiar to anyone in Corinth who was a devotee of the Isthmian Games. Much like our Olympics awards ceremonies, in which the three athletes receive their gold, silver, or bronze medals, athletes in Paul's day stood on the bema seat and received their rewards. So will we.

However, our rewards will not be based on who ran the fastest or jumped the highest. Our rewards will be based on one thing and one thing only—how we lived our lives before our God. Those who have pleased the Lord will be rewarded; those who made disobedient compromises will not. Non-Christians, on the other hand, will stand before the Great White Throne Judgment described in all of its terrifying detail in Revelation 20. These are the individuals who rejected Christ, defied their God, and chose to live their lives apart from Him. Theirs is not a judgment of rewards but one of punishment. Knowing this, living with this reality burning in his heart, Paul devoted himself to trying to persuade all who would listen to turn from their sins and receive Christ, and the cleansing and forgiveness that only He can offer.

## <u>Out with the Old, In with the New</u>

**the big picture**

**2 Corinthians 5:12–21**

The transformation that Jesus makes in the lives of His followers is breathtaking to behold, as Paul describes in this section of Scripture.

We now get a little more insight into the criticisms that were being leveled against the apostle Paul by the pseudo-apostles in Corinth. They accused him of being a radical fanatic. Some would even say that he was *beside* himself—a word that means insane or out of one's right mind.

Actually, truth be told, Paul *was* a fanatic—a man possessed of a mission to proclaim the "message of the cross" to all who would hear. He fancied himself as a man on the bow of a ship tossing life preservers to the drowning masses around him. Paul felt compelled by the "love of Christ" to tell as many people as he could about Jesus. Would that we were as single-focused and fanatical about sharing our own faith!

We've already discussed that the "message of the cross," the gospel, is God's good news—God's *great* news—to the human race. Just how great is that news? Consider the following: Christ takes broken sinful people and transforms them into a "new creation." It's just like starting life all over again. Our sins are forgiven. We are completely new and different people.

Jesus takes a thieving tax collector like Matthew and makes him an apostle. For that matter, He takes a murderous self-righteous thug like Paul and makes *him* into an apostle. He takes the lying adulterer named Abram and makes him into Abraham, the patriarch of the world's three monotheistic religions. He takes a prostitute named Rahab and enshrines her in Jesus's genealogy. Or a homeless widow like Ruth and places her at the epicenter of one of the most endearing love stories ever told. You get the idea.

There is a vast difference between a person's life BC and AD. Before Christ we were enemies of God. We set ourselves against Him and defied Him at every turn. AD, After Dying to our old lives and putting Christ on the throne of our new lives, everything changes. Our values change. Our worldviews change. Our life-purposes change. Our eternal destinies change. No longer God's enemies, we enter into relationship with Him.

**key point**

To use Paul's word, we become *reconciled* to God. As Paul so eloquently wrote in Romans 8:31, "What then shall we say to these things? If God is for us, who can be against us?" (NKJV). As an apostle, Paul saw himself as an ambassador of heaven to a lost and dying world. Would that we would see ourselves in exactly the same way.

All this was made possible because God made His Son, Jesus, who committed no sins of His own, to become sin for us on the cross. As He hung there, God poured out upon Him all of the hellish torment that we each deserved. The moment we invited Christ into our lives, God forgave all of our sins—past, present, and future—and just as He placed all of our sins on Jesus, God placed all of Jesus's righteousness on us. God no longer sees us as filthy sinners. He sees us through the prism of Christ's death on the cross. He sees us as His righteous children!

Being an ambassador of heaven to an unheavenly earth is not an easy task. Paul's life reflected the two worlds in which he operated. Some responded positively to his message; others were violently opposed. Some people loved Paul; others hated him with a passion. Some wanted to honor him as their patron saint; others sought to kill him. Somehow, every servant of God lives in tension between these two competing forces.

**The Smart Guide to the Bible**

## Living Up to God's Grace

*2 CORINTHIANS 6:1–2 We then, as workers together with Him also plead with you not to receive the grace of God in vain. For He says: "In an acceptable time I have heard you, and in the day of salvation I have helped you." Behold, now is the accepted time; behold, now is the day of salvation. (NKJV)*

Many of the Christians in Corinth were new creations all right, but they were not living like it. This sad reality grieved Paul more than we could ever know. Just as he did throughout 1 Corinthians, Paul now pleaded with his readers to live up to the grace that they had received.

Quoting Isaiah 49:8, Paul passionately pressed the point that God was ever longing to save sinners—not just in the fire-insurance sense where people wrongly believe that they can trust in Christ to keep them out of hell, but then go on to live any way they choose without consequence. God longs to walk in relationship with us, and with the Corinthians. But many in the church lived as if God were absent from their lives.

Given the compromising lifestyles of many of his readers, Paul was concerned that they weren't Christians at all. As he will do in 2 Corinthians 13:5, Paul exhorted his readers to make certain that they truly were genuine followers of Jesus, and not to put that off one more day. Twice using the word *behold*—as in "Sit up and take notice, now"—Paul wrote, "Behold, now is the accepted time; behold, now is the day of salvation."

## The Legacy of a Spiritual Leader

### the big picture

**2 Corinthians 6:3-10**

Paul left a lasting legacy as a spiritual leader. This is sobering reading for anyone who is considering assuming the role of spiritual leader. The toll exacted upon the servants of God can be heavy, but the blessings are huge. In this final passage, Paul showed himself to be a man who understood the blessings from the battlefield.

Paul sought to live his life in such a way that no one would ever have a credible reason to cast doubt on his ministry. As one of God's heavenly ambassadors, Paul patiently endured hardships, troubles, and calamities of the worst kind. He acknowledged that he had been beaten, imprisoned, confronted by angry mobs, "worked to exhaustion, endured sleepless night, and gone without food" (2 Corinthians 6:5 NLT). Yet he maintained a lifestyle of purity, patience, and love.

Nevertheless, his critics in Corinth called Paul and his followers "impostors" (2 Co-rinthians 6:8 NLT). Though he had been beaten down, they failed to knock him out. Though they caused him much heartache, he was able to find joy. Even though he was poor monetarily, he was rich spiritually. Even though he owned nothing, he had everything.

Any of God's servants who think they have it tough ought to bury themselves in 2 Corinthians 6:3–10. Conflict is the inevitable and unavoidable result for all citizens of heaven trying to serve as ambassadors to a dark and sinful planet. We can all-too-easily get swept up in the muck and mire that surround us. But as with Paul, there are always God's immeasurable blessings from the battlefield, if only we will allow ourselves to receive them and enjoy them.

# Chapter Wrap-Up

- In this section of 2 Corinthians, Paul does a dramatic turn-around and begins to praise God for all His blessings! This section is a must-read for all students of the Bible, for it's one of the most precious and insightful in the whole canon.

- In many ways, this section is like a "parenthesis," meaning a "turning away" from the subject at hand to address something or someone else. In this case Paul "turned away" from his troubles to proclaim his thanks to God for His blessings!

- Paul became almost profuse in his praise of the Corinthians, in spite of the troubles they had so recently caused him.

- Paul also speaks of the "new covenant" as defined in the thirty-first chapter of Jeremiah—the covenant God promised to make in which He would literally write His laws on our hearts.

- Paul then begins to write about spiritual warfare, insisting that we should not "lose heart," no matter what.

- Paul gives us a wonderful description of physical death, from his perspective, as if we were literally "folding up" our lives as one would fold up a tent, in preparation for the next phase of an adventure.

# Study Questions

1. What are the two steps (or states of being) that Paul said we will go through when we die?

2. In what part of the Bible do we find the main story of God's original covenant with the people who would eventually become known as the Jews?

3. Why do you suppose Paul might have likened death to the "folding of a tent"?

4. How did Paul see himself here on earth?

# 2 Corinthians 6:11–7:16
# The Heart of the Matter

## Let's Get Started

Paul's so-called "severe letter" was now front and center in his mind as he confessed to his Corinthian readers the conflicting emotions he had experienced as he wrote and sent it. On the one hand, Paul was sorry that he had to come down on the church like a hammer. On the other hand, for the most part the church responded well to the letter, for which Paul was most grateful.

We have now come to the heart of 2 Corinthians. And as we are about to learn, 2 Corinthians 6:11–7:16 is written in a tone that should tug at our heartstrings. One almost gets the sense of listening in on a very private conversation between a father and his repentant son or daughter. Disciplining a child is never a pleasant task, as any parent must confess. "This is going to hurt me more than it will hurt you" is not a meaningless cliché.

But when the discipline has accomplished its intended purpose of correcting potentially destructive behavior, there is a desire to take the child in the parent's arms and hold that child close, sad that discipline was necessary but grateful that its goal was achieved. That's the tension you will sense in these verses, as Paul gives us a glimpse into the heart of a spiritual parent now embracing his beloved children.

## Open-Heart Surgery

**2 Corinthians 6:11–13** *O Corinthians! We have spoken openly to you, our heart is wide open. You are not restricted by us, but you are restricted by your own affections. Now in return for the same (I speak as to children), you also be open.* (NKJV)

The *New International Version* of the Bible renders these confusing verses in a slightly different way. It reads, "We have spoken freely to you, Corinthians, and opened wide our hearts to you. We are not withholding our affection from you, but you are withholding yours from us. As a fair exchange—I speak as to my children—open wide your hearts also."

key point

We stand amazed at Paul's godly response to the Christians at Corinth, who viciously and repeatedly wounded him. It would have been understandable if Paul had simply washed his hands. But he didn't. He remained committed to these believers regardless of the pain they had inflicted on him. He refused to withhold his affection from them. He continued to hold them securely in his heart. He was willing—and this is key—to risk loving them even though that love might not have been returned.

Unreciprocated love is one of the most painful human emotions that a person can feel. Yet Paul was willing to put his rather sizable heart on the line and risk just that. All that he asked in return was that the Christians in Corinth would open their hearts to him.

what others say

**James Barrie**

Let no one who loves be called altogether unhappy. Even love unreturned has its rainbow.[1]

## Strange Bedfellows

for your marriage

2 CORINTHIANS 6:14–7:1 *Do not be unequally yoked together with unbelievers. For what fellowship has righteousness with lawlessness? And what communion has light with darkness? And what accord has Christ with Belial? Or what part has a believer with an unbeliever? And what agreement has the temple of God with idols? For you are the temple of the living God. As God has said: "I will dwell in them and walk among them. I will be their God, and they shall be My people." Therefore "Come out from among them and be separate, says the Lord. Do not touch what is unclean, and I will receive you. I will be a Father to you, and you shall be My sons and daughters, says the LORD Almighty."*

*Therefore, having these promises, beloved, let us cleanse ourselves from all filthiness of the flesh and spirit, perfecting holiness in the fear of God. (NKJV)*

This passage has historically been twisted to mean all kinds of things that the apostle Paul never intended. For example, people have passionately interpreted this passage to mean that believers should never marry unbelievers (a viewpoint that I hold, but not based on *this* passage), that Christians should never enter into a business arrangement with an unbeliever, that Christians should never hang out socially with unbelievers, and that Christian young people should never date non-Christians.

I have even heard this passage quoted to buttress the notion that Christians should never read non-Christian books, listen to non-Christian music, or go to see non-Christian movies. Some have even dared to suggest that, based on this passage, Paul would prevent Christians from investing in mutual funds that include non-Christian-owned companies.

Such misinterpretations and misapplications result from a violation of one of the most basic principles of proper biblical interpretation: *Context is everything!* In the context of Paul's letters to the church in Corinth, this particular passage has a dual application both to those outside the church and to those within it.

So, before we go on, let's briefly review the context of 1 and 2 Corinthians. Corinth, as we have well established, was a cesspool of sinfulness. Within the cozy confines of the church in Corinth, every form of debauchery had been present in the former lifestyles of these relatively new Christians. Paul got quite specific when he wrote:

"Do you not know that the unrighteous will not inherit the kingdom of God? Do not be deceived. Neither fornicators, nor idolaters, nor adulterers, nor homosexuals, nor sodomites, nor thieves, nor covetous, nor drunkards, nor revilers, nor extortioners will inherit the kingdom of God. And such were some of you. But you were washed, but you were sanctified, but you were justified in the name of the Lord Jesus and by the Spirit of our God" (1 Corinthians 6:9–11 NKJV).

In our previous discussion of 1 Corinthians 6:9–11, we talked at length about the fact that God reached down into that cesspool and saved scores of people out of their compromised positions. Paul was there in 1 Corinthians 6, and was here in 2 Corinthians 6, concerned about the possibility of those whom God had washed and made holy and acceptable to Himself returning to their former ways. So Paul repeatedly warned his readers and exhorted them not to do so.

Peter did the same thing when he wrote, "They prove the truth of this proverb: 'A dog returns to its vomit.' And another says, 'A washed pig returns to the mud'" (2 Peter 2:22 NLT). Both Paul and Peter—and frankly, every pastor worth his salt today—lives with the same fear. The battle with our fleshly desires is relentless; it never ends. The streets of God's kingdom here on earth are littered with the decaying carcasses of those who experienced God's amazing grace as He forgave, cleansed, and renewed their lives, only to succumb to the pull of the flesh and return to the garbage heap from which they had been rescued. That's the first application of the passage—Paul told his readers not to return to those relationships outside of the church that could result in their going back to their previous lifestyles of sin.

The term *yoke* is an interesting word-choice. It denotes two animals joined (or yoked) together in a harness in order to pull a plow. Obviously, the yoke or harness will work only when the two animals yoked together are the same type, size, and strength. Working in tandem, they can pull the plow together, combining their strength to till the soil. If two different types of animals are yoked together, their individual strength will be compromised rather than combined to maximum efficiency.

In the same way, we compromise our spiritual strength if we yoke or harness ourselves in relationships with unbelievers who are actively pulling in a different direction than we are going. In the context of Corinth, if someone is saved out of a background of drunkenness and determines that he will no longer have any association with anything related to that compromising lifestyle, such sacrifice should be applauded. But if that same individual decides that he can reenter the relationships with the individuals with whom he used to party, that is a surefire prescription for spiritual disaster.

Such a relationship becomes a yoke. One person (the Christian) is seeking to pull away from a drunken lifestyle, while the other unbelievers actively pull toward and fully embrace that lifestyle. While we'd like to believe that nine times out of ten the Christian will influence the non-Christian for the positive, experience shows that most of the time the Christian's days are numbered. The pull of the flesh is just too great to resist in that instance.

Does that mean we should never have friendships with unbelievers? Of course not. How can we be a witness to others if we become like monks in monasteries? Our highest calling, and one of our greatest privileges as Christians, is to share the good news of our faith with others. This obviously demands that we be in relationship with those who believe differently than we do. To the degree that we can be a positive spiritual influence in the lives of our unsaved friends and loved ones, to that degree we are successfully fulfilling the Great Commission of Matthew 28:19–20. This becomes a problem only when we fail to influence others, but succumb to their sinful influences instead.

go to

**provision**
Romans 13:14

**messenger**
2 Corinthians 12:7

what others say

**Martha Grace Reese**

People who share their faith love God and believe that other people's lives would be better if they were in a relationship with God, too. They know why they are doing evangelism: they want to share the driving force in their lives.[2]

We've got to be honest with ourselves about our own unique weaknesses in order to make absolutely certain that we never make any provision for the flesh. There are certain unbelievers, friends of mine, with whom I can hang out without any fear of compromise. They may be into some things that I am not into, but they know where I stand and respect that about me. Their own particular vices are not a temptation to me. They do not try, nor am I tempted, to get involved in some of the things they are into.

However, there are others with whom I cannot have any relationship. They are into things that are very much in line with my areas of fleshly weakness. My association with them places me in tempting situations that I fear I cannot handle. Satan can use those individuals to entice me to a degree that I cannot resist. The possible price of a friendship with them is too great in terms of my spiritual life. Of them I must heed Paul's warning, "Come out from among them and be separate" (2 Corinthians 6:17 NKJV).

apply it

The second of our dual-applications has to do with those inside the church at Corinth. We are now well aware that there were those who infiltrated the church who were false teachers, pseudo-apostles, at least one of whom was a messenger of Satan planted by the enemy in the church at Corinth to beat Paul down. These men should have been removed from the fellowship. They were doing the devil's bidding, and the entire church was suffering because of their evil influence.

**key point**

Paul exhorted the true Christians in Corinth to have nothing to do with these men. They could not fellowship with them because to do so was tantamount to light communing with darkness, righteousness with lawlessness. We must understand that our "Can't we all just go along to get along?" sentimentality in the church, all in the name of unity, will only result in disunity and division. The single most sobering duty of godly church leaders is to protect their flocks from "savage wolves [who] will come in among you, not sparing the flock. Also from among yourselves men will rise up, speaking perverse things, to draw away the disciples after themselves" (Acts 20:29–30 NKJV).

It's tough to discipline disobedient members who have built a following from within the congregation, but that's what needed to happen in Corinth. The church as a whole needed to separate themselves from these men, lest they be enabled and empowered to level even more destruction among the membership.

God promised the Christians in Corinth that He was their God and they were His people. Armed with the assurances of that promise, it was incumbent upon the church and the individuals within it to put into practice Paul's principle of separation. Paul exhorted his readers, "Therefore, having these promises, beloved, let us cleanse ourselves from all filthiness of the flesh and spirit [both inside and outside the church], perfecting holiness in the fear of God" (2 Corinthians 7:1 NKJV).

## The Power of an Uncompromising Life

> 2 CORINTHIANS 7:2–4 *Open your hearts to us. We have wronged no one, we have corrupted no one, we have cheated no one. I do not say this to condemn; for I have said before that you are in our hearts, to die together and to live together. Great is my boldness of speech toward you, great is my boasting on your behalf. I am filled with comfort. I am exceedingly joyful in all our tribulation. (NKJV)*

In contrast to the false teachers from whom the true Christians in Corinth needed to separate, Paul could confidently assert that he and his coworkers "wronged no one, we have corrupted no one, we have cheated no one." This was not a malicious "I told you so" on the part of Paul. He was simply yet strategically driving home the point that some in that church had been deceived into following men who had wronged, corrupted, and cheated others.

Paul was also again asserting his undying love for the Christians in Corinth, many of whom he led to Christ during the eighteen months that he labored there. He loved them so much that he assured them of their secure place in his heart. Indeed, he was willing to live for them and if need be to die for them. It was because of this great love that despite his many trials and tribulations, Paul felt an enormous joy over their repentance and willingness to turn away from those who had hijacked the church and to turn back toward Paul as their true, God-appointed spiritual leader.

## Godly Sorrow

the big picture

**2 Corinthians 7:5-12**

Paul felt encouraged because despite his sufferings, his labors had paid off. Many in the church responded to Paul's appeals with an appropriate sense of repentance and godly sorrow.

Titus was the bearer of good news. The good news was this: "Not only by his coming, but also by the consolation with which he was comforted in you, when he told us of your earnest desire, your mourning, your zeal for me, so that I rejoiced even more" (2 Corinthians 7:7 NKJV).

Prior to hearing that good report, Paul admitted that "we were troubled on every side" (7:5 NKJV). He faced *conflicts* and *fears* that made him feel *downcast*. His spirits revived, however, when Titus filled him in on the good response the Corinthians had to Paul's severe letter.

Paul was encouraged that his letter caused them to feel a godly sorrow that led them to repentance. Godly sorrow is the proper emotional and willful response that one feels in hearing God's truth and being convicted by the Holy Spirit. Jesus promised His disciples that when He returned to heaven He would send them the Holy Spirit.

When He comes, Jesus promised, "He will convict the world of sin, and of righteousness, and of judgment" (John 16:8 NKJV). The word *convict* means to convince someone that something is true.

The ministry of the Holy Spirit is to convince people like us that we are sinful, that we can be made righteous through repentance of our sins, and that if we refuse to repent we will face God's judgment. As the Christians in Corinth read Paul's letter, they were confronted by the truth of what he wrote, and were convicted by the Holy Spirit that what Paul wrote was true; and that, in light of that truth, they were sinning.

They could have responded to the Holy Spirit in several different less-than-positive ways. But they chose to respond by acknowledging their sins and turning from them—specifically, the sins of rebellion against apostolic authority in the church and following false teachers who attacked the truth rather than submitting themselves to it.

Godly sorrow is different from guilt. When we are confronted about our sins, the sorrow we feel in response to the Holy Spirit's convicting ministry is called here "godly sorrow." The purpose of feeling a genuine sorrow over our sins is to prompt us to repent—to change our minds and hearts about our sinful choices.

Guilt, on the other hand, does not come from the Holy Spirit. Satan delights in calling up to our minds the sins from which we have already repented and for which we have already been forgiven. He seeks to hold us spiritually hostage by bombarding us with thoughts like, *You are dirty. You are damaged goods. You are unworthy to serve your holy God.* Guilt is totally inappropriate for the believer, because guilt denies our having been made holy and acceptable to our God.

Guilt is a trap that holds us bound. Godly sorrow liberates the soul when we respond in genuine heartfelt repentance. Many of the Christians in Corinth responded to Paul's letter with godly sorrow and repented, something for which Paul was profoundly thankful.

**what others say**

**Beth Moore**

I want to ask you to do another critical thing if you haven't already come to this step. Muster up every bit of the courage you have within you and ask God to baptize you in a tide of sorrow over your sin. Ask Him to do it for as long as necessary until full repentance comes. I beg you not to be afraid of this kind of sorrow. The Bible calls this "godly sorrow," and it is the most wonderful thing that can happen to you in the next little while. You cannot be restored until it comes.[3]

The end result of genuine repentance is to produce the following in the mind and heart of the one who repents:

1. *Diligence:* An eagerness to turn away from our sinful behavior; a diligence to make doggone sure we do not fall into the same sin again.

2. *Clearing of ourselves:* The earnest desire to rebuild trust with those with whom we have broken trust; to clear our names by demonstrating to others that our repentance is heartfelt and genuine.

3. *Indignation:* Often called "righteous indignation" or a holy anger, the kind of anger Jesus displayed when He cleansed the <u>temple</u>. An anger that one should feel over the circumstances of his or her sin, and over the fact that God's holy name was harmed by our sinful actions.

4. *Fear:* A healthy respect for the righteousness of God, which we violate when we sin, and which often causes God to **chasten** us for our disobedient behavior.

5. *Vehement desire:* A longing to repair any broken relationships—with God and others—that result from our sinful behavior.

6. *Zeal:* The passionate yearning to do right, especially regarding the situations in which we previously did wrong.

7. *Vindication:* The overriding desire to see God's name upheld and His holiness vindicated by our public acknowledgment that what we did was wrong and that we deserve whatever negative consequences come our way because of our sinful choices.

That is what true repentance looks like, the kind of change of mind, heart, and behavior that results from godly sorrow.

## A Friend in Need

2 CORINTHIANS 7:13–16 *Therefore we have been comforted in your comfort. And we rejoiced exceedingly more for the joy of Titus, because his spirit has been refreshed by you all. For if in anything I have boasted to him about you, I am not ashamed. But as we spoke all things to you in truth, even so our boasting*

**temple**
John 2:15

**chasten**
Hebrews 12:6

**chasten**
discipline, much like a loving parent disciplines a disobedient child

**Greek**
Galatians 2:3

**Jerusalem**
Galatians 2:1

**Greek**
non-Jew or Gentile

*to Titus was found true. And his affections are greater for you as he remembers the obedience of you all, how with fear and trembling you received him. Therefore I rejoice that I have confidence in you in everything.* (NKJV)

It's time we met Titus. Oddly enough, we don't know a lot about him. He sort of lurks in the shadows that surround Paul's ministry. But the accolades afforded him are quite impressive.

It's interesting to note that of the twelve times Titus is mentioned in the New Testament, eight of them are here in 2 Corinthians. This is but one indication of the pivotal role that Titus played in Paul's life during this difficult period.

We don't know much, but here's what we do know: Titus was a **Greek** convert to Christianity. Titus apparently accompanied Paul to the Jerusalem council, where the issue of circumcision was discussed at some length, the decision being rendered that non-Jewish converts to Christianity did not have to first be baptized. Titus then apparently accompanied Paul on his second and third missionary journeys.

The apostle Paul lavishes praise upon this unsung hero of the faith. Paul refers to him as "my partner and fellow worker" in 2 Corinthians 8:23 (NKJV). And in Titus 1:4 Paul commends Titus as "a true son in our common faith" (NKJV).

It seems that Paul felt free to parachute Titus into some hot spots when the circumstances demanded someone whom Paul could trust implicitly. We have previously discussed his role in Corinth. When a steady hand was needed at the helm in Crete, Titus was again drafted into service. Of his ministry there we read, "For this reason I left you in Crete, that you should set in order the things that are lacking, and appoint elders in every city as I commanded you" (Titus 1:5 NKJV).

And so it was that when Paul finally hooked up with Titus and heard his report about the goings-on in Corinth, Paul received much-needed comfort, felt refreshed, and was able to rejoice at the good news brought to him by this trusted son in the faith.

Titus shared Paul's heart of love for the struggling Christians in Corinth. "His [Titus's] affections are greater for you as he remembers the obedience of you all, how with fear and trembling you received him" (2 Corinthians 7:15 NKJV). Truly Titus was an amazing servant of Christ, one on whom Paul could count in his darkest hour of greatest need.

# Chapter Wrap-Up

- Paul's "severe" letter to the Corinthians, which is not part of Scripture, was much on his mind as he wrote 2 Corinthians, which was actually his third letter to the church at Corinth.

- Paul was amazingly steadfast in his desire to help the Corinthians through their troubles and establish them as a strong, devout, godly congregation, despite all the organizational troubles and personal hurts some of the members of that congregation had caused him.

- When Paul talked about being unequally yoked with unbelievers, he was not necessarily talking about personal friends, professional colleagues, and business partners. Without such "regular" associations, how would we witness?

- "Guilt" and "godly sorrow" are two different things. The first works against a valid, ongoing relationship with God and is often inspired by Satan himself, while the second is often a vital part of true repentance.

# Study Questions

1. What is the difference between the personal relationships we can safely have with non-Christian friends, and those we cannot have?

2. What three things did Paul say he ("we") had not done, in 2 Corinthians 7:2–4?

3. What kind of report did Paul get from Titus with respect to the "severe" letter he wrote, in which he dealt directly with the Corinthians' major sins?

4. What are the seven characteristics of true repentance that result from godly sorrow?

# 2 Corinthians 8, 9
# The Great Giveaway

**Chapter Highlights:**
- Exceeding Expectations
- A Sincere Love
- Love in Action
- In God's Sight
- A Cheerful Giver

## Let's Get Started

It's time to talk about money again.

In a radical change in the direction of this letter, Paul revisited a topic he broached near the end of 1 Corinthians—the need to take up a <u>collection</u> for the suffering saints in Jerusalem. It seems that a <u>year</u> had passed since his last mention of this desperate need. So Paul reminded his readers that the sufferings continued and encouraged them to give what they could to help alleviate some of the need. In so doing, Paul developed the single most complete blueprint for local church finances to be found in the New Testament.

Paul based his appeal on a fairly straightforward line of reasoning: We who have been the recipients of God's boundless grace ought ourselves to be gracious in meeting the needs of those around us.

go to

**collection**
1 Corinthians 16:2

**year**
2 Corinthians 8:10

## Exceeding Paul's Expectations

**2 CORINTHIANS 8:1–7** *Moreover, brethren, we make known to you the grace of God bestowed on the churches of Macedonia: that in a great trial of affliction the abundance of their joy and their deep poverty abounded in the riches of their liberality. For I bear witness that according to their ability, yes, and beyond their ability, they were freely willing, imploring us with much urgency that we would receive the gift and the fellowship of the ministering to the saints. And not only as we had hoped, but they first gave themselves to the Lord, and then to us by the will of God. So we urged Titus, that as he had begun, so he would also complete this grace in you as well. But as you abound in every-thing—in faith, in speech, in knowledge, in all diligence, and in your love for us—see that you abound in this grace also. (NKJV)*

Three cheers for the churches in Macedonia, the northern Roman province of Greece. There the churches of Philippi, Thessalonica, and Berea—themselves no strangers to tough times—set an amazing example by sacrificially giving to the needs of their suffering Christian brothers and sisters in Jerusalem.

The three cities of Macedonia—Philippi, Thessalonica, and Berea—were all fairly close to each other.

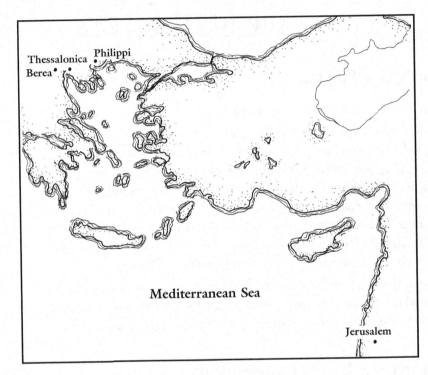

Paul, always one to give credit where credit was due, identified God as the ultimate source of the charity shown by the Macedonian Christians. Indeed, nothing short of a supernatural touch from the Spirit of God would account for the <u>kindness</u> shown by these churches. They had been rocked to the core by a traumatizing combination of Roman oppression (that affected everyone under Roman rule) and persecution (specific to the Christian churches throughout the empire). These were dear saints of God who knew up close and personal both immense suffering and an *abundance* of joy. In the midst of their desperate poverty, their generosity was notable, exceptional, and exemplary.

These believers not only gave according to their ability, but actually exceeded their ability by giving more than their fair share of resources. And it wasn't as if Paul had to badger them to do so. They took the initiative and urged Paul to receive their gifts on behalf of the Jerusalem church.

go to

kindness
Galatians 5:22

The key to their generosity is found in verse 5. Before they gave of themselves to the church in Jerusalem, "they first gave themselves to the Lord" (NKJV). In other words, since they had submitted their lives to Jesus Christ as their Lord, they understood that everything they had was given to them by His grace to be used as He directed. Ultimately, it wasn't their money; it was God's money. They had the unspeakable privilege of being a conduit through which God's resources could flow from His hand to the saints in Jerusalem.

go to

rich
1 Corinthians 4:8

Such giving expressed a phenomenal faith in God. It would be understandable for people in such dire straits to want to hoard their resources—in the fear that with jobs hard to come by, and the possibility of persecution ever lurking in the dark shadows of their troubled minds they might one day need every shekel they could squirrel away. But that's not the calculation made by these precious people of God. They fully understand and embraced the concept Jesus expressed in the Lord's Prayer when He taught His disciples to pray, "Give us this day our daily bread" (Matthew 6:11 NKJV). Just as God was using them to supply the needs of the church in Jerusalem, so God would use others to meet their needs if and when their needs arose.

something to ponder

Indeed, it was *God's will* that they gave to the suffering saints of Jerusalem. They knew it, and they did it. It was that simple.

key point

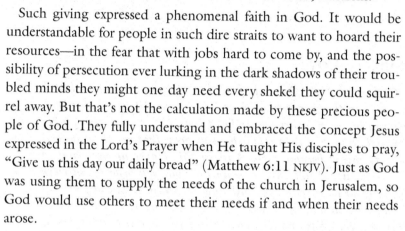

## what others say

### Larry Burkett

For the majority of Christians, serving will never lead to worldwide fame, writing bestselling books, or singing before thousands. But regardless of the work to which we're called, few Christians really cannot afford to give, and when giving is done in love, it exemplifies the greatest sacrifice ever made for mankind—the death of Jesus on the cross.[1]

Trusty old Titus was again pressed into service to complete what he had begun a year earlier when he first urged the Corinthians to take up their collection. You can see a bit of peer pressure being skillfully applied to them by the apostle Paul. Paul laid out his appeal quite nicely. Since the Macedonian Christians gave out of their poverty, the clear implication is that a church as <u>rich</u> as the one in Corinth should do no less than they did by giving sacrificially to meet the needs in Jerusalem.

apply it

But Paul, ever the exhorter, didn't want just the Corinthians' money. He longed that they would manifest all the Christian virtues—*faith* (their deep and abiding trust in God), *speech* (wholesome talk that builds up rather than tears down), *knowledge* (doctrine, their understanding of biblical teaching), *diligence* (an eagerness to follow through on the basic spiritual disciplines of the Christian life), *love* (putting the needs of others ahead of their own), and *grace* (blessing others by giving to others what they don't necessarily deserve, just as God has blessed us by giving to us what we don't deserve.)

## A Sincere Love

2 CORINTHIANS 8:8–15 *I speak not by commandment, but I am testing the sincerity of your love by the diligence of others. For you know the grace of our Lord Jesus Christ, that though He was rich, yet for your sakes He became poor, that you through His poverty might become rich. And in this I give advice: It is to your advantage not only to be doing what you began and were desiring to do a year ago; but now you also must complete the doing of it; that as there was a readiness to desire it, so there also may be a completion out of what you have. For if there is first a willing mind, it is accepted according to what one has, and not according to what he does not have. For I do not mean that others should be eased and you burdened; but by an equality, that now at this time your abundance may supply their lack, that their abundance also may supply your lack—that there may be equality. As it is written, "He who gathered much had nothing left over, and he who gathered little had no lack." (NKJV)*

Paul was pretty up front about the method to his madness where his exhortation to the Corinthians' giving was concerned. He didn't want simply to impose upon them his will. He rather preferred to hold up the Macedonian churches as examples of what genuine Christian charity was all about, in the hope that the church in Corinth would follow suit.

Even more to the point, Paul wanted the Corinthians to emulate their Lord, who, "though he was rich, yet for your sakes he became poor, so that by his poverty he could make you rich" (2 Corinthians 8:9 NLT). Paul reminded his readers that Christ, "being in the form of God, did not consider it robbery to be equal with God, but made

key point

Himself of no reputation, taking the form of a bondservant, and coming in the likeness of men. And being found in appearance as a man, He humbled Himself and became obedient to the point of death, even the death of the cross" (Philippians 2:6–8 NKJV). Think of it—almighty God dying like a common criminal. The rich becoming poor. If He did that for the Corinthians, could they not out of their riches give generously and sacrificially to help those who were truly poor?

Why this need of a reminder? Why didn't the Corinthians complete the process they had started the year before? We can only speculate. The false teachers accused Paul of being a huckster. You might remember that Paul indicated this when he earlier wrote, "For we are not, as so many, peddling the word of God; but as of sincerity, but as from God, we speak in the sight of God in Christ" (2 Corinthians 2:17 NKJV). Could it be that the pseudo-apostles who had infiltrated the Corinthian church were accusing Paul of planning to embezzle the funds that Titus collected on behalf of the church in Jerusalem?

Now that he had regained their trust—this according to the positive report given to Paul by Titus—Paul took up where he had left off and encouraged the Christians in Corinth to complete the task that had been placed on hold for the past year.

## the big picture

### Joel P. Parker

I've heard a lot of pastors quote the bit about sowing and reaping bountifully. They would tell their flock that the more money they gave to the church, the more God would bless them financially. I find it repugnant that a pastor would try to induce anyone to give, promising them some financial reward for their obedience. The command to give was originally given by our Lord, and if someone gives just hoping to receive a greater blessing back, that's just plain wrong. Our motivation to give should come from a heart of love.[2]

Paul chose a great biblical illustration of this principle to amplify what he was saying to the Corinthians. He quoted Exodus 16:18 from the story of God's miraculous and faithful provision of manna to the Israelites as they wandered in the wilderness.

Just as the Israelites pooled their resources to ensure that everyone had something to eat, so too the Corinthians should pool their resources on behalf of the needy in Jerusalem. Those whom God had prospered more should give more; those whom God had prospered less would give less. But put it all together and the needs of God's people would be met, both in Corinth and in Jerusalem.

## Love in Action

key point

If you've hung around the church very long, you've probably heard the phrase "love offering." A love offering is exactly what the name implies, money given to support God's servants out of a heart of love for our God, and for the individual serving our God. A love offering is often given to a guest preacher, a singer, a missionary, or a traveling choir or musical ensemble that ministers during a church service. It's a tangible way in which those who are the recipients and beneficiaries of someone's ministry can give a little back to someone who has shared his or her God-given talents and gifts with them.

The collection taken up by Titus on behalf of the Jerusalem church was in every sense of the word a love offering. The Corinthians were to give according to the way God had prospered them not out of compulsion, but rather out of love—love for God and for the struggling saints in Jerusalem. Paul reminded his readers of this in order to ensure that their motives were proper and pure.

## Honorable in the Sight of God

*2 CORINTHIANS 8:16–24 But thanks be to God who puts the same earnest care for you into the heart of Titus. For he not only accepted the exhortation, but being more diligent, he went to you of his own accord. And we have sent with him the brother whose praise is in the gospel throughout all the churches, and not only that, but who was also chosen by the churches to travel with us with this gift, which is administered by us to the glory of the Lord Himself and to show your ready mind, avoiding this: that anyone should blame us in this lavish gift which is administered by us—providing honorable things, not only in the sight of the Lord, but also in the sight of men. And we have sent with them our brother whom we have often proved diligent in many things, but now much more diligent, because of the great confi-*

*dence which we have in you. If anyone inquires about Titus, he is my partner and fellow worker concerning you. Or if our brethren are inquired about, they are messengers of the churches, the glory of Christ. Therefore show to them, and before the churches, the proof of your love and of our boasting on your behalf. (NKJV)*

Ever mindful of the criticism leveled against him by those who accused him of *peddling* the Word of God, Paul wanted to make absolutely sure that his actions, and those of his emissary Titus, were honorable and aboveboard. We're talking here a rather large sum of money that would be hand-carried over a large distance, in a part of the world in which thieves abounded on land and pirates patrolled the nearby waters of the Mediterranean.

Titus came highly recommended, with glistening credentials established over many years of service to several different churches. He was a man the Corinthians could trust implicitly with their hard-earned funds.

Despite all of the heartache to which the Corinthian believers had subjected the apostle Paul, Titus enthusiastically welcomed the opportunity to visit and serve the church in this way.

Titus was accompanied on his journey by an unnamed colleague, unnamed because he was so well known to the Corinthian assembly that he needed no formal introduction. He too came with unimpeachable credentials, having been appointed by the churches to accompany Paul and Titus with the offering. Paul made it clear that these precautions were being taken "to guard against any criticism for the way we are handling this generous gift" (2 Corinthians 8:20 NLT).

Paul, Titus, and an unnamed brother—such was the level of love that Paul had for the church in Corinth. Paul loved this church, and he requested that in turn they show their love for Titus and his companion when they arrived.

## Promise Keepers

2 CORINTHIANS 9:1–5 *Now concerning the ministering to the saints, it is superfluous for me to write to you; for I know your willingness, about which I boast of you to the Macedonians, that Achaia was ready a year ago; and your zeal has stirred up the majority. Yet I have sent the brethren, lest our boasting of you should be in vain in this respect, that, as I said, you may be*

*ready; lest if some Macedonians come with me and find you unprepared, we (not to mention you!) should be ashamed of this confident boasting. Therefore I thought it necessary to exhort the brethren to go to you ahead of time, and prepare your generous gift beforehand, which you had previously promised, that it may be ready as a matter of generosity and not as a grudging obligation. (NKJV)*

"Put up, or shut up." That's the point where Paul and the Corinthians were at as we come to 2 Corinthians 9. Promises were made. It was now time to collect on those promises.

key point

One can certainly read between the lines that Paul was somewhat doubtful about the Corinthians' follow-through concerning their financial commitments to the church in Jerusalem. This ninth chapter is Paul's attempt to "seal the deal" as it were, to ensure that the Christians in Corinth were now going to fulfill the promises they had made the previous year.

Forgive me for sounding cynical, but when Paul writes, "It is superfluous for me to write to you" (2 Corinthians 9:1 NKJV)—In other words, "I know I don't have to say this but . . ."—I've got to ask, Why the disclaimer if there's no need for it? Paul did indeed need to write to them because, frankly, I don't think he trusted the Christians in Corinth to keep their previous commitment vis-à-vis the offering he was collecting for the church in Jerusalem. And the need there was too great to run the risk that this church would let him down, as they had done on so many other previous occasions.

Once again, Paul applied a little positive peer pressure by indicating (1) that the sacrificial giving by the churches in Macedonia would be supplemented by the generous gifts given by the church in Corinth, and (2) that the Corinthians' participation in the collection motivated the Macedonians to join with them in this financial endeavor. Realizing those two dynamics at play here, the Corinthians did not dare back out now and renege on their commitments.

As if to nudge them a bit farther down the road of sacrificial giving, Paul indicated he was sending Titus and his companion to them to make certain that, when Paul arrived, the money would have already been collected—signed, sealed, and ready to be delivered to the Jerusalem church. I mean, Paul all but admitted that he sent these two trust men ahead of his arrival to make certain that when

Paul finally did arrive, he would not have egg on his face if he found them *unprepared* to take up the promised collection.

If that was the case, Paul would have felt embarrassed because of his "confident boasting" about the Corinthian Christians to those throughout Macedonia. And so Paul wrote, "Therefore I thought it necessary to exhort the brethren to go to you ahead of time, and prepare your generous gift beforehand, which you had previously promised, that it may be ready as a matter of generosity and not as a grudging obligation."

## God Loves a Cheerful Giver

2 CORINTHIANS 9:6–15 *But this I say: He who sows sparingly will also reap sparingly, and he who sows bountifully will also reap bountifully. So let each one give as he purposes in his heart, not grudgingly or of necessity; for God loves a cheerful giver. And God is able to make all grace abound toward you, that you, always having all sufficiency in all things, may have an abundance for every good work. As it is written: "He has dispersed abroad, He has given to the poor; His righteousness endures forever." Now may He who supplies seed to the sower, and bread for food, supply and multiply the seed you have sown and increase the fruits of your righteousness, while you are enriched in everything for all liberality, which causes thanksgiving through us to God. For the administration of this service not only supplies the needs of the saints, but also is abounding through many thanksgivings to God, while, through the proof of this ministry, they glorify God for the obedience of your confession to the gospel of Christ, and for your liberal sharing with them and all men, and by their prayer for you, who long for you because of the exceeding grace of God in you. Thanks be to God for His indescribable gift! (NKJV)*

Paul then developed a theology of giving that is as useful today as it was when Paul first wrote it. He compared our giving to the Lord's work to a farmer who sows seed and reaps a crop. The basic principle is this: He who sows sparingly will reap sparingly, and he who sows bountifully will reap bountifully. Sow a little seed, reap a little crop; sow a lot of seed, reap a bountiful harvest.

**Arthur E. Ball**

In the day of trouble, it is a good thing to be able to come to God as one who has faithfully lived "the offering life." Reminding God of our faithfulness in giving is an important prayer instrument—and it energizes our prayers for others who are in need. Make no mistake. We are not talking about purchasing God's favor. We are talking about coming to God with the evidence of our faith. James writes, "Shew me thy faith without thy works, and I will shew thee my faith by my works" (James 2:18). It is good to be able to show God our faith by our works. Especially in the day of trouble. As the psalmist says, "The Lord hear thee in the day of trouble . . . remember all thy offerings . . . Selah." Think about that.[3]

Even so, God was so concerned that people would corrupt His grace into a give-to-get motivation that He underscored the true motive that should lie behind our giving. He inspired Paul to pen verses 11 and 12, in which God underscored a couple of vitally important principles of giving: "You are enriched in everything for all liberality, which causes thanksgiving through us to God. For the administration of this service not only supplies the needs of the saints, but also is abounding through many thanksgivings to God" (2 Corinthians 9:11–12 NKJV). Let's break these verses apart.

*Principle #1:* God will indeed give bountifully to those who give bountifully, but not so that they might buy more stuff. He gives generously so that we in turn might continue to give generously.

*Principle #2:* Our giving is an act of worship, because those who benefit from our giving will thank God. Just as with every other act of our worship, God should be praised! After all, God is the One "who supplies seed to the sower [the people who give]" (v. 10 NKJV) by providing us with our ability to give. When we do, He promises to provide food for our tables and our other material needs. Therefore, He alone is worthy of praise—both from us because God enables us to give, and from those who receive our gifts, because ultimately our gifts come from His hand.

Part of the benefit to the gift-giver is the fact that the recipients of the gift will "glorify God for the obedience" (v. 13 NKJV) of the Corinthian Christians to the Christian ethic of selfless love. Likewise, the gift-receivers will pray for the gift-givers "because of the exceeding grace of God in you," as manifested by their sacrificial gift.

Here's the bottom line: God demonstrated His great love for us by giving to us "His indescribable gift" (v. 15 NKJV). We demonstrate godliness—godlike love—when we give a sacrificial gift to God's work or God's people. We are never more Godlike than when we give humbly, graciously, and self-sacrificially.

## Chapter Wrap-Up

key point

- Paul thanked the Macedonians for their charity toward the Jerusalem Christians, but gave the ultimate credit to God.
- Paul mentioned the willing charity of the Macedonians to motivate the Corinthians to do the same kind of freewill giving.
- In 2 Corinthians 9:7, Paul gives us one of the Bible's most familiar quotes: "God loves a cheerful giver" (NKJV), meaning that we should support our churches willingly, with joy, rather than grudgingly and with resentment.

## Study Questions

1. What were the six Christian virtues that Paul identified at the beginning of this section of 2 Corinthians?

2. Are Christians in the New Testament formally admonished to tithe?

3. What are the two principles, found in chapter 9 of 2 Corinthians, that tell us how we are to give to others?

# 2 Corinthians 10:1–12:13
# A Survivor's Guide to Suffering

**Chapter Highlights:**
• What You Think
• Building or Destroying
• A Misplaced Standard
• Light or Darkness?
• World-Class Suffering
• Behind the Curtain

## Let's Get Started

An abrupt change in tone occurs in chapters 10–12. It becomes so dramatically different that a debate has raged for years over how the last four chapters of 2 Corinthians relate to the first nine. Some Bible teachers go so far as to say that 2 Corinthians 10–13 form the nucleus of a totally separate letter, one that was circulated independently of 2 Corinthians 1–9. Others suggest that the final four chapters were actually excerpted from Paul's "severe" letter and were later added to the end of 2 Corinthians.

However, nothing in the text suggests anything other than that these chapters form the conclusion to 2 Corinthians, a letter that was both exhilarating and agonizing for Paul to write. Exhilarating, because much of the letter was written in response to the good report Paul received from Titus; agonizing, because as will be evident in our study of these final four chapters, false apostles were still exerting a harmful influence in the Corinthian church that threatened to undermine all that Paul and his companions had tried so desperately to accomplish.

The most accurate way to interpret these chapters is as follows: The first nine chapters were written to the repentant majority in the church who turned away from the pseudo-apostles and submitted to the apostolic authority of Paul. The final four chapters were written to the sinful minority who continued to be held hostage to the teachings of the false teachers, who were still trying to shake the others' confidence in Paul and commandeer the church by assuming positions of power within it.

key point

As we are about to see, this is spiritual warfare of the most blatant nature. Paul is literally fighting tooth and tong for the soul of this church, a battle that is fiercely being waged with the future of the church and the eternal destinies of people hanging in the balance

"The weapons of our warfare are not carnal but mighty in God for pulling down strongholds." So wrote Paul in 2 Corinthians 10:4 (NKJV).

Up to this point in the letter, Paul was talking around the issue of the spiritual warfare taking place in the church. Now he will hit it directly.

## You Are What You Think

*2 Corinthians 10:1–6 Now I, Paul, myself am pleading with you by the meekness and gentleness of Christ—who in presence am lowly among you, but being absent am bold toward you. But I beg you that when I am present I may not be bold with that confidence by which I intend to be bold against some, who think of us as if we walked according to the flesh. For though we walk in the flesh, we do not war according to the flesh. For the weapons of our warfare are not carnal but mighty in God for pulling down strongholds, casting down arguments and every high thing that exalts itself against the knowledge of God, bringing every thought into captivity to the obedience of Christ, and being ready to punish all disobedience when your obedience is fulfilled. (NKJV)*

On one level, spiritual warfare is a battle for the mind—a battle for ideas. Perhaps you have heard the old adage "You are what you eat." That's not quite true when it comes to the realm of spiritual warfare. More accurately, "You are what you think." More often than not, a spiritual attack by the enemy against us is an assault on the way we think. Spiritual warfare is a battle of ideas.

When Lucifer sinned and became Satan, he allowed himself to be duped by his own faulty ideas. He honestly believed that he could make himself God. Armed with that faulty belief, He leveled five verbal assaults against God, culminating in his brazen assertion, "I will be like the Most High" (Isaiah 14:14 NKJV). His self-absorbed, narcissistic belief about himself became his undoing.

He repeated this pattern in the Garden of Eden when he assaulted Eve with a faulty belief system. He first sowed the seeds of doubt in her mind when he slyly asked, "Has God indeed said, 'You shall not eat of every tree of the garden'?" (Genesis 3:1 NKJV). He next completely contradicted God's Word when he declared, "You will not surely die" (3:4 NKJV). The final blow came as he convinced the woman that "you will be like God" (3:5 NKJV). Satan's assault on Eve was a battle of ideas. For the sad fact is this: One's faulty theology will lead to a compromised morality.

key point

Suffice it to say that there was a blatant attempt on the part of some in Corinth to corrupt the thinking of many of the Christians there. The motivation of these false teachers? The same motivation as was behind Satan's eventual demise and his seduction of Eve—power. Their appeal to the immature believers in Corinth was that they possessed the power to live, any way they wanted to live irrespective of the revealed will of God as expressed through the pen of Paul. In an attempt to persuade the people away from the message of their founding apostle, these emissaries of Satan sought to discredit the messenger.

The slam on Paul was that sure, it's easy to sound bold or authoritative when you are writing from a distance. Anyone can hide behind a pen. But face-to-face he is a meek and gentle little lamb, a man of no real conviction or authority. Paul assured them that contrary to that slanderous report, though Paul didn't want to hit them with the full force of his apostolic hammer when he came, he would not hesitate to do so if the situation failed to improve.

Paul acknowledged that the church was embroiled in a spiritual battle that threatened its very soul. He was determined to fight it, to exterminate every last vestige of spiritual opposition coming from those who sought to discredit him. He put this small faction of followers on notice that he would use every weapon at his disposal to expose their leaders and to remove their influence from their lives. This was his promise to these pseudo-apostles and to their small band of followers: "Casting down arguments and every high thing that exalts itself against the knowledge of God, bringing every thought into captivity to the obedience of Christ, and being ready to punish all disobedience when your obedience is fulfilled" (2 Corinthians 10:5–6 NKJV).

**what others say**

**Joyce Meyer**

The Bible presents a lot of detailed instruction on what kinds of things we are to think about. I am sure that you can see from [Philippians 4:8] that we are instructed to think on good things, things that will build us up and not tear us down. Our thoughts certainly affect our attitudes and moods. Everything the Lord tells us is for our own good. He knows what will make us happy and what will make us miserable. When a person is full of wrong thoughts he is miserable, and I have learned from personal experience that when a person is miserable, he usually ends up making others miserable also. You should take inventory on a regular basis, and ask yourself, "What have I been thinking about?" Spend some time examining your thought life.[1]

## Building Up or Tearing Down

*2 CORINTHIANS 10:7–11 Do you look at things according to the outward appearance? If anyone is convinced in himself that he is Christ's, let him again consider this in himself, that just as he is Christ's, even so we are Christ's. For even if I should boast somewhat more about our authority, which the Lord gave us for edification and not for your destruction, I shall not be ashamed—lest I seem to terrify you by letters. "For his letters," they say, "are weighty and powerful, but his bodily presence is weak, and his speech contemptible." Let such a person consider this, that what we are in word by letters when we are absent, such we will also be in deed when we are present. (NKJV)*

apply it

At the tail end of this letter, Paul challenged those who followed the false teachers as to whether they were true followers of Jesus Christ. He warned them to "examine yourselves to see whether you are in the faith; test yourselves. Do you not realize that Christ Jesus is in you—unless, of course, you fail the test?" (13:5 NIV). One of the test questions could well have been, "What is your response to the truth the apostle Paul has taught you?"

That's essentially the question Paul puts to this minority segment of the Corinthian church population here. He basically tells them that a true follower of Jesus will recognize the true servants of Christ. If they reject the truth as revealed by God to Paul, and through him to the Corinthians, then they are giving evidence that they are not Christ's followers at all. As Paul said in 2 Corinthians 10:7: "Do you look at things according to the outward appearance? If anyone is convinced in himself that he is Christ's, let him again consider this in himself, that just as he is Christ's, even so we are Christ's" (NKJV).

The false apostles, of course, were claiming to be the true followers of Christ while denying the authenticity of Paul's apostolic authority. But talk is cheap. Given Paul's unassailable credentials, they could not merely write him off as a phony. For them to deny the authority of what Paul taught was to expose themselves for what they truly were, "savage wolves . . . speaking perverse things, to draw away the disciples after themselves" (Acts 20:29–30 NKJV).

As we mentioned earlier, a part of their attack was to suggest the following: "Paul's letters are demanding and forceful, but in person he is weak, and his speeches are worthless!" (2 Corinthians 10:10 NLT). To those who were saying that, Paul gave this word of warning: "Those people should realize that our actions when we arrive in person will be as forceful as what we say in our letters from far away" (10:11 NLT). In other words, they would soon feel the full force of his Spirit-filled ministry if they did not repent of their false accusations and stop their false teaching.

key point

There's a bit of knife-twisting going on in this passage. When Paul wrote that God gave him his apostolic authority "for edification and not for your destruction" (2 Corinthians 10:8 NKJV), his implication could not have been clearer. The false apostles were using their "authority" to destroy the church; Paul was working tirelessly to preserve the church. That fact alone should have been ample evidence of who was on the side of the angels in this ongoing dispute.

It's a simple matter of examining the fruit of someone's life and ministry. Jesus put it this way in the Sermon on the Mount: "Beware of false prophets, who come to you in sheep's clothing, but inwardly they are ravenous wolves. You will know them by their fruits. Do men gather grapes from thornbushes or figs from thistles? Even so, every good tree bears good fruit, but a bad tree bears bad fruit. A good tree cannot bear bad fruit, nor can a bad tree bear good fruit. Every tree that does not bear good fruit is cut down and thrown into the fire. Therefore by their fruits you will know them" (Matthew 7:15–20 NKJV).

something to ponder

An honest appraisal of the ministries of these infiltrators would have revealed a wide swath of pain and destruction as they came into the church and tore the place apart. The damage these pseudo-apostles did to a true, God-called apostle was unconscionable. They showed nothing but contempt for one of God's choice servants. "His letters . . . are weighty and powerful," they mocked as they accused Paul of trying to terrorize the church by his writings. Adding insult to that injury, they sneered that Paul's "bodily presence is weak, and his speech contemptible."

These evil men built no one up while tearing many down. That should have caused the discerning among them to resist these men and to apply proper church discipline to them, something Paul was now trying to do in their stead.

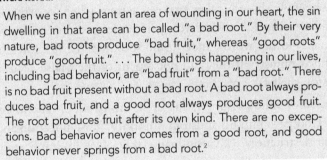

what others say

**Edward Kurath**

When we sin and plant an area of wounding in our heart, the sin dwelling in that area can be called "a bad root." By their very nature, bad roots produce "bad fruit," whereas "good roots" produce "good fruit." . . . The bad things happening in our lives, including bad behavior, are "bad fruit" from a "bad root." There is no bad fruit present without a bad root. A bad root always produces bad fruit, and a good root always produces good fruit. The root produces fruit after its own kind. There are no exceptions. Bad behavior never comes from a good root, and good behavior never springs from a bad root.[2]

## A Misplaced Standard

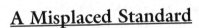

2 CORINTHIANS 10:12–18 *For we dare not class ourselves or compare ourselves with those who commend themselves. But they, measuring themselves by themselves, and comparing themselves among themselves, are not wise. We, however, will not boast beyond measure, but within the limits of the sphere which God appointed us—a sphere which especially includes you. For we are not overextending ourselves (as though our authority did not extend to you), for it was to you that we came with the gospel of Christ; not boasting of things beyond measure, that is, in other men's labors, but having hope, that as your faith is increased, we shall be greatly enlarged by you in our sphere, to preach the gospel in the regions beyond you, and not to boast in another man's sphere of accomplishment. But "he who glories, let him glory in the LORD." For not he who commends himself is approved, but whom the Lord commends. (NKJV)*

We get a real insight into the thinking of truly evil people in this portion of Scripture. Speaking of these false teachers Paul wrote, "They, measuring themselves by themselves, and comparing themselves among themselves, are not wise." In other words, they feel no sense of guilt or shame about their destructive actions because they only compare their behavior with one another's. You know the saying "Birds of a feather flock together." It's also true of false teachers. They dared not compare themselves with Paul and the other true servants of Christ. The differences would have been stark in the extreme. But because they only compared themselves with themselves, they felt justified in their actions and reinforced in their teaching. They set the standards for their own behavior, established their own code of conduct. And the standard that they chose was their own evil behavior. *That* is a dangerous place to be.

go to

**Gentiles**
Romans 11:13

"We are not overextending ourselves (as though our authority did not extend to you), for it was to you that we came with the gospel of Christ" (2 Corinthians 10:14 NKJV). That gave Paul the right to exercise his oversight in the church. He wanted nothing more than to settle the problems in Corinth and stabilize the church so he could extend his ministry beyond Corinth, "to preach the gospel in the regions beyond you" (10:16 NKJV). Paul had the God-given mandate as the apostle to the <u>Gentiles</u> because he was approved by God to carry out that ministry, unlike the false teachers whose only approval they received was their own.

"If he who comes preaches another Jesus whom we have not preached, or if you receive a different spirit which you have not received, or a different gospel which you have not accepted—you may well put up with it!" (2 Corinthians 11:4 NKJV). There it is. The truth exposed. Simple-minded Christians who lack discernment, easy prey for the smooth words and slick packaging of Satan's emissaries. In light of the Corinthians' coming under the sway of these evil men, Paul will now draw an even starker contrast between himself and them, more so than at any other point in 1 or 2 Corinthians.

## <u>Angels of Light or Darkness?</u>

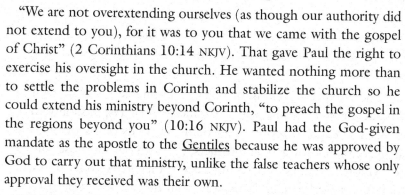

**the big picture**

### 2 Corinthians 11:1–15

While most of the church in Corinth had come to their senses, repented of following the false teachers in their midst, and returned to the teaching of their founding apostle, Paul, a segment of the church held firm to their convictions that Paul was a phony and these pseudo-apostles were the real deal. These deceived Christians were all-too-willing to believe whatever these false teachers taught them, something that Paul found reprehensible. He addressed his concerns in this portion of Scripture.

key point

Paul felt as protective of the church in Corinth as a newlywed husband ought to feel for his wedded wife. But he was constrained to guard tenaciously the purity of this church, and to present her as a "chaste virgin to Christ" (2 Corinthians 11:2 NKJV). But that was not possible. The church had been wooed away from her Savior and His true servants. The same satanic serpent who deceived Eve by his craftiness corrupted the simplicity of the Corinthians' faith in Christ.

**key point**

How did this happen? Many in the church in Corinth—especially their leaders—were willing accomplices. They allowed themselves to become unwitting dupes by tolerating the false teachings of these false teachers.

Thus the conflicts in Corinth were the inevitable result of their leaders' dereliction of duty when it came to their responsibility to guard their flock from those who would sow seeds of discord into the congregation. "I urge you, brothers, to watch out for those who cause divisions and put obstacles in your way that are contrary to the teaching you have learned. Keep away from them" (Romans 16:17 NIV), Paul urged the church in Rome. "Warn a divisive person once, and then warn him a second time. After that, have nothing to do with him" (Titus 3:10 NIV), Paul commanded Titus.

**something to ponder**

We have previously noted that Paul was an average communicator at best. That was one of the charges repeatedly brought against him. He even readily admitted, "I am untrained in speech" (2 Corinthians 11:6 NKJV). The false teachers evidently had a knack for using communication skills. They were entertaining, perhaps spellbinding in their presentations. One indication of the shallowness of the Corinthians was that they were so easily manipulated by the false teachers, and gave them more deference than they did to the teacher of truth.

Unlike the false teachers, Paul ministered to the Corinthians free of charge. He received no salary from the church, working (as we have seen) as a tentmaker to support himself. His truly was a labor of love in the purest sense of the word.

Unlike Paul, the false apostles were "deceitful workers, transforming themselves into apostles of Christ. And no wonder! For Satan himself transforms himself into an angel of light" (2 Corinthians 11:13–14 NKJV). As we have said, they knew the lingo. They knew when to stand up and when to sit down. They answered all the questions correctly and said all the right things. On the outside, they appeared to be the genuine article. But on the inside they were ravenous wolves.

Fortunately God makes us this promise: "[Their] end will be according to their works" (11:15 NKJV). No one can destroy the work of God and continually attack and oppose the servants of God without paying a hefty price. Woe to them. Sure, they may prosper in the short term—the devil always rewards his own, temporarily. But in the end, their end will be just.

## World-Class Suffering

**the big picture**

### 2 Corinthians 11:16–33

Put Paul, the true apostle, side by side with the false apostles and there's no comparison. His résumé, unlike theirs, was written in his own blood. While they were benefiting from their ministries—with power, prestige, and wealth—Paul's ministry took an enormous toll on the beleaguered apostle.

Really, Paul did not want to trumpet his own cause or toot his own horn. But by this point in the letter, he felt he had no choice. So even though he felt foolish doing so, he juxtaposed his experiences with those of the false teachers, in essence to allow his readers to decide for themselves who was the real apostle.

But when you think about it, what did Paul have to lose? He absolutely detested what these false teachers were doing to them. Paul said: "You put up with it if one brings you into bondage, if one devours you, if one takes from you, if one exalts himself, if one strikes you on the face. To our shame I say that we were too weak for that! But in whatever anyone is bold—I speak foolishly—I am bold also" (2 Corinthians 11:20–21 NKJV).

So Paul was weak? I'll say he was weak. But not for the reasons that the false teachers claimed when they mocked him. He was weak for a whole host of other reasons. Check it out:

2 CORINTHIANS 11:23–33 *Are they ministers of Christ?—I speak as a fool—I am more: in labors more abundant, in stripes above measure, in prisons more frequently, in deaths often.*

*From the Jews five times I received forty stripes minus one. Three times I was beaten with rods; once I was stoned; three times I was shipwrecked; a night and a day I have been in the deep; in journeys often, in perils of waters, in perils of robbers, in perils of my own countrymen, in perils of the Gentiles, in perils in the city, in perils in the wilderness, in perils in the sea, in perils among false brethren; in weariness and toil, in sleeplessness often, in hunger and thirst, in fastings often, in cold and nakedness—besides the other things, what comes upon me daily: my deep concern for all the churches. Who is weak, and I am not weak? Who is made to stumble, and I do not burn with indignation? If I must boast, I will boast in the things which concern my infirmity. The God and Father of our Lord Jesus Christ, who is blessed forever, knows that I am not lying. In Damascus the governor, under Aretas the king, was guarding the city of the Damascenes with a garrison, desiring to arrest me; but I was let down in a basket through a window in the wall, and escaped from his hands.* (NKJV)

You want to talk about weak? How humiliating for the then-young disciple to have to escape from a hostile Jewish mob in Damascus via a basket. Paul was, of course, recounting the situation when "after many days were past, the Jews plotted to kill him. But their plot became known to Saul. And they watched the gates day and night, to kill him. Then the disciples took him by night and let him down through the wall in a large basket" (Acts 9:23–25 NKJV).

King Aretas, the Nabatean ruler at the time, was in on the plot, indicating that this relatively new Christian convert was not only an enemy of the Jews but an enemy of the state as well. How ironic that the man who traveled to Damascus to imprison or kill the Christians there ended up a Christian himself, and was hunted much like those he himself had planned to hunt.

Paul continued to press the point that he, and not the pseudo-apostles attempting to commandeer the church, was the true apostle. Paul felt *compelled* (12:11 NKJV) to press his case further by disclosing an event in his life that he normally never referenced, one that took place fourteen years prior to this writing.

**key point**

## A Glimpse Behind the Curtain

2 CORINTHIANS 12:1–6 *It is doubtless not profitable for me to boast. I will come to visions and revelations of the Lord: I know*

*a man in Christ who fourteen years ago—whether in the body I do not know, or whether out of the body I do not know, God knows—such a one was caught up to the third heaven. And I know such a man—whether in the body or out of the body I do not know, God knows—how he was caught up into Paradise and heard inexpressible words, which it is not lawful for a man to utter. Of such a one I will boast; yet of myself I will not boast, except in my infirmities. For though I might desire to boast, I will not be a fool; for I will speak the truth. But I refrain, lest anyone should think of me above what he sees me to be or hears from me. (NKJV)*

Fourteen years prior to his writing 2 Corinthians, Paul saw a vision of heaven. I use the word *vision* loosely because Paul readily admitted that he wasn't sure if he was in the body or out of the body—whether this all took place in his head or if he was actually transported into heaven.

He was so reluctant to talk about it that he did so only in the third person. But when he did, he disclosed to his readers that he was "caught up to the third heaven" (12:2 NKJV). He went through the atmosphere where the birds of heaven fly; through the vast universe where the stars of heaven shine; all the way to God's dwelling place, *Paradise*, the heaven of the heavens.

Some equated this vision with the riot that happened in Lystra in Acts 14:19, where we read that "they stoned Paul and dragged him out of the city, supposing him to be dead" (NKJV). However, that occurrence does not fit with the fourteen-year time line. Whenever it happened, Paul was privileged by God to experience it.

Unlike people today, who supposedly receive a vision and then proceed to hire a publicist, make the Christian radio and television talk-show circuit, and write a best-selling book about it, Paul recoiled at the thought that he would make this public. He did so only because the dire circumstances in Corinth demanded that he do so. And even then, he admitted that "to keep me from becoming conceited because of these surpassingly great revelations, there was given me a thorn in my flesh, a messenger of Satan, to torment me" (2 Corinthians 12:7 NIV). Such visions as experienced by the apostle Paul are extremely rare, and ought to be received in humble gratitude rather than with an attitude of boastful pride.

# Paul's Thorn in the Flesh

*2 CORINTHIANS 12:7–13 And lest I should be exalted above measure by the abundance of the revelations, a thorn in the flesh was given to me, a messenger of Satan to buffet me, lest I be exalted above measure. Concerning this thing I pleaded with the Lord three times that it might depart from me. And He said to me, "My grace is sufficient for you, for My strength is made perfect in weakness." Therefore most gladly I will rather boast in my infirmities, that the power of Christ may rest upon me. Therefore I take pleasure in infirmities, in reproaches, in needs, in persecutions, in distresses, for Christ's sake. For when I am weak, then I am strong. I have become a fool in boasting; you have compelled me. For I ought to have been commended by you; for in nothing was I behind the most eminent apostles, though I am nothing. Truly the signs of an apostle were accomplished among you with all perseverance, in signs and wonders and mighty deeds. For what is it in which you were inferior to other churches, except that I myself was not burdensome to you? Forgive me this wrong! (NKJV)*

Much speculation has been offered over the years as to what exactly Paul's thorn in the flesh might have been. Here are the top contenders:

Some believe that it was a physical infirmity. Suggestions have been made that Paul suffered from boils, sores, migraine headaches, hearing loss, a speech impediment, malaria, exhaustion, or most typically an acute eye problem. Paul did write the churches in Galatia, "You would have plucked out your own eyes and given them to me" (Galatians 4:15 NKJV), and "See with what large letters I have written to you with my own hand!" (Galatians 6:11 NKJV).

Others opt for the idea that Paul's problems were spiritual. They suggest that Paul may have been battling some besetting sin, this because of his admission that "the good that I will to do, I do not do; but the evil I will not to do, that I practice. . . . O wretched man that I am!" (Romans 7:19, 24 NKJV). Still others think it was more emotional in nature, because Paul told the church in Corinth, "I was with you in weakness, in fear, and in much trembling" (1 Corinthians 2:3 NKJV). Some even believe that Paul suffered with clinical depression, as indicated by his statement in Romans 9:2: "I have great sorrow and continual grief in my heart" (NKJV). Yet none of the above explanations fit the context of 2 Corinthians.

**The Smart Guide to the Bible**

The most likely explanation is the most obvious: Paul suffered the unrelenting attack of those determined to discredit and destroy him. The word *messenger* suggests someone in a position of influence empowered by Satan. At the hands of this ringleader of the opposition, Paul was subjected to an ongoing campaign of unrelenting criticism, false accusations, malicious gossips, whiners, and complainers who came against him and sought to discredit him before the whole church. Paul may have even mentioned his name to Timothy: "Alexander the coppersmith did me much harm" (2 Timothy 4:14 NKJV).

Yet he and the people he led against Paul were not ultimately victorious. They never are. Paul wrote, "Concerning this thing I pleaded with the Lord three times that it might depart from me. And He said to me, 'My grace is sufficient for you, for My strength is made perfect in weakness.' Therefore most gladly I will rather boast in my infirmities, that the power of Christ may rest upon me. Therefore I take pleasure in infirmities, in reproaches, in needs, in persecutions, in distresses, for Christ's sake. For when I am weak, then I am strong" (2 Corinthians 12:8–10 NKJV).

Please note that there are times when God answers our prayers with a decisive "No." Three times Paul prayed that God would remove his thorn in the flesh—literally translated as a "stake" driven through his flesh—and three times God refused to grant him his request. But God did assure Paul that He would not abandon His suffering servant to face the pain alone. "My grace is sufficient for you," God reminded Paul, "for My strength is made perfect in [your] weakness." Oftentimes, God's answer to our requests is not to remove our difficult circumstances, but rather to give us the grace to endure them.

key point

**what others say**

**Charles Swindoll**

Now, I need to point out that I'm not qualified to give you the intimate details of how Saul's thorn affected him. However, he does confess that he begged the Lord on three separate occasions to remove it from him (v. 8). And you know what? We would have done the same. You and I would have prayed and prayed and prayed and begged for relief. "Father, please take away the *thorn*. Lord, I beg of You, remove it. Take this pain away from me." That was Saul's response. I see amazing transparency within those lines. The world needs more followers of Christ who embrace pain and hardship rather than deny it. How helpful for us to see all this as God's plan to keep us humble. That can't be taught in Bible colleges or seminaries. Those lessons are learned in the harsh realities of life. What people of prayer we would become! How often we would turn to Him. How fully we would lean on Him. And what insights we would glean.[3]

Paul felt foolish defending himself in this way. But what choice did he have? "You have compelled me," he told them. He added (my paraphrase),

> You should have run to my defense in the face of these "most eminent apostles." You saw firsthand the "signs and wonders and mighty deeds" I did when I was with you. Your recollection of that should have ended their arguments once and for all. And not only did I prove myself to be the genuine article to you; I have done all of this in the other churches that I started as well. The only thing I did differently in Corinth is that I didn't charge you for my ministry. I gave it to you free of charge. Perhaps you would have appreciated it and respected it more if I had charged you a salary. If I was wrong in showing you this extra measure of my kindness and grace, forgive me.

Well, the lines had been drawn, the issues put on the table. Now it was time for the church as a whole, and this group of rebels in particular, to make some tough choices. To further encourage them, Paul assured them that he was now going to make a third visit to them.

# Chapter Wrap-Up

- Paul makes an abrupt change in tone in 2 Corinthians, chapters 10–12. Despite the good news Titus had brought him about the church's eagerness to have him visit, in this section he was forced to deal directly with the sinful minority of members who were still listening to false teachers and were questioning Paul's divinely inspired teachings.

- Paul acknowledged that the church was in the middle of a horrendous spiritual battle, but he was still determined to fight it. Most important, he was not as weak and mild as some believed; on the contrary, he was prepared to assert his full, righteous, apostolic authority, if necessary.

- Paul warned the false teachers to examine themselves; to appraise their own motives and see whether what they were doing was of God or of Satan. But he also warned them not to assess themselves by comparing themselves to others of the same ilk!

- Paul examined his own motives and credentials, and laid them all out for the Corinthians to see, including his own "thorn in the flesh" that they were probably familiar with, but which has never been conclusively identified to modern scholars.

# Study Questions

1. Can you name three specific physical sufferings that Paul said he had endured?

2. At one point, Paul had either a vision or a literal, out-of-body experience in which he was shown many divine things. Regardless of how this was accomplished, where was he taken?

3. What do you believe Paul's "thorn in the flesh" might have been?

# 2 Corinthians 12:14–13:14
# Ready or Not, Here I Come

**Chapter Highlights:**
- Positive Parenting Skills
- Mourning Song
- A Final Heartfelt Plea
- Summary Statement
- A Final Farewell

## Let's Get Started

We have finally entered the end game as far as Paul's correspondence to the Corinthians is concerned. Here he shifted his focus away from the immediate problems in the church to his upcoming visit, during which he sincerely hoped once and for all to stabilize the church and get them back on track as far as their mission in their community was concerned.

Paul certainly hoped that "three time's a charm." His first visit was his extended stay, during which he founded and sought to establish the church in Corinth as recorded in Acts 18. Subsequent to that, Paul made his "painful" visit. Now he laid out his plans for his third visit, one that he sincerely hoped would be quite different from the last.

key point

## Positive Parenting Skills

**2 CORINTHIANS 12:14–18** *Now for the third time I am ready to come to you. And I will not be burdensome to you; for I do not seek yours, but you. For the children ought not to lay up for the parents, but the parents for the children. And I will very gladly spend and be spent for your souls; though the more abundantly I love you, the less I am loved. But be that as it may, I did not burden you. Nevertheless, being crafty, I caught you by cunning! Did I take advantage of you by any of those whom I sent to you? I urged Titus, and sent our brother with him. Did Titus take advantage of you? Did we not walk in the same spirit? Did we not walk in the same steps?* (NKJV)

Paul began this last section of his letter by writing as if he were an estranged parent. And to one small segment of the Corinthian congregation he was. Nevertheless, in his undying efforts to hold the family together, he assured his readers that when he came he did not intend to be financially *burdensome* to them; as before, this third visit would be from start to finish a labor of love. Perhaps still feeling the

something to ponder

sting of the accusation that he was motivated by money—huckstering the gospel—he made it clear that he wanted nothing from them. "I do not seek yours," he told them. He sought not their resources; he sought them.

**key point**

And just like a parent reaching out to an estranged child, he was prepared to do whatever it took, pay whatever price required in terms of his personal sacrifice and effort—"I will very gladly spend and be spent for your souls," is how the New King James Version puts it—in order to ensure that those in this rebel faction were true followers of Christ. After all, he was going to visit Corinth with the urgency of one who understood that the eternal destinies of these people's souls was very much on the line.

Yet despite these assurances, some in this faction of the church had been so deluded in their thinking by the accusations of their false teachers that Paul had to resort to saying this: "Be that as it may, I did not burden you. Nevertheless, being crafty, I caught you by cunning! Did I take advantage of you by any of those whom I sent to you? I urged Titus, and sent our brother with him. Did Titus take advantage of you? Did we not walk in the same spirit? Did we not walk in the same steps?" (2 Corinthians 12:16–18 NKJV).

There wasn't a hint of truth to what the leaders of this rebel band were saying. Paul and Titus conducted themselves in an absolutely honorable fashion. These people rejected Paul and followed the others through no fault of his. Those who chose to reject him did so in response to the devil's deceptions, through his messengers sent by him to infiltrate this church and wreak havoc on its members. Obviously, Satan's minions were still having a field day—a tragedy of inestimable proportions given the immensity of the spiritual need in the community they were responsible to reach.

## Mourning Song

2 CORINTHIANS 12:19–21 *Again, do you think that we excuse ourselves to you? We speak before God in Christ. But we do all things, beloved, for your edification. For I fear lest, when I come, I shall not find you such as I wish, and that I shall be found by you such as you do not wish; lest there be contentions, jealousies, outbursts of wrath, selfish ambitions, backbitings, whisperings, conceits, tumults; lest, when I come again, my God*

*will humble me among you, and I shall mourn for many who have sinned before and have not repented of the uncleanness, fornication, and lewdness which they have practiced. (NKJV)*

Paul's singular motivation was to build up the people of the church in Corinth, despite the enormous pain and suffering he had experienced because of many of them. Dare I say it? Paul was fearful. He was fearful that when he came he wouldn't like what he found. He was fearful that he would have to witness firsthand their quarreling, jealousy, anger, selfishness, slander, gossip, arrogance, and disorderly behavior. He was fearful that he would discover that some in the church had yet to give up their old immoral sins.

> **what others say**
>
> **Robert Benson**
>
> We have far more in common than we often think we do. The things that keep Christians apart from other Christians are not nearly so important to me these days as are the things that bind us to one another. It is curious how we seem to talk so much about the former and pay so little attention to the latter.[1]

In his bones Paul knew the truth—that the problems plaguing the church in Corinth were caused not so much by the truly converted Christians there, but by those church members who were not truly Christians at all. Jesus's ominous words at the conclusion of His Sermon on the Mount would certainly apply to the church in Corinth: "Not everyone who says to Me, 'Lord, Lord,' shall enter the kingdom of heaven, but he who does the will of My Father in heaven. Many will say to Me in that day, 'Lord, Lord, have we not prophesied in Your name, cast out demons in Your name, and done many wonders in Your name?' And then I will declare to them, 'I never knew you; depart from Me, you who practice lawlessness!'" (Matthew 7:21–23 NKJV). There were those in the congregation who would hear those words, "Depart from me . . . I never knew you." Paul felt compelled to warn them of their dire destiny.

## A Final Heartfelt Plea

2 CORINTHIANS 13:1–6 *This will be the third time I am coming to you. "By the mouth of two or three witnesses every word shall be established." I have told you before, and foretell as if I*

*were present the second time, and now being absent I write to those who have sinned before, and to all the rest, that if I come again I will not spare—since you seek a proof of Christ speaking in me, who is not weak toward you, but mighty in you. For though He was crucified in weakness, yet He lives by the power of God. For we also are weak in Him, but we shall live with Him by the power of God toward you. Examine yourselves as to whether you are in the faith. Test yourselves. Do you not know yourselves, that Jesus Christ is in you?—unless indeed you are disqualified. But I trust that you will know that we are not disqualified. (NKJV)*

Paul left no doubt that he would come bolstered by his full apostolic authority to set things in order in Corinth. With those who were still in a spiritual state of unrepentant sin Paul was going to deal finally and decisively. "I will not spare you," he told them. Implication, *Like your leaders who have been unwilling to do what needs to be done.* What needed to be done was good old-fashioned church discipline as outlined in Matthew 18 and 1 Corinthians 5. Those who were unrepentant needed to be put out of the church, in the hope that then they would finally come to their senses, repent, and then be restored to the fellowship.

key point

Remember what we just read in 2 Corinthians 12:21: "I am afraid God will make me ashamed when I visit you again. I will feel like crying because many of you have never given up your old sins. You are still doing things that are immoral, indecent, and shameful" (CEV). Well, they wouldn't be permitted to do "immoral, indecent, and shameful" things once Paul arrived.

If the slam on Paul was that "'his letters,' they say, 'are weighty and powerful, but his bodily presence is weak, and his speech contemptible'" (2 Corinthians 10:10 NKJV), and so they blew him off as an inconsequential bag of wind, they were in for a shock. For just as Jesus was crucified when He was weak and bloodied, but now "lives by the power of God," so Paul was beaten into a weakened state but would soon arrive in the power of God. No longer would it be business as usual in the church in Corinth.

apply it

It has been an undercurrent of thought throughout 1 and 2 Corinthians that there are times when church discipline is mandated. Whenever church leaders choose to appease the sinners in their church by essentially giving them a pass on their sins, the inevitable result will be to re-create Corinth in all of its sin-sick impotence.

The core issue was this: There were too many members of the church in Corinth who thought they were saved, when truly they were not. So Paul put them to the test. "Examine yourselves as to whether you are in the faith. Test yourselves. Do you not know yourselves, that Jesus Christ is in you?—unless indeed you are disqualified" (2 Corinthians 13:5 NKJV). Since many of these individuals were living as if Christ were absent from their lives, Paul feared—rightly so—that they weren't Christians at all.

As Paul also wrote to the church in Corinth, "In the name of our Lord Jesus Christ, when you are gathered together, along with my spirit, with the power of our Lord Jesus Christ, deliver such a one to Satan for the destruction of the flesh, that his spirit may be saved in the day of the Lord Jesus. . . . But now I have written to you not to keep company with anyone named a brother, who is sexually immoral, or covetous, or an idolater, or a reviler, or a drunkard, or an extortioner—not even to eat with such a person" (1 Corinthians 5:4–5, 11 NKJV).

---

**what others say**

**John MacArthur Jr.**

Our Lord's words about eternal life were invariably accompanied by warnings to those who might be tempted to take salvation lightly. He taught that the cost of following Him is high, that the way is narrow and few find it. He said many who call Him Lord will be forbidden from entering the kingdom of heaven (see Matthew 7:13–23). Present-day evangelicalism, by and large, ignores those warnings. The prevailing view of what constitutes saving faith continues to grow broader and more shallow, while the portrayal of Christ in preaching and witnessing becomes fuzzy. Anyone who claims to be a Christian can find evangelicals willing to accept a profession of faith, whether or not the person's behavior shows any evidence of commitment to Christ.[2]

---

## Summary Statement

**2 CORINTHIANS 13:7–10** *Now I pray to God that you do no evil, not that we should appear approved, but that you should do what is honorable, though we may seem disqualified. For we can do nothing against the truth, but for the truth. For we are glad* *when we are weak and you are strong. And this also we pray, that you may be made complete. Therefore I write these things being absent, lest being present I should use sharpness, according to the authority which the Lord has given me for edification and not for destruction. (NKJV)*

In most of his letters, Paul wrote a declarative statement in which he defined his purpose in writing his letter. You could call it Paul's theme. For example, the theme verse of Romans is Romans 1:16, "I am not ashamed of the gospel of Christ, for it is the power of God to salvation for everyone who believes, for the Jew first and also for the Greek" (NKJV). Everything in the book of Romans explains, applies, illustrates, or amplifies that verse. As another example, when Paul wrote Timothy, he stated his purpose in 1 Timothy 3:15: "If I am delayed, I write so that you may know how you ought to conduct yourself in the house of God, which is the church of the living God, the pillar and ground of the truth" (NKJV).

By the same token, Paul's theme verse for all of 2 Corinthians can be found in 2 Corinthians 13:10, where Paul wrote, "I write these things being absent, lest being present I should use sharpness, according to the authority which the Lord has given me for edification and not for destruction" (NKJV).

In light of that desire, Paul literally prayed that the Corinthians would not do what was wrong by refusing his correction as spelled out in this letter. As we have seen, even though Paul was planning to confront any sin issues he found in the church, he truly didn't want to. His hope was that when he arrived he would discover, much to his delight, that he would not need to demonstrate his apostolic authority. "Do the right thing before we come" (2 Corinthians 13:7 NLT), he pleaded. Only time would tell if his prayers would be answered.

## A Final Farewell

2 CORINTHIANS 13:11–14 *Finally, brethren, farewell. Become complete. Be of good comfort, be of one mind, live in peace; and the God of love and peace will be with you. Greet one another with a holy kiss. All the saints greet you. The grace of the Lord Jesus Christ, and the love of God, and the communion of the Holy Spirit be with you all. Amen. (NKJV)*

Paul was about to bid adieu to the church in Corinth, and sadly, so are we. But the bottom line to all of this is summarized quite nicely by the good apostle himself. God desperately desires that His church become *complete*, or *mature*. God longs for all of us to be of one mind, to live in peace, with God intimately involved with, and deeply connected to, the lives of our churches.

Indeed, this is so vitally important to God that every member of the Trinity shares in this deep desire that our churches manifest to our communities the obvious truth that God loves us, that Jesus Christ is gracious toward us, and that the Holy Spirit directly communes with us. That's what "church" is all about; that's what church has always been about.

key point

## Chapter Wrap-Up

- In spite of everything, Paul indicates that he is now ready to return to Corinth.

- Paul makes it clear that he does not intend to be a financial burden to the Corinthians.

- Paul is still somewhat apprehensive about the kind of reception he will receive. Nonetheless, he was still preparing to come and would not be swayed from doing whatever God directed him to do to reestablish the Corinthian church within the divine will of God.

- Paul ended 2 Corinthians with a typical blessing on the Corinthian church, asking that the "grace of the Lord Jesus . . . the love of God, and the communion of the Holy Spirit" be with the entire congregation.

## Study Questions

1. How many times does Paul say that he had already visited the Corinthian church?

2. In what particular way did Paul indicate he did not want to be a burden to the Corinthians?

3. What is the basic theme of 2 Corinthians?

4. What five things did Paul tell the Corinthians to do in 2 Corinthians 13:11–12?

# Appendix A—The Answers

**1 Corinthians 1:1–16—Fracturing the Family**

1. It was incredibly immoral, favoring every sin known to ancient man. Many words might describe it; for example, decadent, corrupt, and perverted.

2. *Aphrodite* was the Greek name, but in Egypt she was known as *Hathor*; in Rome as *Venus*; in the Holy Land, *Astarte*. She was also known as *Ashtoreth* in the Bible.

3. Sosthenes.

4. Very high—indeed, they often have been. And, they continue to plague the churches of today.

**1 Corinthians 1:17–31—When Fools Rush In**

1. Its citizens worshiped the same false gods, pursued the same perverted pleasures, and thought the same "philosophical" thoughts about "higher things."

2. Because it requires them to trust in God rather than in themselves, and most people are simply not willing to do that.

3. This question can only be answered individually, according to your own understanding.

4. This question, also, can only be answered individually, according to your own understanding.

**1 Corinthians 2—Reveling in Revelation**

1. In the very first verse of the second chapter he says that he "did not come with excellence of speech" or in his own wisdom.

2. He exhorts them to be mature, and cautions them that only the spiritually mature can truly understand the things of God.

3. The Holy Spirit

4. By revelation, inspiration, and illumination.

**1 Corinthians 3—Floundering in the Flesh**

1. Paul and Apollos.

2. A plant, which must be watered so it will grow from the original seed, and a building, which must be built on a solid foundation.

3. God wants us to do well in all legitimate things, but we are not saved by "doing" things—only by accepting His forgiveness and salvation.

4. Spiritual maturity would have to be at or close to the top of the list.

**1 Corinthians 4—Corinthians at a Crossroad**

1. "The church is the only army that shoots its own wounded."

2. This is really an opinion question, but we must recognize that even such things as deplorable as sarcasm, correctly used in certain situations, can be very effective.

3. Paul wrote in a spirit of love, and he was acting just like a concerned father.

4. Paul had mentored Timothy and knew that he was more mature, spiritually, than the Christians at Corinth. Could it also be possible—assuming that Timothy was

above corruption—that his very youth could serve as a rebuke to the Corinthians?

## 1 Corinthians 5—An Unpleasant Business

1. It's simply not appropriate for a professing member of any Christian church, modern or ancient, to be allowed to pollute the witness of the church to the rest of the world by his sinful actions. The church *must* not be compromised by such a public posture.

2. No—if they are not professing believers our mandate as Christians is not only to associate with them as necessary in the normal conduct of our lives, but to witness to them as well.

3. This is strictly an opinion question.

4. The six categories are sexually immoral, covetous, idolater, reviler, drunkard, and extortioner. Reread this section if the meaning of any of these terms is not clear to you!

## 1 Corinthians 6—Who and Whose We Are

1. Suing in open court, especially over relatively petty matters, reflects badly on all of Christianity—those who cannot settle their disagreements honorably and amicably, in private, give unbelievers all kinds of ammunition to use against Christians.

2. This is an opinion question only.

3. The ten categories included fornicators, idolaters, adulterers, homosexuals, sodomites, thieves, coveters, drunkards, revilers, extortioners.

4. Because when we join ourselves together physically we also join ourselves to one another spiritually, which we are intended to do only through marriage.

## 1 Corinthians 7—On Matters of Marriage

1. Apparently, the members of the church at Corinth were asking questions about singleness, marriage, divorce, remarriage, adultery, homosexuality, and related subjects. They were also asking about whether they should renounce Judaism itself.

2. Absolutely not! Paul has been grossly misunderstood on this point; this chapter explains how and why.

3. It's always sad and unfortunate, but God does recognize the need for divorce in cases of infidelity.

4. No. Absolutely not!

## 1 Corinthians 8–10—What Is Christian Liberty?

1. This is strictly a "personal experience" question.

2. This is strictly a "personal experience" question.

3. The examples in the book are obvious. These include sports obsessions and drinking alcohol. Others might include a consuming fascination with movies and television, overeating, and even driving too fast on an everyday basis.

4. This is a "personal experience" question.

## 1 Corinthians 11—Conduct in the Church

1. This is a "personal experience" question.

2. Most people seem to leave out the obligation of men to function as Christ functions as the head of His church. The behavior of husbands is the second half of an equation that's not complete if wives are the only ones who meet their obligations.

3. They were overeating and getting drunk on wine.

4. They were doubly or triply wrong because (1) they debased an integral part of Christianity, based on Christ's example; and (2) they were shaming the poor by refusing to share their food with them; and (3) in all ways they were presenting a horrid example of so-called "Christianity" to the rest of the world.

## 1 Corinthians 12–14—What About Spiritual Gifts?

1. The nine spiritual gifts included (1) word of wisdom, (2) word of knowledge, (3) faith, (4) healing, (5) miracles,

(6) prophecy, (7) discerning of spirits, (8) tongues, and (9) interpretation of tongues.

2. Paul stipulated that (1) unbelievers must be present in the worship service when tongues are used; (2) there can be no more than two or three people speaking in tongues in any given service; and (3) an interpreter must be present.

3. This is an opinion question that you must answer for yourself after prayerful consideration.

4. Paul wanted us to understand that while the spiritual gifts will one day cease, our *faith, hope,* and *love* will endure forever.

## 1 Corinthians 15—The Resurrection: Hoax or History?

1. The three central elements of the gospel are (1) that we are sinners; (2) that Christ died to save us from our sins; and (3) that He arose from the dead and is alive today, just as we will one day be.

2. He was seen by Peter, by the twelve disciples, by more than five hundred other people all at once; He was seen by James, He was seen by all the apostles, and He was seen by Paul also.

3. That word would be *sleep*, and Paul used it because it captures the essence of what death is really all about for those who are truly counted among the children of God.

4. That word would be *rapture*.

## 1 Corinthians 16—The Joy of Giving

1. (1) He taught them doctrine; (2) he reproved and rebuked them; (3) he corrected them; and (4) he instructed them in how to live righteously.

2. These people were suffering from a famine.

3. He told them (1) to watch out for spiritual danger, (2) to stand fast in the faith, (3) to be brave, (4) to be strong, and (5) to do everything they did with love.

4. Aquila and Priscilla were tentmakers. Paul did the same and, indeed, often worked with and even lived with them!

## 2 Corinthians 1:1–7—The Purpose of Pain

1. Paul's first letter had not solved all the Corinthians problems, and he was being attacked, both in physical terms and by other negative spiritual forces in other ways as well.

2. "Tribulation" is more commonly applied to the suffering that all who live upon the earth must endure during the end times.

3. Paul's sufferings might be compared to those of Job.

4. He needed comforting himself, so he reached out to the Corinthians and comforted *them.*

## 2 Corinthians 1:8–2:13—A Rationale for Restoration

1. Paul basically put his trust in God, hunkered down, and let God sustain him through whatever troubles came along.

2. He asserted his own fundamental innocence, as one who was simply doing exactly and precisely what God required of him.

3. First, Paul said that he was firmly *established* in Christ, with Him as the foundation of his own life. Second, he said that God had *anointed* him and set him apart for a special purpose. Third, he said that God had sent the Holy Spirit to live in his heart, as both a seal and a guarantee that he was truly God's own.

4. Paul never identified the man, but we know he caused a lot of trouble for Paul personally, in addition to fomenting a great deal of disorder and dissatisfaction within the church.

## 2 Corinthians 2:14–6:10—Blessings from the Battlefield

1. While here on earth we are in temporary tents (our bodies) and are absent from the Lord. But (2) the minute we fold our tents (at death) we are absent from our bodies and in the presence of Christ.

2. The main story of God's covenant with His people takes place at Mount Sinai in the book of Exodus.

3. Paul himself was a tentmaker; it would be perfectly natural for him to use such a reference!

4. Paul saw himself as an ambassador of heaven to a lost and dying world.

## 2 Corinthians 6:11–7:16—The Heart of the Matter

1. If the non-Christian has no respect for your relationship with God and repeatedly tries to turn you away from Him, the relationship is not healthy. But if that same person respects your beliefs and does not try to subvert them, the relationship can be quite healthy.

2. Paul said he had not wronged, corrupted, or cheated anyone.

3. Titus' report was greatly encouraging, for it seemed that the Corinthians were receptive to Paul's chastisements and longed to see him in person.

4. These include (1) diligence against sin, (2) a desire to rebuild trust with others, (3) "righteous anger" over your own sins, (4) a healthy, renewed respect for the righteousness of God, (5) a strong desire to repair any broken relationships, with God and with others, (6) zeal for righteousness, and (7) a desire for vindication of God's name.

## 2 Corinthians 8, 9—The Great Giveaway

1. Paul exhorted the Corinthians to manifest (1) faith, (2) speech (i.e., wholesome talk), (3) knowledge of doctrine, (4) diligence, (5) love, and (6) grace.

2. No, tithing is mentioned in the Old Testament only.

3. God gives bountifully so that we, in turn, can continue to give generously. Our giving is also an act of worship, for those who benefit from our giving will thank God. And just as with every other act of our worship, God should be praised!

## 2 Corinthians 10:1–12:13—A Survivor's Guide to Suffering

1. These would include being jailed, flogged with thirty-nine lashes, beaten by Roman rods, pummeled with rocks, shipwrecked, having to fend off robbers, being immersed in the open sea, losing sleep, and missing countless meals.

2. Paul was taken up to what he called the "third heaven."

3. This is an open question that has not been conclusively answered. So, ultimately, this becomes an opinion question; did Paul suffer from weak eyes, a speech impediment, or something else entirely?

## 2 Corinthians 12:14–13:14—Ready or Not, Here I Come

1. Do not be tricked by this question! His third visit was upcoming, so he'd already been there just two times.

2. He did not want to burden them financially.

3. Paul made it clear that he did not want to use his apostolic authority if he didn't have to, but that he would do whatever was necessary to restore the church to its righteous position before God.

4. Paul told them to (1) become complete, (2) be of good comfort, (3) be of one mind, (4) live in peace, and (5) to greet one another with a holy kiss.

# Appendix B—The Experts

**Arthur, Kay**—well-known Bible teacher and best-selling author, cofounder of Precept Ministries.

**Ball, Arthur E.**—a pastor and church planter with more than thirty years of ministry in the United States, Canada, and England.

**Barclay, William**—professor of divinity and biblical criticism at Glasgow University, best-selling author, broadcaster on radio and television, and a regular contributor to widely circulated newspapers.

**Belleville, Linda**—an ordained minister and associate professor of biblical literature at North Park Theological Seminary in Chicago

**Benson, Robert**—Christian writer and seminar/retreat leader.

**Boa, Kenneth**—president of Reflections Ministries, with a ministry in relational evangelism and discipleship, teaching, writing, and speaking.

**Boice, James Montgomery**—Reformed theologian, pastor of Tenth Presbyterian Church in Philadelphia, radio broadcaster on *The Bible Study Hour*, speaker, and author.

**Bonhoeffer, Dietrich**—German Lutheran pastor, theologian, participant in the German Resistance movement against Nazism, and a founding member of the Confessing Church.

**Boone, Wellington**—an author and speaker who has been instrumental in the development of numerous national ministries, including New Generation Campus Ministries.

**Bruce, F. F.**—a founder of modern evangelical understanding of the Bible; author of *New Testament Documents: Are They Reliable?*

**Burkett, Larry**—founder (now deceased) of Christian Financial Concepts, well-known author and host of a nationally syndicated radio talk show.

**Callahan, Kennon**—church consultant, motivational speaker, pastor, teacher, researcher, theologian, and workshop/seminar presenter.

**Card, Michael**—contemporary Christian music artist and author of fourteen books.

**Carraway, Bryan**—an author who holds an M.A. in practical theology and ministers in churches throughout the body of Christ.

**Carson, D. A.**—an evangelical Christian scholar; also a research professor of the New Testament at Trinity Evangelical Divinity School in Deerfield, Illinois.

**Craig, William Lane**—a philosopher, theologian, New Testament historian, Christian apologist, author, and lecturer.

**Elliot, Elisabeth**—wife of martyred missionary Jim Elliot, well-known speaker, and author.

**Farrar, Steve**—president of Point Man Leadership Ministries and author of several books including *Standing Tall: How a Man Can Protect His Family.*

**Farrel, Pam**—a pastor's wife, popular women's conference speaker, and author of many books including *Woman of Influence.* She and her husband, Bill, are founders of Masterful Living.

**Fee, Gordon**—professor of New Testament at Regent College, Vancouver, British Columbia, Canada, and author of numerous books.

**George, Denise**—longtime Christian church woman, teacher, speaker, and author, with many books to her credit.

**Graham, Billy**—world-famous evangelist and best-selling author of several books.

**Green, Wilda**—now retired, was a well-known curriculum writer for the Southern Baptist Convention Press.

**Hybels, Bill**—pastor of Willow Creek Community Church in South Barrington, Illinois, and an author of Gold Medallion award–winning books.

**Hybels, Lynne**—wife of Pastor Bill Hybels; also a writer and speaker.

**Jeffers, James**—author and associate professor in the Torrey Honors Institute at Biola University; also teaches ancient history at California State University in Dominguez Hills, California.

**Kaiser, Walter C., Jr.**—senior vice president of education, academic dean and professor of Old Testament and Semitic languages at Trinity Evangelical Divinity School, and author of several books.

**Kent, Carol**—an author and a popular international public speaker, a former radio show cohost and a featured speaker at *Time Out for Women* and *Heritage Keepers* arena events.

**Kurath, Edward**—an author, a professional counselor, and a marriage and family therapist.

**Leman, Kevin**—internationally known psychologist, author, and speaker.

**Lotz, Anne Graham**—founder of AnGeL Ministries, and Anne is an award-winning author.

**Lowery, David K.**—a church planter, associate pastor at a Dallas-area church, and a frequent author

**MacArthur, John F., Jr.**—author and radio preacher, and pastor of Grace Community Church in Sun Valley, California; also president of the Master's College.

**Martin, Ralph P.**—a scholar in residence for the Haggard Graduate School of Theology; has been a visiting lecturer in several countries, and has maintained an impressive writing career.

**McGee, J. Vernon**—Bible teacher of the *Thru the Bible* radio broadcast, pastor, and college lecturer.

**Meyer, Joyce**—charismatic Christian author, speaker, and proponent of Word-Faith teachings; has written more than seventy books on Christianity and theology.

**Moore, Beth**—writer and teacher of best-selling Bible studies whose public speaking engagements carry her all over the world. Her books include *Things Pondered, A Heart Like His*, and *Praying God's Word*.

**Nystrom, Carolyn**—a writer who has authored more than fifty books and Bible study guides.

**Ogilvie, Lloyd**—author of more than forty books and former chaplain of the United States Senate; former senior pastor of Hollywood Presbyterian Church in Hollywood, California.

**Packer, J. I.**—author and British-born Christian theologian in the Calvinistic Anglican tradition; Board of Governors' Professor of Theology at Regent College in Vancouver, British Columbia,

**Peterson, Eugene**—author, pastor, scholar, and poet who has written more than thirty books.

**Phillips, John**—retired former assistant director of the Moody Correspondence School, director of Emmaus Correspondence School, professor, radio Bible teacher, and author.

**Powell, Mark Allan**—author, and professor of New Testament at Trinity Lutheran Seminary, Columbus, Ohio.

**Radmacher, Earl**—professor at Western Baptist Seminary, Portland, Oregon; author and speaker.

**Reese, Martha Grace**—author, and president of GraceNet, Inc., a not-for-profit corporation specializing in the training of clergy.

**Richards, Lawrence**—teacher and writer of Sunday school curriculum for every age group; has published more than two hundred books; is also general editor of this series of Smart Guides to the Bible.

**Rienecker, Fritz**—was a well-known and highly respected German journalist, teacher, theologian, and author.

**Rogers, Cleon**—author and lecturer in biblical and exegetical studies at the New Life Seminary in Altenkirchen, Germany, and at the Bible Seminary in Bonn, Germany.

**Schonfield, Hugh**—author and British Bible scholar specializing in the New Testament and the early development of the Christian religion and church.

**Singleton, Charlyn**—author and president of the God's Woman Conferences in Rialto, California.

**Stanley, Dr. Charles**—senior pastor of the 12,000-member First Baptist Church of Atlanta and popular speaker for *In Touch*, a national television and radio program.

**Storms, Sam**—author of several books, founder of Enjoying God Ministries in Kansas City, Missouri, former pastor, and professor at Wheaton College.

**Stott, John R. W.**—famous lecturer, author of numerous devotional books, and the rector of All Souls Church in London.

**Swindoll, Charles R.**—president of Dallas Theological Seminary, host of the nationally syndicated radio program *Insight for Living*, and author of many books.

**Thomas, Ian**—author, and founder of the Torchbearers of the Capernwray Missionary Fellowship, now known as Torchbearers International.

**Thomas, Robert L.**—author, professor of New Testament.

**Vine, W. E.**—well-known biblical scholar and author; renowned as a classical scholar, a skilled expositor, and an acute theologian.

**Wilkinson, Bruce H.**—the founder and president of Walk Thru the Bible Ministries, an international ministry dedicated to providing the very finest biblical teaching, tools, and training.

**Wilson, Sandy**—author, counselor, conference speaker, and instructor of counseling at Western Seminary, Portland, Oregon.

**Yancy, Philip**—executive editor of *Campus Life Magazine*, editor of Campus Life Books and an author.

**Zacharias, Ravi**—Indian-born, Canadian-American author and evangelical Christian philosopher, apologist, and evangelist.

# Endnotes

## 1 Corinthians 1:1–16—Fracturing the Family

1. Bruce Wilkinson and Kenneth Boa, *Talk Thru the Bible* (Nashville: Thomas Nelson, 1983), 381.

2. Fritz Rienecker, *Linguistic Key to the Greek New Testament* (Grand Rapids: Zondervan, 1980), 385.

3. Westminster Shorter Catechism, in response to the question, "What is the chief end of man?"

4. James Montgomery Boice, *Romans: Volume 3, God and History, Romans 9–11* (Grand Rapids: Baker, 1993), 1476.

5. Michael Card, *Immanuel: Reflections on the Life of Christ* (Nashville: Thomas Nelson, 1990).

6. Wilda Green, *The Disturbing Christ* (Nashville: Broadman, 1968), 116.

7. *Revell Bible Dictionary* (Old Tappan, NJ, Revell, 1990), 886.

## 1 Corinthians 1:17–31—When Fools Rush In

1. Jonathan Swift, *A Critical Essay Upon the Faculties of the Mind* (1707).

2. Walter C. Kaiser, Jr., *Archaeological Study Bible* (Grand Rapids: Zondervan, 2005), 1802.

3. Ravi Zacharias, "September 11, 2001: Was God Present or Absent?," *Just Thinking* (Winter 2002), 7.

4. John R. W. Stott, *Basic Christianity* (Grand Rapids: Eerdmans, 1958), 21.

5. *Reflection on the Psalms* (Fort Washington, PA: Harvest Books, 1965), 110.

## 1 Corinthians 2—Reveling in Revelation

1. "What Is Presbyterianism?" An address delivered before the Presbyterian historical society at their anniversary meeting in Philadelphia, on Tuesday evening, May 1, 1855. By the Rev. Charles Hodge, D.D. (Michigan Historical Reprint Society, 2006), 65.

2. William Barclay, *The Letter to the Hebrews* (Philadelphia: Westminster 1957), 3.

3. William Barclay, *The Letter to the Hebrews* (Philadelphia: Westminster 1957), 4.

4. Blaine Pascal, *Pensées* (1670), 288, tr. W. F. Trotter

## 1 Corinthians 3—Floundering in the Flesh

1. http://www.biblestudy.org/maps/pauls-third-journey-map.html.

2. St. John of the Cross, *The Dark Night of the Soul*, excerpted in Richard Foster and James Bryan Smith, *Devotional Classics* (San Francisco: Harper, 1990), 36.

3. Ravi Zacharias, "Let My People Think," Radio Broadcast, March 10, 2002.

4. F. F. Bruce, *The New International Commentary on the New Testament: The Epistle to the Hebrews* (Grand Rapids: Eerdmans 1990), 49.

5. Lawrence Richards, *Victor Bible Background Commentary: New Testament* (Wheaton, IL: Victor, 1994), 554.

## 1 Corinthians 4—Corinthians at a Crossroad

1. Earl D. Radmacher, Salvation (Nashville: Word, 2000), 3.

2. Dietrich Bonhoeffer, *Life Together*, excerpted in Foster and Smith, 296.

3. Ravi Zacharias, *Can Man Live Without God?* (Nashville: W Publishing, 1994), 179.

4. D. A. Carson, *How Long O Lord* (Grand Rapids: Baker, 1990), 73.

## 1 Corinthians 5—An Unpleasant Business

1. J. I. Packer and Carolyn Nystrom, *Never Beyond Hope* (Downers Grove, IL: IVP, 2000), 76–77.

2. Billy Graham, *How to Be Born Again* (Waco, TX: Word, 1977), 128.

3. Charles R. Swindoll, *The Living Insights Study Bible* (Grand Rapids: Zondervan, 1996), 1258.

4. Ralph P. Martin, *Ephesians, Colossians, and Philemon, A Bible Commentary for Teaching and Preaching* (Atlanta, GA: John Knox Press, 1991), 47.

5. Rienecker and Cleon Rogers, *Linguistic Key to the Greek New Testament* (Grand Rapids: Zondervan, 1980), 400.

## 1 Corinthians 6—Who and Whose We Are

1. Pam Farrel, *A Woman God Can Use* (Eugene, OR: Harvest House, 1999), 133.

2. Thomas Edwards, *Commentary on First Corinthians* (Minneapolis: Klock and Klock, 1979), 139.

3. Gordon Fee, *The First Epistle to the Corinthians* (Grand Rapids: Eerdmans, 1987), 234.

4. W. E. Vine, *Expository Dictionary of New Testament Words, vol. 2* (Old Tappan, NJ: Revell, 1966), Volume II, 280.

5. Wellington Boone, *Breaking Through* (Nashville: Broadman, 1996), 68.

6. John Phillips, *Exploring 1 Corinthians* (Grand Rapids: Kregel, 2002), 126.

7. Steve Farrar, *Point Man* (Sisters, OR: Multnomah, 1990), 138.

8. Charles R. Swindoll, *Growing Deep in the Christian Life* (Sisters, OR: Multnomah, 1986), 344.

## 1 Corinthians 7—On Matters of Marriage

1. Beth Moore, *Believing God* (Nashville: LifeWay Press, 2002), 11.

2. Kevin Leman, *Keeping Your Family Together When the World Is Falling Apart* (Colorado Springs, CO: Focus on the Family, 1983), 76.

3. Bill and Lynne Hybels, *Fit to Be Tied* (Grand Rapids: Zondervan, 1991), 38.

4. James Jeffers, *The Greco-Roman World of the New Testament Era*, 229.

5. Jan Frank, *A Graceful Waiting* (Ann Arbor, MI: Servant, 1996), 128.

## 1 Corinthians 8–10—What Is Christian Liberty?

1. Anne Graham Lotz, *Just Give Me Jesus* (Nashville: Thomas Nelson, 2002), 166.

2. Pam Farrel, *A Woman God Can Use* (Eugene, OR: Harvest House, 1999), 219.

3. Carol Kent, *Becoming a Woman of Influence* (Colorado Springs, CO: NavPress, 1999), 154.

4. Charles Stanley, *A Touch of His Freedom* (Grand Rapids: Zondervan, 1991), 35.

## 1 Corinthians 11—Conduct in the Church

1. *Life Application Bible* (Wheaton, IL: Tyndale, 1988), 1752.

2. William Barclay, *The Letters to the Galatians and Ephesians* (Louisville, KY: Westminster John Knox, 1954), 140.

3. Rienecker, 538.

4. William Barclay, *The Letters to the Galatians and Ephesians* (Louisville, KY: Westminster John Knox, 1954), 174.

5. Elisabeth Elliot, *Discipline, the Glad Surrender* (Old Tappan, NJ: Revell, 1982), 89.

6. Beers, 1752.

7. J. Vernon McGee, *Ephesians* (Pasadena, CA: Thru the Bible, 1977), 96.

8. Lloyd Ogilvie, *Enjoying God* (Dallas: Word, 1989), 46.

## 1 Corinthians 12–14—What About Spiritual Gifts?

1. Robert L. Thomas, *Understanding Spiritual Gifts* (Grand Rapids: Kregal, 1998), 22.

2. Sam Storms, *The Beginner's Guide to Spiritual Gifts* (Ventura, CA: Regal, 2002), 77.

3. Bryan Carraway, *Spiritual Gifts: Their Purpose and Power* (Enumclaw, WA: Winepress Publishing, 2005), 107–8.

## 1 Corinthians 15—The Resurrection: Hoax or History?

1. Eugene Peterson, *Living the Resurrection* (Colorado Springs, Co: NavPress, 2006), 102.

2. Hugh Schonfield, *The Passover Plot: Special 40th Anniversary Edition* (Disinformation Co, 2005), back cover.

3. William Lane Craig, "The Absurdity of Life Without God," http://spruce.flint.umich.edu/~simoncu/165/craig.htm.

4. Gordon Fee, *The New International Commentary on the New Testament: The First Epistle to the Corinthians* (Grand Rapids: Eerdmans, 1987), 765.

5. Phillips, 364.

6. See 1 Corinthians 15:40, footnote 7, NKJV.

7. Billy Graham, *Death and the After Life* (Nashville: W Publishing, 1994), 82.

## 1 Corinthians 16—The Joy of Giving

1. John MacArthur Jr., *The MacArthur Study Bible* (Nashville: Word, 1997), 1791.

2. Mark Allan Powell, *Giving to God: The Bible's Good News about Living a Generous Life* (Grand Rapids: Eerdmans , 2006), 53.

3. Kennon Callahan, *Giving and Stewardship in an Effective Church: A Guide for Every Member* (San Francisco, CA: Jossey-Bass, 1997), 3.

## 2 Corinthians 1:1–7—The Purpose of Pain

1. David K. Lowery, *The Bible Knowledge Commentary, vol. 2* John F. Walvoord and Roy B. Zuck editors, (Wheaton, IL: Victor, 1983), 551.

2. Charlyn Singleton, *The Journey from Pain to Purpose* (Denver: Legacy, 2002), 137.

3. Denise George, *Tilling the Soul: Prayer Penetrates Our Pain* (Grand Rapids: Zondervan, 2004), 35.

4. Philip Yancey, *Where Is God When It Hurts?* (Grand Rapids, MI: Zondervan, 2002), 91.

## 2 Corinthians 1:8–2:13—A Rationale for Restoration

1. Major Ian Thomas, *The Indwelling Life of Christ: All of Him in All of Me* (Sisters, OR: Multnomah, 2006), 120.

2. Kay Arthur, *Lord, Give Me a Heart for You: A Devotional Study on Having a Passion for God* (Colorado Springs, CO: WaterBrook, 2001), 62.

3. Linda Bellevill, *2 Corinthians: IVP New Testament Commentary Series* (Downer's Grove, IL: InterVarsity, 1996), 69.

4. Sandy Wilson et. al., *Restoring the Fallen: A Team Approach to Caring, Confronting, and Reconciling* (Downer's Grove, IL: InterVarsity, 1997), 71.

## 2 Corinthians 2:14–6:10—Blessings from the Battlefield

1. Philip Yancey, *What's So Amazing About Grace* (Grand Rapids: Zondervan, 2002), 13.

2. Billy Graham, *Death and the Life After* (Nashville: Thomas Nelson, 1994), 20.

## 2 Corinthians 6:11–7:16—The Heart of the Matter

1. Quoted by John R. Hoyle, *Leadership and the Force of Love* (Thousand Oaks, CA: Corwin, 2001), 1.

2. Martha Grace Reese, *Unbinding the Gospel: Real Life Evangelism* (St. Louis, MI: Chalice Press, 2007), 4.

3. Beth Moore, *When Godly People Do Ungodly Things* (Nashville: Broadman, 2002), 209.

## 2 Corinthians 8, 9—The Great Giveaway

1. Larry Burkett, *Giving and Tithing* (Chicago, IL: Moody, 1998), 25.

2. Joel P. Parker, *Tithing in the Age of Grace* (New Bern, NC: Trafford, 2006), 110.

3. Arthur E. Ball, *Let Us Give* (Grand Rapids: Kregel, 2003), 36–37.

## 2 Corinthians 10:1–12:13—A Survivor's Guide to Suffering

1. Joyce Meyer, *Battlefield of the Mind* (Nashville: FaithWords, 2002), 68.

2. Edward Kurath, *I Will Give You Rest* (Post Falls, ID: Divinely Designed, 2005), 34–35.

3. Charles Swindoll, *Paul: A Man of Grit and Grace* (Nashville: Thomas Nelson, 2002), 100.

## 2 Corinthians 12:14–13:14—Ready or Not, Here I Come

1. Robert Benson, *The Body Broken: Answering God's Call to Love One Another* (New York: Doubleday, 2003), 11.

2. John MacArthur, Jr., *The Gospel According to Jesus* (Grand Rapids: Zondervan, 1994), 27.

# Index

rewards of being, 59, 61, 257
sons and daughters of Christ, 8, 264
spiritual growth, 45, 53
test yourselves, 18, 100, 184, 290, 306, 307
church, 5, 10, 15, 19, 40, 58, 81, 87, 156, 177, 222, 238, 304
church of God, 10, 159, 160, 187, 216
church of Jesus Christ, 59, 86
circumcised, 30, 121, 122, 142
circumcision, 272
citizen of heaven, 255, 260
city
  holy, 44, 154
  of Jerusalem, 202
city wall of Jerusalem, 201
Claudius Caesar, 202
clearing of ourselves, 271
code of conduct, 293
Colossae, 254
Colossi, 124
commandment, 103, 121, 123, 133, 177, 278
commitment
  to Christ, 222, 307
  to spouse, 130
  to the church, 282
communing, 268
communion
  cup, 247
  getting drunk by, 5, 62, 151
  of Holy Spirit, 308, 309
  table, 152, 159, 160, 162, 163
  wine, 5, 62, 151
compromises, 18, 111, 257
condemned, 74, 162, 251
confess, 160, 299
confession, 32, 167, 283

confidence, 29, 30, 59, 207, 232, 240, 254, 287, 288
confident, 42, 133, 256, 268, 282
confident boasting, 282, 283
conflicting emotions, 263
conflicts, 97, 100, 239, 269
confrontational
  style, 188
  tone, 9, 40
congregation
  in Corinth, 5, 21, 39, 53, 67, 83, 166, 181, 240
  split, 19, 39, 134
consequences, 86, 87, 104, 209, 271
consolation, 73, 220, 222, 239
  and salvation, 222
contempt, 7, 126, 291
contemptible, 41, 290, 291
contented people are thankful people, 127
contentment, 55, 127, 128
conundrums of Scripture, 48
convicting, 138, 270
conviction of a father, 126, 129
convictions, 194, 207, 222, 293
Corinth
  Aphrodite worship flourished, 8
  cesspool of carnality, 6
  cesspool of sinfulness, 265
  church of, 15, 94, 105
  contaminated culture, 10
  cultural corruption, 6, 19
  economic powerhouse, 6
  harsh, cruel culture, 155

spiritual and moral decline, 6
Corinthian Christians
  defiant sin among members, 81
  hearers of the Word, 15
  purified people of God, 11
  saints, 10
Corinthian congregation
  appalling behavior, 5
  defiant sin among members, 81
  disobedient members, 5, 268
  divisions, 5, 18, 19, 56
  hopelessly divided, 5
  proper church discipline, 5, 292
  splintering the congregation, 19
Corinthian fashion, 236
corruption of our bodies, 195
corruption of our culture, 8
covenant(s)
  of marriage, 118
  new, 161, 247, 248, 249, 251
  old, 248, 249, 250, 261
  original, 248, 249, 250, 261
Craig, William Lane, 189
creation, 13, 26, 185, 257, 259
Creator, 27, 98
Crispus, 20, 21
cross, the, 17, 25, 35, 37, 42, 161, 247, 249
cross of Christ, 17, 25, 35, 78, 169, 247
crown
  imperishable, 144
  of righteousness, 59, 144
crucifixion
  and resurrection, 188, 189
  of the Lord, 162
crucify, 46, 89
cry, 44, 102, 167, 221, 256

cry of adoration, 167
cults, 7, 8, 20, 21
cultural corruption, 6, 19
cultural faux pas, 152
cultural practices, 152
Cyrene, 178

# D

daily bread, 146, 277
Damascenes, 296
Damascus, 31, 140, 154, 187, 296
darkness, 29, 55, 92, 227, 252, 253, 293
David, 244
Davidic
  definition of, 244
  Dynasty, 30
  psalms, 244
day of judgment, 60
day of our Lord, 16, 87, 203, 307
Day of Pentecost, 21, 171, 202
day of salvation, 259
dead
  in Christ will rise, 16, 190, 194
  and is alive today, 185, 186, 199
  Jesus arose from the, 185, 186, 188, 195, 199
  Savior, 186
  in trespasses and sins, 13, 165
death,
  Christ's, 5, 14, 17, 161, 258
  life after, 189, 193, 194, 198
  pain of, 12, 42
  physical, 199, 261
deceitful workers, 217, 294
deception, 188, 252, 304
decimate Judah, 249
decree, 191, 235
deep and abiding trust in God, 278
deep concern, 219, 296
deep divisions, 96, 173

deep sleep, 41
defiant, 18, 81, 82, 84, 86, 88, 91, 95
defiant sin among church members, 81
defilement, 61
deliverance, 34, 219, 231, 254
Demas, 145
Demetrius
incited a crowd and stirred them into a rage against Paul, 193
demon-contaminated meat superstition, 136
demonic spirits, 135, 169
demon possession, 135
deportment of the church, 161
Derbe, 142
descendants of Abraham, 30, 204
descendants of Levi, 204
destroyer, 146
Deuteronomy, 44
devil, 62, 95, 227, 234, 304
devil's bidding, 234, 267
devil's deception, 304
devotion, 126, 129, 130, 174, 245
devotional, 174
devout men, 177
die, 21, 34, 141, 193, 195, 269
dip or immerse, 170
disaster, spiritual, 266
disasters, natural, 210
discerning of spirits, 168, 169
disciples, 20, 21, 34, 74, 83, 87, 96, 141, 202, 255, 269, 296
disciplined, 81, 94, 145, 289, 218
discipline unrepentant sinners, 5, 84, 87, 88, 94, 268
discredit Paul, 228, 232, 234, 243, 289, 299
dishonest gain, 246

dishonor, 72, 195
disobedience, 26, 288, 289
disobedient, 5, 74, 235, 257, 268, 271
disorderly and chaotic world, 157
disorderly behavior, 305
disorderly church, 76
dissension, 123, 209
distract or influence others, 149
distress, 126, 127, 223, 298, 299
distresses, 223, 298, 299
divine judgments, 209
divine Spirit, 47
divine will of God, 209
division and conflict, 237
divorce
biblical, 86
and infidelity, 117, 118
of Mary and Joseph, 117
and remarriage, 111, 112, 116, 125, 131
doctrinal and historical heresy, 188
doctrinal and organiza-tional unity, 227
doctrinal error, 123, 173, 216
doctrinal purity, 173
doctrinal roots, 86
doctrine
definition of, 15
"Progressive Revelation," 44
do-it-yourself salvation, 32
doubts about God, 8
downcast, 239, 269
drunkard, 91, 100, 102, 265, 307
drunken debauchery, 7
drunkenness, 104, 105, 139, 160, 162, 167, 266

## E

early believers, 10, 201
earthen vessels, 253

edifying, 72, 165
Edward, Kurath, 292
Edwards, Thomas, 97
Egypt, 89, 113, 149, 248
Egyptian military, 68
eilikrineia, 231
ekklesia, 10
"church," 10
Elamites, 177
Eliphaz, 220
Elliot, Elisabeth, 143, 157
emissaries, 12, 233, 289, 293
emissary, 281
emulate, 278
enables, God, 50, 51, 284
end of the age, 171, 190
enemies
Christ's, 33, 192
Paul's, 254
enmity, 56
Epaphroditus, 170
Ephesian believers, 230
Ephesians, 205
Ephesus, 5, 7, 15, 35, 72, 87, 193, 205, 209, 230
epistle, 9, 48, 76, 90, 112, 238, 246
Erastus, 206
eschatology
definition of, 185
essence of the Gospel, 250
eternal destiny, 6, 17, 258, 287, 304
eternal security, 17, 18, 144, 189
Eucharist, 161
euphoria, 244
Eutychus
Paul raised from the dead, 41
evangelism, 267
evangelist, 21, 172
everywhere present
meaning of, 27
evil
angels, 97, 98
behavior, 293
company corrupts good habits, 192, 194
influence, 267

intent, 89
one, 194
exhaled disobedience, 26
exhaustion, 260, 298
existential
definition of, 23
exposed, 180, 293
exterminate, 289
extortioner, 90, 91, 100, 102, 265, 307
eye, 5, 46, 149, 246, 298
eye problem, 298
Ezra, 44

## F

failed Messiahs, 35
failed the test, 100
failed to be faithful, 16
faith
in Christ, 28, 43, 184, 187, 189, 191, 193, 197, 294
Christian, 202, 208
faithful, 16, 57, 68, 69, 199, 234, 284
faithfulness, 16, 244, 284
fallen angels, 97
fallen asleep, 184
fallen world, 221
false accusations, 231, 254, 291, 299
false apostles, 217, 219, 287, 290, 291, 294, 295
false brethren, 219, 296
false doctrine, 188
false gods, 101, 135, 136, 147, 168
false prophets, 291
false religion, 32
false sense of security, 202
false teachers, 183, 188, 194, 216, 233, 268, 279, 287, 293, 294, 295
Farrar, Steve, 103
Farrel, Pam
on being the children of light, 137
on relying on God's power rather than our own, 96

reproof, 45, 201
reputation, 40, 55, 71, 83, 91, 102, 279
resist an evil person, 99
resist sexual impulses, 131
restore the church, 179
restore the repentant man, 239
resurrection,
  bodily, 183, 189
  of Jesus, 6, 183, 186, 188, 193, 199
Resurrection Day, 203
resurrection of Jesus, 6, 183, 186, 188, 193, 199
return, the imminent, 16
returns, Christ, 190, 191, 197, 232
revelation, 15, 24, 33, 44, 47, 177, 203, 296, 298
"revelatory periods," 43
Revell Bible Dictionary, 18
reverence under God, 157
reviled, 72, 74, 75
reviler, 91, 100, 102, 265, 307
rewards not punishment, 59, 61
rewards of the battle, 243
Richards, Lawrence O., 62
righteous indignation, 271
righteous Judge, 59, 144
right with God, 36, 24, 186
ritual feasts, 136
road to Damascus, 140, 154, 187
"Rock of Ares," 24
Rock-of-Gibraltar, 58
rod of discipline, 78
roles of men and women in the church, 151, 155
roles within the church, 152, 153, 171
Roman emperor, 14, 87
Roman Empire, 24, 68, 107, 124, 160

Rome
  Christians in, 18, 26, 170
  escaped to, 124
  Nero as emperor of, 14, 87
root
  good, 292
  produces fruit after its own kind, 292
R-rated movies, 146
ruler, 10, 43, 45, 46, 128, 191, 192, 296
rulers of this age, 43, 45
Ruth, 44, 113, 258

# S

Sabbath, 122, 203
sacred, 11, 69, 160, 163, 191
  celebration, 160
  definition of, 11
sacrifice, 88, 89, 135, 136, 160, 161, 193, 277, 304
  animal, 135
  of Christ, 89, 160, 162
  greatest, 277
  pagan, 136
  personal, 304
  on the cross, 89
sacrificial death, 186
sacrificial giving, 282, 285
sacrificially, 173, 275, 277, 279, 285
Sadducees, 33
saint, 21, 223
saints, 10, 11, 13, 20, 21, 95, 96, 201, 230, 275, 277, 281
  Corinthian Christians, 11
  purified people of God, 11
sake, Christ's, 72, 223, 298, 299
salary, 140, 294, 300
salt, 266
salvation, 16, 17, 18, 32, 37, 100, 119, 222, 259
  "getting saved," 17

Samuel, 63
sanctification, 36
sanctified, 10, 100, 103, 111, 119, 120, 265
  heavenly purposes, 11
  "to glorify God and enjoy Him forever," 11
  "to separate (or set apart)," 120
sanctifying, 36, 216
sanctity, 83, 162, 163
Sarah, 113, 120
sarcasm, 73, 74, 77, 79, 176
Satan, 87, 114, 222, 267, 288, 299, 304
satanic
  serpent, 294
  temptation, 115
Satan's assault on Eve, 288
Satan's emissaries, 293
Satan's eventual demise, 289
Satan's minions, 304
Saturday, 203, 204
Saul, 202, 296, 299, 300
saved, 25, 32, 37, 39, 50, 57, 102, 103, 135, 185, 199, 244, 266, 307
save us from our sins, 154, 185, 186
"save us now," 34
saving faith, 184, 307
Savior, 19, 20, 21, 25, 34, 50, 122, 186, 195, 251, 294
schism, 19, 227
schisma, 19
  cleft, 19
  divisions, 5, 18, 19, 21, 39, 40, 56, 63, 70, 75, 153, 165, 183, 294
  rent, 19
  tearing a piece of cloth in half, 19
scribe, 32, 209
Scripture, 45, 48, 53, 70, 97, 103, 134, 137, 142, 169, 185, 195, 201, 203, 204, 243

Scriptures, 20, 31, 36, 39, 50, 89, 92, 94, 184, 186, 256
Sea
  Adriatic, 6
  Aegean, 6
  city-by-the, 6
  Mediterranean, 276
  Red, 146
sealed, 76, 216, 234, 235, 249, 282
seaport, 6, 22, 23, 68, 116
second-born son, 30
second-class Christians, 118
second-class citizens, 107
secular
  definition of, 11
secure, 17, 58, 127, 155, 249, 264, 269
security, 16, 17, 18, 68, 198
seduction of Eve, 289
seductive, 104
Selah, 284
self-absorbed, 56, 172, 288
self-appointed apostles, 221, 233
self-appointed false prophets, 219
self-appointed pseudo-apostles, 234
self-centered, 174
self-control, 114, 115, 145, 146
self-controlled man, 157
self-focused, 56, 174
self-gratifying, 231
self-indulgence, 6, 8
selfish, 56, 174, 304
selfishness, 305
selfless commitment, 175
selfless love, 115, 284
selfless service, 72, 73
self-righteous, 73, 224, 258
self-sacrificing, 157, 258
self-serve, 37
self-serve religion, 32
self-willed sinners, 118
seminaries, 300
sentence of death, 205, 228, 229, 230

struggling financially, 202

stumbling block, 24, 33, 35, 122, 138, 142

submission, 154, 158, 163, 192

of wives to husbands, 120, 158, 163

submissive, 120

submit, 31, 118, 126, 154, 156, 158, 180, 216

Sunday, 56, 138, 151, 203, 223

Sunday school, 42, 126

super apostle, 68

superhuman strength, 236

superstition, 135, 136

superstitious beliefs, 135

supreme act of love, 154

supremely gifted, 166

Swift, Jonathan, 23

Swindoll, Charles R.

on prayer, 299

on the body of Christ, 107

on the church's model, 86

symbol, 158, 160, 249

symbolize, 61, 158

synagogue, 10, 21, 31, 61, 122

in Corinth, 10, 21

in Damascus, 31

Syria, 31, 216, 248, 249

# T

Tabernacle, 190, 204

tares, 234, 252

definition of, 234

tax collector, 86, 250, 258

temple, 7, 15, 55, 62, 101, 106, 107, 134, 141, 148, 167, 204, 264, 271

of Aphrodite, 7, 15

of God, 62

prostitutes, 7, 167

of the Holy Spirit, 55, 62, 106, 107

temples, 24, 62, 107, 135

temptation, 8, 113, 114, 115, 127, 138, 146, 229, 267

tempting, 148, 267, 296

Ten Commandments, 133, 146, 248, 249

disrespect for, current, 260

ten plagues, 89

tentmakers, 208, 255, 294

tent-making, 9

ten tribes, 30

Tertius, 209

Tertullian, 222

tested as genuine, 232

tested by fire, 53, 60

testing, 33, 229, 278

thanksgiving, 13, 53, 283, 284

thanksgiving offering to God, 190

theologians, 27

theology, 77, 201, 202, 221, 283

Thessalonica, 41, 141, 190, 196, 205, 275, 276

thieves, 100, 102, 265, 281

Thomas, Major Ian, 230

Thomas, Robert L., 167

thorn in flesh, 12, 87, 133, 297, 298, 299, 301

three cities of Macedonia Berea, Philippi, and Thessalonica, 276

Timothy, 43, 76, 87, 145, 156, 173, 206, 209, 210, 222, 232, 234, 253, 308

pastored the church in Ephesus, 76, 156

Paul's pastoral protégé, 12, 76, 78, 87

tithe, 141, 204, 285

Titus, 43, 217, 239, 245, 272, 279, 281, 303, 304

tongues, 165, 168–70, 172–73, 175–79, 181

tongues of angels, 173

tongues of men and of angels, 172

Torah, 31, 44

definition of, 31

touch of woman, 113, 131

touch our spirits with discernment, 143

traditions, 31, 155

trial, 10, 59, 124, 161, 219, 221, 223, 229, 236, 244, 269, 275

trial of mockings, 219

trials and tribulations, 244, 269

tribe of Benjamin, 30

Tribulation, 185, 215, 218, 219, 220, 224, 225, 268, 269

Trinity, 47, 51, 185, 309

Triune

definition of, 47

Godhead, 47

Troas, 41, 203, 217, 239

troublemakers, 237, 238

troubles, 225, 241, 253, 260, 261, 273

true follower, 16, 17, 18, 86, 165, 167, 290

of Christ, 16, 17, 18, 165, 290

true God, 24, 31, 91, 135, 147, 168, 248

trumpet, 16, 178, 190, 196, 197, 295

trumpet of God, 16, 190

trust, 32, 49, 67, 76, 147, 169, 205, 228–31, 259, 278, 282, 306

trustworthy messenger of his God, 234

truth, 15, 23–24, 29, 44–50, 85, 91–92, 133, 159, 169, 180, 252, 266, 269–70, 290

God's, 50, 85, 259

suppression of, 26

twenty-four elders, 60

two shall become one flesh, 116

# U

unbelief, 26

unbelievers, 92, 98, 100, 121, 147, 170, 178–79, 234, 264–67, 273

marriage to, 112, 116, 119

should be present in the worship services where the gift of tongues is used, 179

who masqueraded as believers, 234

unbelieving spouse, 111, 119, 120, 121

unclean, 119, 120, 264, 305

unconditional commitment, 128

undeniable proof God exists, 28

unfulfilled sex drive, 126

unholy act, 106

unity, 39, 50, 72, 136, 160, 171, 201, 227

of the church, 136

universe, 46, 62, 156, 297

unmarried, 114, 116, 118, 129, 130, 203

unrepentant, 81, 82, 83, 84, 88, 89, 90, 91, 93, 94, 101, 306

unrepentant sinning church member, 81, 93, 94

unreturned love, 106, 264

unruly mob, 193

unshakable foundation, 17

unspiritual person, 49, 50

unwanted diseases, 106

unwelcomed suffering, 218, 223

unworthy manner, 162

usefulness to God, 134

usefulness to the kingdom, 84

# V

value, 23, 100, 115, 131, 144, 155–57, 160, 162, 193, 258

vehement desire, 271
veil or head covering, 151, 158, 251, 256
Venus, 7
victims, 34, 154
victory, 183, 196–98
vindication, 271
vineyard, 140
virgins, 126, 127
never been married, 129, 130

# W

wages of sin is death, 250
war, 19, 98, 140, 198, 288
warfare, 18, 71, 74, 145, 215, 227, 230, 243, 252–53, 261, 287–88
washed, sanctified, 103, 107, 111
watch, 95, 99, 100, 115, 136, 154, 159, 207, 224, 230, 246
water, 6, 53, 57–58, 65, 146, 151, 166, 219, 250, 281, 296
weaknesses, 82, 138, 144, 207, 215, 231, 253, 267
what would Jesus do, 153
wholeness, 84, 89
wholesome talk that builds up rather than tears down, 278
wicked choices, 29
wickedness, 88, 89, 145
sinful lifestyle choices, 89
wicked pharaohs, 146
widow, 114, 258
wife, 9, 30, 53, 82–83, 105, 113–20, 126, 157–58, 294
of Abraham, 113
of Aquila, 9
Christian, 120, 140, 266
of Jacob, 30
wilderness, 145, 146, 219, 279, 296

willfully defiant, 84, 86, 88, 123
will of God, 9, 103, 123, 216, 289, 309
Wilson, Sandy, 240
wisdom of God, 29, 32, 33, 43, 159
wisdom of the age, 43
wisdom of the wise, 25, 29
wisdom of this world, 29, 32, 63
wives, 114, 117, 120, 128, 129, 140, 156, 157, 163
wolves in sheep's clothing, 233
woman of God, 156
women's liberation crept into the church, 156
wonders, 46, 169–70, 298, 300, 305
word of God, 6, 48, 76, 180, 246, 252, 279, 281
is living and powerful, 76
word of knowledge, 168
word of the Lord, 29
word of warning, 291
word of wisdom, 168, 169
work, 29, 33, 57, 60, 77, 198, 216
works, 18, 57, 61, 62, 65, 73, 97, 100, 156, 177–78, 207, 256, 273, 284, 295
worldly, 23, 29, 30, 32, 33, 45, 46, 48, 63
worldly wisdom, 23, 29, 30, 32, 45, 48, 63
worldview, 31, 33, 245, 252, 258
worship, 5, 7, 8, 91, 135, 147, 152, 167–68, 179, 203, 284
of God, 147
of idols, 167, 248
writing with the authority of an apostle, 54

# Y

Yancey, Philip
on grace, 250
on Job, 223
yielded to the lordship of Christ, 157
yoked, 121, 264, 266, 273

# Z

Zacchaeus, 102
Zacharias, Ravi
on living with God as revealed in the Incarnation of Jesus Christ, 73
on sin against God, 56
on spiritual intimacy, 28
zeal, 30, 125, 240, 269, 281
zero tolerance, 128
Zion, 191

CPSIA information can be obtained
at www.ICGtesting.com
Printed in the USA
LVOW06s1551260616

494073LV00003B/6/P